Making Equity Planning Work

LEADERSHIP in the PUBLIC SECTOR

Conflicts in Urban and Regional Development

A SERIES EDITED BY JOHN LOGAN AND TODD SWANSTROM

Norman Krumholz and John Forester

with a Foreword by Alan A. Altshuler

TEMPLE UNIVERSITY PRESS
Philadelphia

Making Equity Planning Work

LEADERSHIP in the PUBLIC SECTOR

Temple University Press, Philadelphia 19122
Copyright © 1990 by Norman Krumholz and John Forester
All rights reserved
Published 1990
Printed in the United States of America

Library of Congress Cataloging-in-Publication Data
Krumholz, Norman.
    Making equity planning work : leadership in the public sector /
Norman Krumholz and John Forester ; with a foreword by Alan A.
Altshuler.
        p.   cm. — (Conflicts in urban and regional development)
    ISBN 0-87722-700-4 (alk. paper). — ISBN 0-87722-701-2 (pbk. :
alk. paper)
    1. City planning—Ohio—Cleveland—Case studies.   2. Urban policy—
Ohio—Cleveland—Case studies.   I. Forester, John, 1948–   .
II. Title.   III. Series.
HT168.C54K78   1990
307.1'216'0977132—dc20   89-39116
                                                                    CIP

To Virginia Krumholz and our children—
Daniel, Laura, Andrew

and

To Betty Falcão

CONTENTS

━━━━━━

PART TWO
LESSONS

FOREWORD

I first encountered Norman Krumholz at Cornell in 1963, shortly after my own arrival as a neophyte faculty member. Then in his mid-thirties, with a wife and children to support, Norman had just abandoned a decade-long career in business to become a graduate student in city planning. A mature, street-savvy professional, he was already an acute student of politics (the field I was supposed to be teaching him). It soon developed that he was also a quietly intense dreamer, one who hoped against the history of his chosen profession that he might seriously contribute to racial integration and the alleviation of poverty.

The combination was immensely winning, if (in the light of planning experience) more than slightly implausible. Moreover, it gave us a lot to talk about. I had recently completed a dissertation, which I was in the midst of revising for publication, on the forces that typically drive American planners to serve propertied interests and established patterns of power. Norman was eager to absorb my argument, and whatever else I had to offer. He did not argue much, in my recall, but he was endlessly probing, determined to figure out what other possibilities the world might have to offer.

As it turned out, our discussions were occurring at the outset of an era of turmoil and reform in urban politics—and in city planning. As civil rights and poverty moved to the center stage of American politics, city planners at first found themselves on the sidelines. Their techniques, their standard nostrums, and their apolitical modus operandi were at best irrelevant to these new issues, at worst perverse. It soon became apparent to perceptive observers that even the most "neutral" planning was inescapably political in failing to question, and tending to reinforce, the existing distribution of power and wealth in society. And a reaction got under way, in the journals and on the campuses if not in many city halls, pointing toward a new era in which some planners, at least, would serve (in

Paul Davidoff's term) as advocates for the poor and the politically weak.

So, by the time Norman graduated in 1965 (the year Davidoff's landmark article on advocacy planning was published), one could not dismiss the possibility that a new planning era had dawned, and that Krumholz just might find ways to realize his dream.

What I could not then imagine, however, was that he would prove unique among the practicing planners of his generation—in the consistent purity of his vision, in his tactical brilliance on its behalf, and in his eloquence as an advocate, not just to local audiences but to his colleagues across the nation as well.

In hindsight, it is now apparent that the moment in which Norman launched his career, when the causes of redistribution and racial integration were ascendant, was fleeting. Soon, even before he reached Cleveland (a year into the Nixon administration), the tide would turn. Fortunately, it did not turn everywhere at once. Norman got his chance to become planning director of Cleveland because Carl B. Stokes, the first black to be elected mayor of an American city with a population larger than half a million, for the moment dominated its politics. Within two years, though, Stokes was gone. The remarkable thing is that Norman then pursued his agenda successfully through six years of a conservative Republican mayoralty (before concluding with two more years under still a third mayor).

Now, a decade after leaving government, Norman, who describes himself as still an activist but also an "uneasy academic," has joined with John Forester in writing a superb book on the Cleveland experience. However awkward his academic hat may feel, Norman wears it with flair. He takes full, reflective advantage of the perspective that distance can bring, and of the hard questioning that students and faculty colleagues can provide. In a series of chapter-length vignettes he portrays the swirling interplay of political, professional, and personal considerations in high-stress planning practice in vivid colors, and with remarkable candor about his planning encounters with the seamy underside of big city politics. Forester concludes with three chapters of highly insightful commentary on the implications of the Cleveland story for planning theory and practice.

The professional choices that Norman made in Cleveland

were invariably controversial at the time, and few readers (myself included) are likely to agree with every one. Was it appropriate for him to lobby against his own mayor's proposal for a Downtown People Mover? Was it foolhardy to propose massive, regionwide public housing when there was no visible constituency to support it? Did Norman and his colleagues devote too little attention to eliciting active participation by their ostensible low-income clients, and to mobilizing their potential allies? Were they unduly hostile to the private marketplace, and indifferent to the city's need for taxpaying developments? All of these strike me as legitimate topics for debate. But no planner, I predict, will be able to consider his or her education complete during the next decade or so who has not grappled vicariously with the dilemmas Norman faced. And few planning seminars will be more lively than those organized around his account, and Forester's perceptive commentary, in the following pages.

Alan A. Altshuler
Harvard University

PREFACE

For a decade between late 1969 and 1979, the city of Cleveland was the site of a quiet but important experiment. What would happen if a group of professional planners, working for the city, devoted themselves to serving the needs of the poor even while the national mood, federal dollars, and local politics chased other priorities? This book explores the experience and the lessons of that experiment in equity planning.

This book is an experiment as well. It reflects a collaboration between colleagues whose professional histories and styles of work are quite different. Krumholz, born shortly before the Great Depression, is a planning director turned uneasy academic, an activist involved intimately with Cleveland's neighborhoods and urban issues for the past twenty years. Forester, born after World War II, is an academic interested in the politics and ethics, the limits and possibilities, of planning practice. Together, though, we share a deep sense of the unrealized possibilities of the city planning profession.

This book argues that planners can indeed work to serve those most in need. They can publicize issues that threaten or may benefit the people of the city. They can resist public giveaways. They can work effectively, if always within limits, in the face of power. Their work can produce tangible benefits for their clientele. Yet planners alone, even with the best of efforts, will not be able to alter the structure of the political economy. They may diminish, but not abolish, inequality. They will not end injustice, even if they can strengthen democracy, weaken exploitation, empower citizen organizations, and resist injustice. Should they do nothing, though, because they cannot do it all, or should planners try to do as much as they can? Just what can they do? In this book, we try to show how much more planners can do than many of us have thought.[1]

---

[1]We are grateful for the help of many readers and critics who read portions of this manuscript and helped us to improve it. We remain solely responsible for its flaws, but our thanks go to Seymour Adler, Judith Allen, David Allor,

The chapters that follow are divided into two parts. In Part One we review the high and low points of the Cleveland planning staff's work under Norman Krumholz's guidance. In Part Two we explore the implications of this experience, the lessons we may draw for planning, public management, and administrative practice more generally.

Part One begins with two introductory chapters. The first provides a historical background to contemporary city planning in Cleveland. (See Map 1 of contemporary Cleveland, p. 2.) We learn, for example, that the very inactivity of city planning in the 1960s may, by way of contrast, have enhanced the subsequent reputation of Krumholz's activist and articulate staff. We then move directly to Krumholz's experience upon arriving in Cleveland during the administration of Mayor Carl B. Stokes, this country's first black mayor in a city with a population over 500,000. He found a demoralized staff, too many of whom were "putting in time" with little sense of public purpose.

How did they develop an activist, poverty-focused, public-educating style of practice? The remaining ten chapters in Part One provide case material to answer these questions and tell the story.

In the early years, Krumholz and his staff learned the hard way. They won many points handily at the Planning Commission only to lose disastrously in the City Council. They developed rational, well-argued analyses of policy options—involving transportation services, for example—only to find powerful interests oblivious to their work. They took principled and risky positions to support the construction of low-income housing, only to face hatred, racism, and a death threat for doing so.

Howell Baum, Ernest Bonner, Linda Chu, Pierre Clavel, Linda Dalton, Harry Fagan, Eric Ferguson, Raphaël Fischler, Allen Fonoroff, David Goss, Patsy Healey, Charles Hoch, Michael Hoffman, Jerome Kaufman, Robert Letcher, Helen Liggett, John Linner, Susan Olson, Ruth O'Leary, Mary Niebling, William Norris, Alvin Schorr, Bruce Stiftel, Todd Swanstrom, Diana Tittle, and Layton Washburn. For generous interviews, we thank Tom Andrzejewski, Roldo Bartimole, Rosetta Boyd, Janice Cogger, James B. Davis, Dennis Kucinich, Craig Miller, Ruth Miller, Ralph J. Perk (telephone only), Carl B. Stokes, the late Wallace Teare, Homer Wadsworth, Layton Washburn, Bernice Krumhansl, and Kathryn Jaksic. Many of the quotations in Part One come from these interviews. For help with the manuscript itself, we thank Beatriz Rodriguez, Nancy Hutter, and Marie Simmons. We are grateful for the financial support of David C. Sweet, dean of the College of Urban Affairs, Cleveland State University.

Yet they prevailed and won on many other issues. Beginning with studies of local housing problems, the staff's work led ultimately—but directly—to a change in the state of Ohio's property law. Ohio cities could now quickly land-bank tax-delinquent properties and assemble large parcels for desirable uses. Working with other city agencies, the planning staff helped to improve public service delivery. Working on transportation issues, the staff protected transit services for the transit-dependent population most in need. Working on land-use issues over many years, the staff helped to survey, plan, and rescue city parklands and beaches. Part One reviews cases that show the breadth, richness, frustrations, and satisfactions of the Cleveland city planners' work during the decade of the 1970s.

Working as professionals, the staff confronted a complex, ambiguous, and fully political world. Part Two of this book asks, "How did they do it?" We first explore the institutional opportunities the staff seized and built upon. Here we point to openings and opportunities we believe planners across the country often have, yet often overlook, to serve the urban populations most in need. Then we examine the planners' practical judgments and strategies. Just how did the planners deal with the political world? Finally, we conclude Part Two by exploring how we might evaluate the Cleveland planners' work. Their strategies recognized political complexity, exploited intrinsic ambiguity, and engaged rather than shunned its political reality. They identified problems, shaped public agendas, produced technical analyses, organized task forces, protected some interests, and fought others. Their work was complex and instructive, but it provides no simple model, no simple recipes to follow.

Instead, the work of the Cleveland planning staff provides a series of practical lessons. Faced with no clear charge from elected politicians, the planners shaped their professional work plan to serve the poor. Rather than taking an ambiguous mandate as a source of confusion, they took it as a source of opportunity. The equity-serving goal of the staff—expand choices for those who have few; serve populations most in need—provided a sense of direction, mission, even solidarity for the planners; it provided no technical decision rule. But the persistent and careful articulation of the goal gave the planning staff a crucial visibility, so that others throughout the city, in neighborhoods and in agencies alike, could ally themselves with the planners as opportunities and issues arose. The planners also used information as a source of influence, of course, but they did so in very interesting ways. Information does not act by itself. The planners cultivated close and mutually beneficial ties with the media. The Cleveland planners could use their analyses and information influentially only because they had developed a reputation for credibility, for producing both timely and well-focused professional work.

Throughout this book, then, we explore how the political and professional aspects of practice may be integrated rather than isolated from each other. We show how a staff may take a committed equity-promoting posture, fully recognize and work through (and against) the political–economic processes in the city, and still maintain and nurture, indeed strengthen, a public-service-oriented and professional style of work. This book points toward a new conception of professionalism in planning, a professionalism no longer apolitical by definition—not a professionalism immediately threatened with practical irrelevance—but one that is politically sensitive, engaged, and practically pitched.

We hope the cases and analysis we present make one point vividly. A successful planning practice depends on the committed and cooperative efforts of many people, not just the planning director, however central she or he may be. The cases we report are very poorly explained by an emphasis on any one person's personality. Our point is not that personality is irrelevant; quite the contrary—the personalities of many, many actors in the city are relevant to the quality and character of the coalitions and working relationships the planning staff can nurture and build upon as they work. We wish, in the very beginning, to reject any reading of the Cleveland experience that attributes such special qualities to the individual planning director, Krumholz, that it obscures the opportunities that planners across the country face every day to pursue a professionally effective, politically astute, progressive practice.

As a committed, if ever-changing, group, not as charismatic individuals, the Cleveland planners had successes and failures. Their collective work is as instructive for its defeats as for its victories. If we can continue to document and study equity-oriented efforts in public, not-for-profit, and other settings too, we will learn still more about the richness and possibilities of contemporary planning practice.

This is a book, too, about the problems of sustaining political vision in professional practice in a liberal democracy that rewards self-interest and sometimes ridicules public service. It is a book about a committed planning staff that worked in the face of substantial odds to do serious public serving professional work. The question we must inform is not whether, but how, to plan to improve the quality of urban life for all citizens, to improve services and the availability of jobs and housing, to strengthen neighborhoods, to resist "take the money and run" speculation. How can we plan so that we can respond seriously to, rather than willfully neglect, the real and painful issues surrounding poverty, racism, profiteering, power and powerlessness?

While they were hardly revolutionaries, the Cleveland planners were certainly advocates. Planners, of course, have often been advocates for the business and middle-class communities of their cities. In Cleveland, though, the planners chose to be advocates not for the business community but for "those people in Cleveland who had few if any choices," for poor and working-class city residents. What was distinctive here was not the fact of advocacy, which might have been expressed only rhetorically or ideologically, but the pragmatic equity-planning agenda that the planners pursued so energetically.

The Cleveland planners had reasonably simple goals. They wanted the city's citizens to have jobs so they could feed their kids; transportation to get to whatever jobs existed; the opportunity to rent or own an affordable house without the terror of finding a cross burning on the front lawn. They wanted the city's and the nation's resources to be used prudently, not to subsidize millionaires in the development industry, but to upgrade services and infrastructure for the neediest populations in the city. So the Cleveland planners were quite traditional in many respects. They wrestled directly with democratic ideals: protect all citizens, provide opportunities and care for those most vulnerable, consider public and not just private welfare.

We hope that this book will encourage other planners and students of planning to write about their work, addressing issues of poverty, equity, and inequality. If we are only partially successful, this book will show how similar the challenges faced in Cleveland were to those in other cities, towns, and regions throughout this country and, we suspect, in many other countries too. We have been able only to tell one version of a complex history spanning ten years of work. We hope that others will build upon our work, telling the story differently in places, extending it here, revising and arguing with it there, continuing in any case to clarify the possibilities of a progressive and engaged planning practice.

We have tried to present a brief for a politically astute, professionally sound model of planning devoted to the needs of the relatively poor and powerless in our cities. We do not present a distanced evaluation of such planning and its prospects—future evaluations of our argument will do that. We want here to prompt research, to set agendas for discussion, to put questions of planning commitments, strategies, and skills forward for attention and debate. We are less committed to carving answers into stone than we are to posing a question: how can planners work effectively in the face of power and poverty?

We provide a history that is inevitably limited, calling for further study and analysis. In writing this book, Krumholz drafted the case histories of Part One and responded to Forester's requests for detail and explanations along the way. Forester worked in Part Two to derive lessons, to point to the broader implications for planners in other localities, at other times.

Our history is partial, of course; a complete history is impossible. Other actors in Cleveland and across the country will, we hope, offer conflicting interpretations of the cases. Other members of the Cleveland planning staff will no doubt have partially assenting, partially dissenting views. This sense of potential controversy heartens rather than dismays us, for the questions about the pragmatic limits and possibilities of planning practice need much more attention, debate, and analysis.

We are happy to raise more questions about leaking information, for example, or organizing coalitions, or shaping public agendas than we could possibly answer definitively. In realms of practice, realms of ethics (what should be done?), "definitive" answers will be more illusory than real. We wish instead to point to careful, critical, and pragmatic answers that will inform practical judgments. We distrust the search for recipe-like answers, for these are too often today's false promises of "solutions" that will be threatened by obsolescence come daybreak. Tomorrow morning's challenges, tomorrow morning's meetings, will always call upon us to rework, appropriate, and adapt today's answers in the face of new and particular circumstances. So we do not argue that leaking information, for example, is always justifiable or never justifiable. Instead, we hope our discussion of cases will clarify what considerations should be made when a course of action like leaking information appears to be a practical option.

So we deliberately risk giving some readers a sense of having left a series of practical questions unanswered. We propose pragmatic approaches and welcome the proposal of alternative—and still more fruitful—approaches to the practice of equity-oriented planning.

We intend this book to be both scholarly and committed, both objective—reflecting past arguments and building upon them—and passionate: we inevitably pay attention to issues of equality, access, power, and strategy, but we downplay or neglect others; we worry about public sector planning strategies more and private sector strategies less. We wish to raise questions, to pose problems, to set an agenda for discussion and research—all with the purpose of clarifying possibilities for the more effective service of human needs.

We suspect that much good work in planning has gone unreported. It needs to be recognized, appreciated, built upon. We suspect also that too many opportunities for improving shelter, providing jobs, fixing streets, rebuilding neighborhoods, have gone unrecognized, have not been seized. We suspect that the risks of an equity-planning posture have been exaggerated, that openings for effective work have been unnecessarily ignored, indeed that earlier professional aspirations to transcend "politics" have seriously, if unintentionally, weakened the planning profession. So we hope to provide not a cookbook for action, but agendas to explore, stories whose richness will point us toward further opportunities. Where we have not succeeded in doing so, we hope the criticisms of this book will clarify further possibilities of equity-oriented practice—rather than deepening a cynical resignation in the face of needless human suffering.

Ultimately, we wish to defend a progressive, practical, and

critical planning practice that will not succumb to dogmatic criticisms of either the right or the left. From the right, planning is attacked as paternalistic, ineptly centralized, and inevitably authoritarian—as if the decision to trust the free market did not reflect another expansive theory of society, a theory in which relatively few do very well and many suffer. From the left, planning is often seen as complicit with the forces of capital, as inevitably tainted with the stains of unnecessary compromise, as too little, too late—as if more radical organizers could merely announce the contradictions of capitalism and find a revolutionary class snapping out of its liberal slumber and arising to take power. These criticisms from the right and left have elements of truth to them, yet the problem before us is to reconstruct and revive publicly committed planning, not to kill it.

American city planning is not without its own problems. It is often too slow, lethargic, and passive, despite flashes of brilliance and vision. It suffers from bad advice and recently borrowed, hopelessly technocratic illusions; more data and better analysis by themselves will solve precious few problems. It suffers too from the hangover that followed the profession's intoxication with the drink served by the "hidden hand" of the market. But now, after two terms of national inebriation with the "free market," we have more poverty, more hunger, and many hundreds of thousands of homeless adults and children sleeping in our cities' streets.

In this book we present no miracle cure. We present the experiences of a hard-working, turbulent, chaotic planning staff, in a real city with real problems, more like than unlike other major metropolitan areas around the United States. We wish to situate ourselves not halfway between the political right and left, but forward. We must all face problems of action and inaction. We have no recourse to professional neutrality. History gives planners no special box seats on the sidelines from which to watch the action. Instead, history forces a question upon us all: how now? This question is far too often lost from sight in studies of planning history, theory, or political economy. How now? This book seeks less to provide a single answer—for that must always be done anew, in each situation, assessing needs, drawing from history, adapting vision—than to resurrect this question for the planning profession. When planners work to counteract severe inequalities, what influence can they have? What problems and opportunities are they likely to face? How are they to work at the intersection of politics, professionalism, and realism? These are the central questions we address in this book.

The Cleveland planners advanced an aggressive and compassionate sense of the public welfare and the common good. They appealed to planning tradition and tried to change it, to reconstruct the vocation of planning, as well. They learned the rules of the political game as well as they could and tried to change those rules too. They built relationships with other city actors, agency staff, neighborhood activists—in addition to redoing the maps of the city. Caught between the idealism of the 1960s, their professional mission, and the constraints and corruption of city politics, the Cleveland planners amassed a record, in fits and starts, wins and losses, that suggests the real limits, but also the real possibilities, of public-serving city planning practice.

PART
ONE

EXPERIENCE

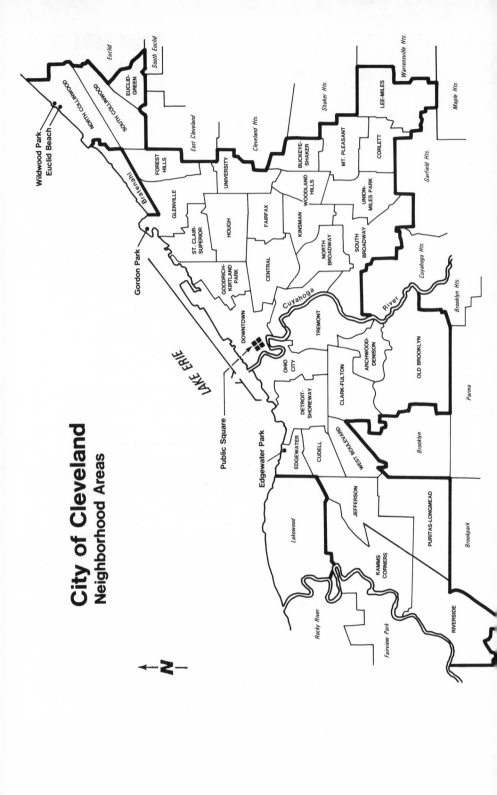

City of Cleveland
Neighborhood Areas

1

Planning in Cleveland

Cleveland has the problems of an old industrial city. It also has the most acrimonious government in Christendom.

—George Will (1978)

Cleveland . . . is the ethnic family trapped in a flat and going to the dogs. . . . It is neighborhood after neighborhood after neighborhood. . . . Cleveland is industry: huge complexes that create steel and a Central Avenue that shouts. . . . Cleveland is Euclid Avenue, a neighbor named Krtchmareck. Cleveland is expressways and narrow alleys. . . .

Yet somewhere in this—between the Cleveland Tower and the melancholy neighborhoods and the pleasing suburbs decked out in early American Formica and the factories and all the people these items feast upon—exists the dream, the beauty, and the anger that is Cleveland.

—Dick Perry, *Ohio: A
Personal Portrait of the
Seventeenth State* (1969)

The city of Cleveland (see Map 1) was founded in 1796. Like so many other cities, it was founded as a speculative real estate venture. The city's founder, Moses Cleaveland, was an investor in the Connecticut Land Company, which hoped to reap a tidy profit by selling all the lands it owned in what then was called Connecticut's Western Reserve. The town was surveyed in 1796 by a team under the direction of Augustus Porter. Porter's was the earliest plan for Cleveland, a simple grid design around a town square on the New England model. It was the only model the surveyors knew. The early plan turned its back on the river and lake, but it was neat and orderly, and it facilitated land sales, a compelling motive of land planning then as now.

With the opening of the Ohio Canal in 1827, expanding trade supplied the town of Cleveland with a solid commercial basis for economic prosperity, and the beginnings of manufacturing suggested its industrial destiny. An expanding manufacturing-based economy would be the key to Cleveland's development over the next century, with iron, steel, machine tools, chemicals, oil, and shipbuilding leading the way. Business, industry, and commercial development came first in the early days and still come first in Cleveland. Any public-serving planning that has taken place has always been secondary to the needs of business.

For the next century, while the city grew from a single log cabin by the Cuyahoga River to one of the mightiest industrial cities of the world, the physical development of the city went forward without anything that could be called public-serving city planning. As Cleveland's population rocketed from 17,034 in 1850 to 381,768 in 1900, public planning for services fell sharply behind problems of congestion, sanitation, crime, and disease. A great deal of private planning did take place, of course, as the great industries and commercial enterprises planned their growth. But successive city governments simply built capital improvements—the roads, bridges, and sewers—in response to the demands of burgeoning business activities. Meanwhile, the growing population crowded into what the Cleveland *Leader* in 1873 described as "small, dirty and wretched" housing.

The first plan that could be termed "public-serving" (although mightily endorsed by downtown businessmen) took place at the turn of the twentieth century. In 1903, on the wave of Progressivism that was promoting the grand schemes of the "city beautiful" movement along with such good-government reforms as civil service, nonpartisan elections, and city planning, Daniel Burnham, the great Chicago architect, designed the Mall Group Plan in Cleveland's downtown. The plan, with strong support from Progressive Mayor Tom L. Johnson, cleared forty-four acres of downtown land crowded with small businesses, shops, and homes and constructed in its place, on a north–south axis, a formal mall of public buildings and rows of lawns and trees modeled after the Place de la Concorde in Paris. Cleveland's Mall Plan, clearing and displacing small homes and businesses in favor of civic buildings in a park, foretold the U.S. Urban Renewal Program of the 1950s and 1960s.

Cleveland waited another twelve years after the Mall Plan before Mayor Newton D. Baker appointed the city's first planning commission in 1915. The eleven-person commission's duties included overseeing the city's works of art, reviewing public works projects, and preparing a city plan. Since the commission had no staff and no budget, it is not surprising that the first city plan did not appear until 1949, fully thirty-four years after the commission was created and twenty years after the City Council passed Cleveland's first zoning ordinance.

During the Great Depression, planning in Cleveland was simply routine zoning administration done by the city engineer. Slum clearance and low-rent housing received some attention from Ernest J. Bohn, who wrote the state's first public housing law, which was passed by the Ohio General Assembly in 1933. Bohn, a Cleveland city councilman who became first director of the Cleveland Metropolitan Housing Authority, and later the chairman of the City Planning Commission for twenty-four years (1942–1966), also helped set up Cleveland's Regional Planning Association in 1937.

In 1942, following the recommendations of the prestigious Mayor's Advisory Committee on Planning Organization under the chairmanship of Walter L. Flory, the city passed a series of charter amendments reorganizing the planning function. City Council finally provided for a planning staff, and John T. Howard began as planning director with a staff of seven and a budget of $26,000. Howard's staff completed the city's first General Land Use Plan in 1949. When he left in 1949 to take a post as planning professor at the Massachusetts Institute of Technology, his place was filled by James M. Lister. Lister in turn left in 1957 to take the post of director of the city's new Department of Urban Renewal and Housing.[1] Eric A. Grubb then filled the planning director's post from 1957 to 1969, when I became director under Mayor Carl B. Stokes.

In the 1950s and 1960s, federal grants for urban renewal and highway projects sparked new interest in city planning, and budgets and numbers of city planning staff increased. Much of the new activity was related to urban renewal developments, since federal money was now available to support approved projects. Private institutions, working with local foundations, saw an opportunity to harness this federal money

---

[1]In 1968, amid a backlash against Cleveland's disappointing urban renewal program, the Department of Urban Renewal and Housing was renamed the Department of Community Development.

in behalf of their own redevelopment needs. They set up private, nonprofit development corporations, such as the Cleveland Development Foundation and University Circle, Inc., to "guide" the city's renewal planners. In that way, private interests actually prepared the Title I urban renewal plans for such projects as the St. Vincent's and University–Euclid projects, which the city then approved and executed. These plans, especially the St. Vincent's plan, destroyed thousands of homes occupied by poor black residents and replaced them with institutional land uses. However, even with the power of eminent domain and federal funding behind many of Cleveland's renewal plans, they were ignored in substantial detail or poorly executed. A major problem was the fact that most of the plans wildly overestimated the demand for the new land uses they proposed. At one time in the mid-1960s, Cleveland had more land in certified urban renewal projects (6,060 acres) than any other city in the country. The follow-through, however, was so weak that the urban renewal program was temporarily shut down by the federal government in 1966. "Cleveland," an official of the Department of Housing and Urban Development (HUD) told a local reporter in 1969, "is our Vietnam. We want to get out but we don't know how."

In spite of about ninety years of planning history in Cleveland and consistent, vocal support for planning from local newspapers and from business, it is difficult to find examples of sustained political enthusiasm for anything above the scale of project planning. But if Cleveland's city planning has its contradictions, so does its politics.

Cleveland is a study in political contradictions. In this century it has been the home of Marcus Hanna and Tom L. Johnson. Hanna was an iron master who went into politics to protect his business interests and made it his life's work. For a quarter of a century, he and George B. Cox, a former saloon-keeper from Cincinnati, controlled Ohio, Cox running the southern part of the state and Hanna controlling the northern part. Between them they named Ohio's officials and national representatives, and maintained the steady hand of self-interested control over Ohio politics. When Hanna's protégé William McKinley was elected president of the United States in 1896, it could be said that Hanna was boss of the whole country. As John Gunther remarked of Hanna in his book *Inside U.S.A.*, "he wore a President like McKinley as a watch fob."

But Cleveland was also the crucible for Mayor Thomas L. Johnson's brand of municipal socialism. Tom L. Johnson was a millionaire street railway magnate and a leading Progressive politician who was converted to the reform movement by Henry George's book *Progress and Poverty*. As mayor from 1901 to 1909, Johnson fought vigorous campaigns against "privilege." He began the Municipal Electric Light Plant (Muny) to compete with the Cleveland Electric Illuminating Company (CEI), instituted a three-cent transit fare, and supported innovative programs for neighborhood parks, schools, and bathhouses as well as the Cooley Farms to rehabilitate convicts. Johnson took garbage collection and street cleaning out of private hands and made them municipal services. His name continues to be invoked in the name of the "little people" in Cleveland politics, and his statue in Cleveland's Public Square is the site of liberal and progressive rallies to this day.

In his book *The Shame of the Cities*, muckraker Lincoln Steffens judged Cleveland to be the "best run city in America" and Tom Johnson to be the nation's best mayor. Yet knowledgeable political analysts point to a long history of political corruption.

Cleveland had a black councilmember before Chicago (Thomas W. Fleming, elected in 1915), and was the first large American city to elect a black as mayor (Carl B. Stokes in 1967), even though blacks represented only a 39 percent minority at the time. Yet the black population of the city and surrounding suburbs is deeply segregated, and its history of race relations up to the present is stained with conflict and violence.

Voter registration in the city is about eight-to-one Democratic. Yet between 1971 and 1989 a Republican was mayor for all but two years, while the legislative body was overwhelmingly Democratic.

The contradictions are readily seen. Understanding the system requires familiarity with politicians, their race and ethnicity, and local party politics as it interacts with business.

POLITICAL POWER

In textbook terms, Cleveland has a strong-mayor–council government. That is, the mayor can appoint his or her own people as department heads without Council's approval and can veto budget items. This was not always the case. From 1924 to 1931, Cleveland had a city manager, but this arrangement was dispensed with in 1931, when the people voted to reinstate the mayor–council system. Up until 1982, all thirty-three Cleveland councilmembers were elected on a ward basis every two years. The mayor also had a two-year term, an impediment, it was said, to long-range planning, since all political decision-makers were constantly running for re-election and could not consider longer-term issues. In 1982, voters reduced the size of Council from thirty-three to twenty-one and extended the term of councilmembers and mayor to four years.

In 1932, Cleveland gave Franklin D. Roosevelt a solid majority. Yet in 1933 the Republican candidate for mayor was handily elected, and until 1941 all the mayors were Republicans. Since then, all the mayors, whether Republican or Democrat, have been "independent" of strong party control. Meanwhile, regardless of the politics of the mayor, City Council has remained overwhelmingly Democratic. As of 1988, for example, all twenty-one councilmembers were Democrats, but relations with the Republican mayor could not have been better.

To say that Cleveland has a strong-mayor form of government that centralizes all powerful executive functions in the mayor's office is to simplify the issue. The mayor may appoint and dismiss the directors of all operating agencies without Council's approval and may appoint individuals to various boards and commissions with or without the consent of Council, depending on the appointment. Members of the Planning Commission, for example, are appointed by the mayor only with the Council's consent. The mayor prepares and submits for Council's approval an annual budget called the Mayor's Estimate, and has the power to veto Council's decisions.

It would be a mistake, however, to assume that the system in Cleveland conveys controlling power to the executive branch; the president of City Council is at least as strong as the mayor and, depending on the individuals involved, may be stronger. In the Stokes administration (1967–1971), Council President James V. Stanton fought the mayor to a bitter standstill on many issues. From 1973 to 1990, Council President George Forbes was the undisputed ringmaster of Cleveland politics, with Mayors Ralph J. Perk and George V. Voinovich playing second fiddle.

The city charter strictly separates the legislative from the executive and mandates noninterference in administrative matters in this precise language: "No member of Council shall, except in so far as is necessary in the performance of the duties of his office, directly or indirectly, interfere in the conduct of an administrative department." Yet interference, manipulation, and bartering are actually the order of the day.

As the city's legislative branch, Council controls all appropriations. No money may be applied for by any city agency and no money may be spent without Council's specific authorization. Every expenditure of more than $3,500 requires a separate ordinance by Council. Many cities will give a responsible executive department "blanket authorization" to execute the precise details of a long-term, complex undertaking such as an urban renewal plan. Other cities have their Council simply authorize an autonomous urban renewal authority to proceed with a plan that councilmembers have reviewed and generally approved. Once that blanket authority is granted, the renewal authority proceeds on its own to implement the plan. Not so in Cleveland, where Council, jealously guarding its prerogatives, insists on acting by separate ordinance on every land acquisition, every land sale, every change of plan or change of zoning. Departments operating with federal or state money must also get Council authorization to accept and then expend those monies. In practice, this means that the passage of every ordinance is potentially a lengthy procedure with bargaining every step of the way. At any given time, the Department of Community Development, which executes renewal plans and plans the expenditure of the city's annual $20 million-plus Community Development Block Grant, may have forty or fifty ordinances before Council. A routine community development ordinance may be assigned for hearings and action to Council's Finance Committee, Community Development Committee, and City Planning Committee before action by Council as a whole. Each committee chair, who alone establishes what will be on the agenda for committee hearings, may delay a piece of legislation while working out a deal with the department—that is, extracting some concession. The concession may have to do with the acquisition and price of a specific parcel of land either in the project or elsewhere, or it may involve an entirely unrelated matter such as the hiring or salary of an individual employee (possibly a client or relative of the councilmember) or the renting of a storefront owned by a favored constituent or some other condition.

Since administrative agencies cannot act without Council's authorization, and since each committee chair can delay or jeopardize that authorization, agency staff, especially at the commissioner and director level, are anxious to help Council out and help their program move along in the legislative process. When I was appointed community development director in 1977, I spent the first two days of my tenure listening to various councilmembers tell me the names of their relatives and friends, who were liberally sprinkled throughout my 270-person staff and whose jobs I "had to protect" if I didn't want "trouble" with the legislation I had before Council.

Because this haggling can become chaotic and inordinately time-consuming if uncontrolled, businessmen and powerful institutions who need favors, and administration officials who need action on legislation, prefer to do business with a strong Council president who controls the action by virtue of the working majority that elected him.

A strong Council president controls his majority by a reputation for clout, rewards, and sanctions. George Forbes, who took over as president of Council in 1973, enriched his reputation for clout when, under indictment, he enlisted the white establishment to make statements of support (and got a significant number of them to appear in City Council in an unlikely tableau, linking hands and singing "We Shall Overcome"). The downtown business establishment also raised a fund to pay for Forbes's defense and got the city's premier law firms and best criminal attorneys to provide that defense. Forbes was acquitted of all charges on a directed verdict in 1979. Developers and the corporate community also provided strong support for Forbes in all his political campaigns.

The rewards Council presidents dispense to their Council supporters include a share of the campaign contributions that the president has collected for his or her own re-election campaigns; tacit permission to control all zoning changes and the many permits issued in each ward; assignments to powerful committees that offer other "business" opportunities; jobs for friends or family members; a fair share of the city's capital improvements and street repaving; and contracts for favored social service agencies. If a supportive councilmember is defeated for re-election, the president can usually place him or her in another job.

Sanctions include pressure on a straying councilmember. In 1981, a black councilman, Lonnie Burton, put together twelve votes—ten white and two black—enough to strip the Council presidency from George Forbes and elect himself. A day later, Forbes had summoned the biggest guns in the business community to his aid as well as—more importantly—key black ministers and the *Call & Post*, Cleveland's black newspaper, putting unendurable pressure on the two black members of the insurgency, who shortly recanted.

In maintaining his power over his colleagues and holding the bargaining within reasonable limits, the Council president centralizes power in himself. As a result, while good-government advocates complain of the "fragmentation" of Cleveland City Council, it is a myth; the Council president controls, and he controls with a grip that is at least as strong as the mayor's. On most important legislation, commissioners, the highest level of the permanent civil service and part of the mayor's administration, will negotiate deals directly with the Council president, relying on the fact that the Council president often has more longevity than the mayor and controls more favors.

It is common to describe official party organizations as "machines" and leaders as "bosses." In Cleveland, the terminology verges on the ludicrous. Party discipline is nonexistent. Democrats support and contribute to Republicans who run for office or seek patronage favors, and vice versa. Carl Stokes (Democrat) had much more influence with the U.S. Congress than he had with his own City Council, which was, for most of Stokes's term, 31–2 Democratic but engaged in constant warfare with the mayor. Ralph J. Perk and George V. Voinovich (both Republicans) enjoyed a cozy and harmonious relationship with a similarly top-heavy Democratic Council as they swapped favors and patronage. Democratic (or populist) Mayor Dennis J. Kucinich, on the other hand, was continually and bitterly embroiled with his Democratic Council, which chose to help local banks drive the city into default in 1978 rather than negotiate with him. Party partisanship is so weak that local leaders of both political parties sometimes combine into law firms to dispense political influence from both sides of the aisle. In fact, the formal political organizations in Cleveland are only loose agglomerations controlled by no guiding philosophical principles and restrained by little visible party discipline.

THE BUSINESS OF POLITICS

There is a commonly held view in Cleveland that businessmen run the town. In 1981, when Council President Forbes nominated James C. Davis, managing partner of the prestigious law firm of Squire, Sanders, & Dempsey and one-time president of the Growth Association, to the state-mandated fiscal revenue board that controlled the city's budget as it worked its way out of default, he remarked, "He's always run the place from behind the scenes; he might as well make it public."

My staff and I decided that it was actually an oversimplification to presume that businessmen run Cleveland; actually they intervene only in that part of the public business that is important to their private enterprises. Of course, when businessmen intervene, as they did in Cleveland's 1978 default, they tend to get what they want.

The most important planning or development initiatives come, not from the city, but from developers, utility companies, the Growth Association, and major law firms. Developers contribute to political campaign chests, employ legal retainers, and provide jobs and other gifts in return for the millions in public development subsidies dispensed by the city. The gas and electric utilities employ "government relations" executives who spend much time with City Council. Much of their apparent work has to do with picking up councilmembers' luncheon checks, buying them gifts, and otherwise making them comfortable. This is perceived to be good business, since the city routinely but ineffectually intervenes whenever the utilities file for a rate increase with the Ohio Public Utility Commission. Also, the Cleveland Electric Illuminating Company has spent much time and effort over most of this century trying to take control of its Municipal Light Plant competitor and drive it out of business. For such purposes, a tight relationship with local government was important to CEI objectives.

It seemed clear to me from my earliest days in the city that the initiatives of the business community were uniformly directed toward new development and growth in Cleveland, whose slogan is "The Best Location in the Nation." When the regional planning organization proposed a system of highways cutting a path through the city's neighborhoods, and displacing about 19,000 Cleveland residents, the business community nonetheless saw the highways as improvements to downtown accessibility and general mobility. The suburbanization of the city's housing, jobs, and industry was not a problem to the Growth Association, since its objective was development wherever it took place in the Greater Cleveland region. For the same reason, city–suburban fiscal disparities, which are among the most extreme of any metropolitan area in the country, are not an issue to the business community. Any development proposal— especially one that can be built largely at someone else's expense—is sure to get the enthusiastic endorsement of the business community. In twenty years in City Hall and out, I do not recall a single development proposal that the Cleveland business community opposed, and this includes all highway and urban renewal projects, proposals for a bridge across Lake Erie to Canada, a Domed Stadium, a Rock 'n Roll Hall of Fame, and a $3 billion jetport in Lake Erie. The Growth Association is, as its name implies, fixated on "growth and development."

Business interests are also happy to recommend and support programs that will cost them little or save them taxes while adding to the tax burden of others. This is called "improving the business climate so that business investments may provide jobs and taxes" (even if the taxes are to be abated). Thus, the city freely offers business subsidies in the form of grants, long-term low- or no-interest loans, capital improvements, its powers of eminent domain, and tax abatements in the hope that business will in turn provide investment. The net impact of these subsidies on the city's fiscal vitality or on the number of jobs for the city's residents or unemployed is unknown. Many studies suggest that the impact of such inducements is negligible or nonexistent. Meanwhile, other city property owners have to pay for any public costs and services incurred by these new developments.

Just as businessmen may participate in local politics to serve their own commercial ends, so may some politicians. This is not a recent phenomenon; Fred Kohler, who served as mayor, sheriff, and police chief in the 1920s, left an estate of over $400,000, although he never earned more than $15,000 a year. In the same way, some current politicians are less focused on serving the public interest than their own personal financial interests. Not surprisingly, a cozy, reciprocal relationship links them with business. Thus, it is common knowledge that zoning changes might be sold for cash or business favors. Council-members are sometimes charged, indicted, convicted, and jailed over zoning matters. Some city permits may be available for cash. In 1978, eight Council members, including the Council president, were indicted for getting cash kick-backs from a carnival owner whom they permitted to operate in their wards. They were all cleared. Members of Council who have the good fortune to be lawyers or insurance vendors are not above directing private entrepreneurs who seek public business to their own establishments as a quid pro quo. A councilmember who is a lawyer, for example, may steer a public job to an architect, who in turn may contribute a percentage of the fee to the councilmember's re-election campaign and employ the councilmember's law firm. Multi-million-dollar municipal bond issues whose legality must be certified before they can be sold may be steered to favored law firms who collect fat fees in the same way. All of this takes place in an open, free-wheeling, catch-as-catch-can style. Each mayor is expected to have a "favorite" architect, accounting firm, management consultant, and legal counsel, all of whom are selected for city contracts without bids. Councilmembers and appointed officials may frequently act as fronts for developers.

What, my staff and I asked, did all this mean for city planning? First, there was probably little interest in city planning above the level of project planning. Any deals that had been cut between developers and politicians would be difficult or impossible for planners, speaking the language of "consistency with the general plan," "long-range significance," or "the public interest," to modify. Second, Council took a great interest in zoning because it might be marketable. But the role of the planners in zoning might be inconsequential, since Council reserved to itself the right to introduce all zoning changes and was able (because of bloc voting and backscratching) to override any Planning Commission disapproval. Third, there was little interest in general medium- to long-range planning, since its implications and marketing opportunities were unclear. As George Forbes said when I gave him copies of *The Cleveland Policy Planning Report* in 1974, "Sheeet! I ain't got time for planning!" Fourth, appeals to "rationality" had little capacity to stir action or support. Who cared how rational a policy was if it didn't produce patronage? Finally, new physical developments of all kinds were welcomed, and if the city had some subsidies to offer, they would be made available on generous terms.

Given the political economy and culture of Cleveland politics, planners might well despair. But, as the cases that follow make clear, there is much that planners can do.

INDUSTRIAL AND ECONOMIC DECLINE

Perhaps more destructive to rational city planning than a political process with little commitment to planning was the sharply declining local economy. Cleveland is a prototypical product of industrial America. It is more an agglomeration of jobs than a deliberately located and planned community. At one time, the whole world was anxious to buy the durable goods and other products made in Cleveland. The city was growing, self-confident, and powerfully assertive. That has all changed. Today, planners scramble to hold onto the assets the city still has while offering the widest range of public inducements to developers of new properties.

Like most other older, industrial cities in the Northeast and Midwest, Cleveland has experienced population loss, waves of plant closings, rising unemployment and poverty rates, and the growing deterioration of an aging housing stock. Cleveland's population fell from 914,000 in 1950 to an estimated 530,000 in 1985. It fell by 177,081 during the 1970s, a drop of 24 percent, and it continues to fall by about 7,000 a year in the 1980s. From 1950 to 1975, Cleveland lost 50 percent of its white population; in the 1960s, the city lost 25 percent of its families with incomes over the median for the Standard Metropolitan Statistical Area. A new planning study projects continued population decline through the year 2000, with the loss ranging from 42,000 to 101,000, depending upon various factors. A rising share of the city's population is economically dependent. In 1986, about 20 percent of the city's families received Aid to Dependent Children. From 1969 to 1974, the city's assessed value base fell 5 percent while the Consumer

Price Index rose 34.5 percent. Local general fund operating revenues declined 37 percent during the same period.

Cleveland's traditional economic base of manufacturing industries eroded significantly after World War II. Manufacturing employment in the city declined by 59 percent between 1947 and 1982. Between 1976 and 1984 alone, Cleveland lost 18,000 manufacturing jobs. Service industry employment, nearly one-third of which is located downtown, has picked up some of the slack, although the new jobs created in this category have either been in high-skilled business and professional/technical services or in low-paying personal support services. A 1984 congressional study found that only the residents of three other central cities in the United States were needier than those in Cleveland.

The decline of Cleveland as a regional steel center highlights these trends. In the immediate postwar era, the city boasted three large, integrated steel mills—Republic Steel, U.S. Steel, and Jones & Laughlin Steel Corporation. Republic Steel had its national headquarters in the city. Employment at these three mills reached 18,000 during the 1960s. Steel production in Cleveland declined, amidst growing foreign and domestic competition and the weakening of key markets such as autos and machine tools in the 1970s and a national economic recession in the 1980s. The current period in steel is characterized by plant abandonment and industrial restructuring. By the early 1980s, U.S. Steel had dismantled its Cleveland blast furnace, and Republic Steel and Jones & Laughlin were laying off thousands of workers. In 1984 Jones & Laughlin, then a subsidiary of LTV Corporation, merged with Republic Steel to form LTV Steel, which consolidated its Cleveland operations into one central, reduced-capacity production facility on the banks of the Cuyahoga River. The 1987 bankruptcy of LTV threatened the prospects for this plant and jeopardized the pension benefits of nearly five thousand LTV retirees residing in Cuyahoga County.

From 1980 to 1987, Cleveland's poverty rate increased by over one-third. As of July 1986, its poverty rate was 39 percent, but within three black neighborhoods on the east side, more than 65 percent of the population was in poverty.

Growing poverty rates have combined with deteriorating housing conditions and widespread tax delinquency and abandonment to create a housing crisis in many Cleveland neighborhoods. An exterior conditions survey by the Cuyahoga County Regional Planning Commission during 1984–1985 identified 24,000 substandard one- to four-unit structures, representing 19 percent of the total housing stock in Cleveland. When interior conditions are also considered, the city's Department of Community Development estimates that nearly one-third of the housing stock is substandard.

Concentrated poverty, my staff and I thought, linked with racial discrimination, lay at the root of most of Cleveland's problems. Merely to scratch the surface of many of these problems—crime, inadequate education, unemployment, rotting housing and neighborhoods—was to reveal pervasive racial discrimination. The ghettoization of blacks in America was clear beyond dispute. The 1970 census, which my staff and I were studying at the time, made it obvious that more than 98 percent of all the suburban growth of the 1960s was white; that, virtually without exception, the twenty largest metropolitan areas of the United States had lost white population and gained black population; that in 1970 black Americans represented only 4.5 percent of the suburban population, an increase of less than one-half of one percent over 1960. The decade of concerned involvement and civil rights militancy had not made much of a dent.

In Cleveland, blacks were intensely segregated; less than 2 percent of the county's 255,000 blacks were in the suburbs in 1960. The Cuyahoga River divides the city into east and west sides. In 1970, 98 percent of the west side's 280,904 residents were white; 61 percent of the 469,963 east side residents were black. Blacks were segregated in other ways as well. In 1952, 57 percent of Cleveland's black children went to public schools with more than 90 percent black enrollment; in 1962, 82 percent attended such schools; in 1969, 85 percent attended such schools.

The price of racial discrimination and segregation was paid in lost jobs, lower incomes, crime, higher poverty rates and welfare costs, worse housing, fewer opportunities of all sorts, and the bitterness and humiliation such enforced conditions exact. Yet, in spite of these and many other destructive effects on the people, politics, and physical city of Cleveland, segregation has been remarkably persistent. A 1987 report ranked blacks as the most segregated minority in the United States and Cleveland as the second most segregated city in the nation.[2]

In the face of such social and physical conditions and political opportunism, city planners in Cleveland have their work cut out for them. What can planners do in such situations? More than we might expect.

I came to Cleveland in 1969 and worked in City Hall as planning director for ten years. This book reports on our planning efforts and some of the more significant planning events of that time. It also begins to analyze our successes and failures so that other planners, in no less political and turbulent circumstances, can do still better work to serve those most in need in our cities.

Despite the conflict and frustration described from time to time in the cases that follow, I think of the years I spent in Cleveland City Hall with fondness; I enjoyed being a public servant. I recall reading Dean Acheson's *Present at the Creation*, in which he speaks of public life as fulfilling the Aristotelian ideal of happiness: the exercise of vital powers along lines of excellence in a life affording them scope. I agree; being a good public servant is a challenging and deeply satisfying thing.

For planning students and practitioners, I hope to point out that the kind of planning my staff and I adopted from time to time generated conflict with powerful institutions and individuals who had vested interests in the status quo. Yet this conflict was less frequent than one might think, and was always manageable. In the ten years I served as planning director, under three mayors who could not have been more dissimilar, the agency's staff and budget grew along with its influence, prestige, and success.

By their very nature, the materials contained in this volume touch upon values and expectations regarding the goals of planning and the conduct of public officials. To the best of our ability, John Forester and I have attempted to present these materials fairly. It is, however, impossible to know in every detail the strategies and calculations used by other participants

---

[2]Douglas S. Massey and Nancy A. Denton, "Trends in the Residential Segregation of Blacks, Hispanics, and Asians: 1970–1980," *American Sociological Review* 52 (1987): 802–25.

in each of the case studies except as they were related to us or as we deduced them. We, of course, acknowledge the values that inform this work. We feel that city planning focused to improve the lives of the most distressed people of the city is appropriate and possible and can strengthen the potential of city governments to address their most vexing problems. We hope the presentation of this book will contribute to a greater understanding of the potential of such planning and will encourage students and planning practitioners to attempt their own approaches to redistributive justice.

2

Inheriting a Staff and Building a New One

It might be nice if a new planning director with new ideas and a new work program could bring in an entirely new staff and set to work. Nice but impossible. Planning agencies have on-going responsibilities that predate the arrival of a new director. Inherited assignments, traditions, people, and politics all must be dealt with. Just how they are dealt with may determine the success or failure of the new director's program.

I was ready for the job as planning director of the city of Cleveland when it came along in 1969. I had just turned forty and was increasingly interested in the challenge of a director's position, having spent the mid-1960s as assistant director for planning and programming in the city of Pittsburgh and, before that, working as a senior planner in Ithaca, New York, while I pursued a master's degree in city and regional planning at Cornell. Before becoming interested in city planning, I graduated with an undergraduate degree in journalism in 1954 and spent the intervening years in a variety of businesses, including advertising, furniture, carpeting, and travel. I was confident that I could "meet a payroll" and run my own shop because I had already done so. I also thought I had some good ideas on how to run a planning agency and make its work more useful to the people of the city, especially those who had few advocates in City Hall. These ideas—more directly focused on city residents with the greatest needs and on more involvement of the people in the preparation of the plans that affected them—were not of great interest to the directors I had served, but I believed in them, and I wanted to try them out. The 1960s were an especially opportune time for developing new ideas about proper and ethical planning practice. The ghettos of America were burning, and equity was becoming a more central issue in all governmental institutions.

In the summer of 1969, I was contacted by Allen Fonoroff, a planning professor at Case Western Reserve University in Cleveland and a member of the Cleveland Planning Commission. Fonoroff was leading the search for a new director, and he asked me if I wanted to apply for the job. I jumped at the chance! Cleveland was the city that had elected Carl B. Stokes as mayor. I thought Cleveland would present an interesting, challenging environment for planning and would be open to new ideas other than the traditional planning concepts of zoning, land use, and design.

Following Fonoroff's contact, I met with members of the search committee, was offered the job, and accepted it. That is, I accepted it on one condition. Stokes was running for a second term as mayor against a Republican challenger, Ralph J. Perk. I decided I would come to Cleveland only if Stokes was elected; otherwise I was content to stay in Pittsburgh. Stokes won narrowly in 1969, and I came to Cleveland and worked for him for two years. Ironically, Stokes then decided not to seek re-election, and Perk won the mayor's office in 1971, 1973, and 1975. I ended up working for him for six years. Although our ideologies and politics differed widely, the planning staff enjoyed as solid a working relationship with Mayor Perk as it had with Mayor Stokes, and we achieved some very substantial victories in Perk's administration.

It is hard for me—even now, twenty years later—to express how deeply I felt the importance of being planning director in the Stokes administration. I had grown up poor as the youngest of three sons of a widowed mother in the industrial mill town of Passaic, New Jersey. My father, a foreman in a large textile mill, died when I was three years old. Without my thinking about it much, politics was the backdrop to my youth. My mother, a seamstress in a sweatshop (when she could find any work at all), was a precinct worker for the local Democratic party. She was the glue that held our little family together. Both she and my father, immigrants from Rumania, were members of the "Workmen's Circle," a fraternal organization devoted to the needs of working-class people. Although we had little money, we never thought of poverty as a problem, or thought it demeaning. I was aware of what having no money meant, but

I never thought I would be stopped from doing whatever I wanted to do because of it.

Two of my mother's sisters played a particularly important role in my early growth and development. Since my mother's health was not good, I spent long periods of time—especially during the summers—living with one or another of two aunts. One of them, Clara Krumholz, lived in the Brighton Beach section of Brooklyn. She offered not only her hospitality, but spirited discussions of national and international politics. Her heart was with the working man and woman, and she donated a good deal of her time to support labor organizing activities. Her husband, my Uncle Dave, was a labor organizer and a surrogate father to me. Their household included three daughters; it was a warm and lively place, full of visitors, suitors, and interlopers, all of whom were free to offer their opinions loudly on any political subject, at any time, without any coaxing.

My other aunt, Sally Axelrod, was a quieter and more contemplative person. She had helped set up a cooperative community in a rural area named Stelton, in New Jersey. She was committed to her ideals, living in Stelton and raising her four children in an old farmhouse. The board of the Stelton community assigned residents to the jobs that they could do best—farming, teaching, working in town for cash, and so on. Aunt Sally taught school. I have pleasant memories of learning how to run a printing press, set sticks of type, and build a dam in the small lake behind the commune's Modern School. I also remember picking and eating stringbeans morning, noon, and night during the season. Though Sally and her husband, Adolph, had little, they were always happy to share their home, their table, and their library, which was well stocked with political books and tracts, with me and my two brothers. I had no way of knowing it, but Stelton is "the longest experiment in anarchist education and communal living in American history."[1]

My thinking was also shaped by the courage of my father-in-law, the Reverend Robert A. Martin, an Episcopal priest, who took a strong stand on racial justice in the 1940s as rector for an all-white congregation in rural Louisiana. His courage

---

[1]Paul Avrich, *The Modern School Movement* (Princeton, N.J.: Princeton University Press, 1980), p. 221.

cost him his position, and he was effectively barred from re-ligious work in the South thereafter. Later, the Reverend Martin was chosen by an all-black Episcopal congregation in Kansas City to be its priest, and he worked tirelessly there to dismantle the segregated society of the 1950s.

The only U.S. president I knew up until the time I entered the U.S. Navy at the tail-end of World War II was Franklin D. Roosevelt, and everyone I knew as a child idolized FDR. Of course, I knew very little about FDR's program of emergency jobs, old-age insurance, unemployment compensation, support for union organizing, and the rest of the New Deal liberal agenda. What I did know is that my family always made a point of listening to FDR's Fireside Chats on the radio. His voice reassured us of his friendship and support against the "economic royalists" (whoever they were) who didn't care about people like us. We never doubted that, with FDR's help, we would get out of our situation. In a way, I considered him responsible for the first jobs my older brothers got with the Work Projects Administration and the National Youth Administration while they were still in high school. Even today, I describe my politics as "Franklin D. Roosevelt liberalism."

So, in 1969, I went to Cleveland. I had always been involved in liberal issues. I had hoped for and worked for a racially integrated society, and I was strongly sympathetic to the civil rights movement. I was and am deeply devoted to our country, but I did not believe America as a nation had solved all its problems or achieved all its important objectives. Stokes's election had been of huge importance to large segments of the black and liberal communities, and I felt deeply honored to be part of his administration.

INHERITING A STAFF

I arrived in Cleveland with great enthusiasm, but I knew that enthusiasm alone would not be enough to run a decent planning program. A director needs more than that. I would need a first-rate staff, and I wondered what kind of staff I had inherited. I knew there were thirty-two employees on the payroll, but I had no indication of how qualified they were except for copies of their resumes and assignments that I had requested and some hearsay from local observers. As it turned out, the group I inherited was a mixed bag.

There were a few enormously competent veterans on the staff in the persons of Layton Washburn, John Wilkes, and Rosetta Boyd. They had been with the commission for decades, were overworked, and were not given the recognition they deserved. They produced solid, professional work that I learned I could depend upon, and they also provided an invaluable institutional memory and an entree to the network of their friends and associates throughout City Hall. Wilkes ran the zoning section in a way that was reassuring to City Council and the Planning Commission. His handling of zoning was professional and smoothly routine. By creating a problem-free environment for processing zoning cases, Wilkes provided space and time to devote to other matters.

Boyd, a secretary, became the able office manager. When her husband, James, was elected to City Council, Rosetta also became an invaluable liaison to that body. Washburn, in charge of current planning, had a special interest in parks and recreation. He had been with the City Planning Commission since the 1930s and had participated in the making of Cleveland's 1949 Land Use Plan. Washburn, in particular, was a most valued associate in much of the work we were to undertake in the next ten years.

The rest of the staff I inherited reflected the up-and-down fortunes of a planning agency surviving within big city politics.

During the decade of the 1960s, the planning function in Cleveland was in virtual eclipse. When Jim Lister was planning director in the 1950s, the City Planning Commission was, in fact, the city's urban renewal agency. Layton Washburn recalled that Lister had enjoyed the status of a top advisor to Mayor Anthony Celebrezze (1953–1962). Lister's prestige rubbed off on his planners, who were given great respect and cooperation in City Hall. When he left in 1957 to become director of the new Department of Urban Renewal and Housing, his prestige (and some of his staff) left the City Planning Commission with him.

Although fifteen staff members had professional job descriptions, only two had a master's degree in city planning or a related field. No one knew much about the computer work or sophisticated analytical techniques that were then coming into their own in the planning field. Some had problems expressing themselves verbally or in written form; some had difficulty working out math procedures; some with supervisory responsibility had difficulty providing leadership; some were poorly trained; and most were locked into their jobs by civil service rules.

The planners I inherited were working on a great variety of projects. Several were collecting real property and social and economic data for various districts of the city in order to prepare redevelopment plans for these areas. In some cases, these district studies were years old because there was really no "client" for their work. That is to say, there was no person or group in the city that was particularly interested in either the planning process or the plans themselves. Nonetheless, despite this vacuum, this group did site plans, site studies, and neighborhood plans, as well as site plan reviews for the few new development proposals that came before the commission.

Some planners were assigned as liaison people with other planning agencies around town. Others prepared the city's capital improvement program, a responsibility mandated by the city's charter. Some served on the team that evaluated and criticized the project plans of the Department of Community Development—a sharp comedown from the early 1950s, when the planners directly prepared and helped implement their own urban renewal plans. The commission also met federal requirements for public notification and hearings on all urban renewal plans, and rubber-stamped its approval of them. According to Ernie Bohn, former chairman of the City Planning Commission, rubber stamping was all the planning staff could do at that time, since it lacked the resources needed to contribute to the actual planning process or to make a critical analysis of the proposals.

Members of the planning staff were under no illusions. They seemed depressed at their agency's loss of status and authority, but at the same time they were resigned to that reality. A few planners on the staff seemed to be merely putting in their time until retirement.

The director who preceded me, Eric Grubb, was a competent planner who may have been traumatized by the high level of political activity in Cleveland, the difficulty of following in the footsteps of Jim Lister, who was the "fair-haired boy of planning" in the 1950s, and the failure of his first major planning effort. Grubb's first plan for Cleveland, the carefully prepared *Downtown Cleveland: 1975 Plan,* was presented with great fanfare in 1959, but was overshadowed completely only two years later by the *Erieview Urban Renewal Plan.* Although the *Downtown Cleveland* plan had been prepared by John T. Howard, Edmund N. Bacon, planning director of Philadelphia, Walter H. Blucher, and other planning luminaries, it did not generate any local commitment and was quickly shelved. Ironically, the 1959 plan highlighted Public Square and the waterfront; after decades of neglect, current planning in Cleveland is focused on the same two points.

Erieview, by contrast, was hailed at its inception in 1961 as the "most ambitious project so far undertaken under the federal urban renewal program." Designed by I. M. Pei for the Department of Community Development, it called for new office buildings, luxury apartments, malls, and fountains at a cost of $45.5 million, two-thirds of which was to come from federal subsidy. While land was being cleared for the *Erieview* plan (which shifted the center of gravity away from Euclid Avenue, the city's best shopping street, and Playhouse Square, an important office/entertainment area), all attention was focused on the community development staff. Meanwhile, the City Planning Commission's plan for downtown, which emphasized Euclid Avenue, was ignored, and the planners languished. Relations between the planners and the Community Development Department—two sister agencies—were virtually nonexistent.

It was said that Eric Grubb had been disheartened not so much by the rejection of his plan for downtown as by Mayor Celebrezze's enthusiastic sponsorship of *Erieview* while the City Planning Commission's plan was still brand new. Grubb, a dignified, shy man, reacted defensively. Staff members recall that Grubb took to avoiding the second floor of City Hall (where the offices of City Council and the mayor were located), coming in late, eating a solitary brown-bag lunch in his car, and leaving early for his rural home in order to avoid the rush hour. The impact on the staff, as recalled by one staff member, was devastating: low morale, widespread absenteeism, and agency drift.

I was determined to avoid that fate. I thought there were at least two ways to do this. First, I had to make planning, myself, and my staff all visible. Whereas my predecessor avoided the mayor and Council, I almost immediately became a regular at Mayor Stokes's cabinet meetings. I had not been invited to attend these meetings; nor was I disinvited. I simply attended, introduced myself, and began participating along with the other directors. No one expected this kind of behavior from a planning director, but they welcomed it! I was immediately accepted; in no time, I was getting information and assuming roles and assignments arising from the cabinet meetings.

The second way to develop planning influence where none existed was to recruit a competent staff and pay attention, not only to their prompt, capable action on the immediate issues at hand, but to the staff's visibility around town and to its reputation for high-quality and timely work. I hoped the deal I had worked out with Mayor Stokes would help me accomplish this.

One of the commitments I had gotten from Mayor Stokes before agreeing to come to Cleveland was a promise to allow me to fill six new slots on the City Planning Commission staff with people of my own choosing. But the city's civil service requirements seemed both to limit my choices and to stretch out the time involved in the hiring process.

Before we could hire anyone, according to the rules, the civil service staff and I would have to agree on the qualifications for each new employee; then civil service would have to publish the opening and the qualifications, develop a list of applicants, and announce, administer, and grade examinations. City residents, veterans, and city employees with seniority would be given bonus points. Applicants who scored lower than they had expected to would be allowed to appeal. At the end of the testing, weighting, and appeals process, the appointing authority—I, in this case—would be allowed to make a choice from the three applicants scoring highest on the weighted test. Given the rules, a high school graduate who lived in the city and had fifteen years of City Hall seniority could easily beat out a well-educated planner new to the city but with great promise. I was deeply fearful that these civil service procedures would make it impossible to staff the planning agency with the kind of well-trained, well-motivated new people that I wanted. If we let the civil service rules dictate who the new planners would be, we might not be able to improve the quality of the staff at all. My discussions with the civil service staff confirmed my worst fears: if we hired within existing job classifications, we would be bound by the letter of the regulations.

I had no wish to skirt the civil service commission or its regulations; I just wanted to hire the best staff I could find. After much deliberation, we decided to drop the traditional classifications for planners and establish new job classifications, such as "project director," for which no applicant list or salary band was available. Or we hired the person we wanted as a "temporary" employee, since such applicants were not subject to the rigid screening of "permanent" employees. Of course, the "temporary" employees lacked the job security awarded to the "permanents," but none of the people we were looking for were likely to be interested in doing a full thirty-year tour of duty in Cleveland City Hall. We wanted people who were caring, well-trained, bright, and eager to work very hard on serious issues. Since they were going to be used in many different roles, their talents would probably be marketable in any city in the country.

Our hiring strategy worked well. The system's informal flexibility gave us all the maneuverability we needed with regard to new personnel appointments.

BUILDING A NEW STAFF

The first person hired, an incredible find, was central to most of what happened for the next few years. Ernie Bonner was a planner with an economics background whose career had taken him over some of the same ground as mine. Ernie had taken a master's degree in city planning at Cornell, worked at the Ithaca planning commission, and in the mid-1960s was in Pittsburgh pursuing his Ph.D. in economics at the University of Pittsburgh when I was with the Pittsburgh City Planning Commission. We met in Pittsburgh and became fast friends.

By 1969, Ernie was teaching planning and urban economics at the University of Wisconsin in Madison. He had decided to leave the university and was considering an offer to work for the United Nations in Valpariso, Chile, when I asked him to come to Cleveland and help me work for Carl Stokes. Ernie found the offer full of possibilities. He came and immediately took hold of essential and broad responsibilities.

Ernie, bearded, wiry, and immensely thoughtful, had been deeply moved by the civil rights and antiwar movements of the 1960s and was seriously committed to change that would produce more choice and opportunity for all Americans, but particularly for those people in our society who had few, if any, choices. He thought city planning could play a role in nudging our society in a more progressive direction. I agreed and encouraged him to run as fast and as far as he could with his ideas.

Bonner, often clad in bell-bottomed trousers and sandals with his pack of cigarettes twisted into the short sleeve of his T-shirt, became a familiar figure in the corridors of Cleveland City Hall. Among the three-piece polyester suits with white patent-leather belts affected by many of his fellow bureaucrats, he was unique, a hippie peacock among crows. His liberal, redistributionist ideas were carried to other city departments, where they attracted the interest of other liberals who had come to Cleveland to work for Stokes. That helped improve the visibility of the planning agency as well as recruit allies with whom we could work on many issues.

Bonner had excellent connections with many university professors of planning. We used these to help recruit the first five or six new members of the planning staff, a few of whom were his former students. Bonner also helped conceptualize the framework for the *Cleveland Policy Planning Report* and, in the process, helped establish the format and mind-set of the agency.

As chief of the new comprehensive planning division, Ernie helped set up and guide the staff in preparing housing, transportation, and employment and income studies, some of which were unique among planning agencies. For example, because we felt it would be crucial to Cleveland's unemployed and underemployed, we analyzed President Richard Nixon's proposed Family Assistance Program. When, after analysis, we concluded that its effects would be favorable, we persuaded the mayor and others to support the bill. To a certain degree, Bonner became Mr. Inside to my Mr. Outside. While I faced "upward and outward," maintaining relationships with the mayor, cabinet members, the city council, planning bureaucracies such as the American Planning Association and the Northeast Ohio Areawide Coordinating Agency (NOACA), the media, and some of the mayor's voting constituency, Bonner looked "inward and downward," developing the work program, relating to City Hall agencies, and managing the staff on a day-to-day basis in the execution of plans, policies, and programs. Both of us, usually working together with a few of the newly hired planners, established the new staff's work program by cooperatively deciding what we had to do, what we wanted to do, and who should do it.

We also complemented each other in terms of style. We tried to be available to anyone who wanted to talk to us; we were both very informal and flexible, preferring meetings and group decision making to top-down directives. Both of us preferred to assign work to those who volunteered and to monitor the progress of assigned work gently and infrequently. The professional drive on the part of our new recruits was usually enough to produce excellent and timely material. This informal, group-based decision structure probably stood in stark contrast to the bureaucratic chain of command of most large planning agencies, but it worked very well for us.

Bonner also had the notion (which I came to share later) that our work in Cleveland might help reform the entire planning profession and move it in the direction of greater concern for equity. Accordingly, we wrote papers for professional conferences as well as five or six speeches for Mayor Stokes, who was in great demand nationally as a speaker. When the word got out that we were drafting speeches for the mayor, our stock in City Hall went up sharply. The speech that we wrote for Mayor Stokes to deliver at the 1971 convention of the American Society of Planning Officials in New Orleans, "On Reordering the Priorities of the Planning Profession," sums up our point of view:

A great part of this urban crisis centers on such questions as the redistribution of income and services, yet how many institutions can you name which have as an important goal the redress of grievances among the powerless and disenfranchised? How many take a strong advocacy stance in favor of the poor? How many pursue a more equitable distribution of the wealth and power in our society in the simple name of justice? In fact, few institutions—if any—do, and this lack of purpose almost assures a lack of attention to the poor and powerless.

The goals of most city plans clearly indicate this lack of focus and concern. Rarely do they challenge the present distribution of the rewards in our society. Rather, planning goals are based on accepted notions of "efficiency" and "objectivity" organized around concepts of land use. Since planners have assumed that they have no legitimate responsibility to direct the goals of their efforts in any egalitarian sense, planning activity has, at best, maintained the status quo and, at worst, contributed to the "crisis." . . .

It seems to me that the name of the planning game (and the political game, as well) must be to ensure that the rewards of our society are more equally allocated and shared.

Bonner remained with the Cleveland City Planning Commission until the fall of 1973, when he left to become planning director in Portland, Oregon. At this writing, he is in charge of energy conservation for the Bonneville Power Company in Portland, where he maintains an active interest in regional planning.

One of the first new people Bonner helped recruit for the staff was Janice Cogger. She was one of his star pupils at the University of Wisconsin at Madison and had another master's degree in public administration to go with her master's in city planning. In many ways Cogger was the most thoughtful and caring of the new planners we hired. She believed, quite simply, that she could by her work make things better for people. It was, she said, part of her psychic baggage. She was also immensely talented and was emotionally outraged that many people in our society never win and others never lose; and that the benefits of many public programs almost inevitably, it seemed, flowed away from those who needed help (and in whose behalf the programs were ostensibly initiated) and toward those who lacked nothing. Besides grinding her teeth in frustration, Cogger used her substantial skills in policy analysis to try to redress some of the imbalances in our system.

As was true for many of the new planners, Cogger's assignments were all over the place. She revised our approach to capital improvement programming and was the indispensable analyst in several important negotiations, including lease arrangements with the Cleveland Browns for the Cleveland Memorial Stadium, as well as the Port Authority and Regional Transit Authority (RTA) negotiations (Chapter 8). Cogger also pulled together all the elements for, and then wrote, the *Cleveland Policy Planning Report*, and was the joint or sole author of a large number of speeches and professional papers. Later, she and another new planner, Joanne Lazarz, led the planning staff into deep but welcome involvement in support of Cleveland's emerging neighborhood movement. Early on, for example, both served on the board of the Buckeye–Woodland Community Congress, the first of Cleveland's neighborhood-based advocacy organizations.

Cogger was immensely frustrated by the juxtaposition of

Cleveland's rich and poor, the concerns of elitists who commented on Cleveland's problems and the concerns of those residents who actually suffered from them. In a major paper for the University of Wisconsin, she compared the two worlds of Cleveland by printing back-to-back a letter to Mayor Perk from a Cleveland resident trapped in an inner-city neighborhood and a column on downtown development by the editor and publisher of the Cleveland *Plain Dealer*.

The resident wrote of the "violence, deterioration and filth" in her neighborhood, and asked the mayor to find the thief who burglarized and burned her home and knifed her son. The *Plain Dealer* editor, in contrast, discoursed about the project manager for a downtown development plan, "who looks like a movie version of a man from San Francisco. He wears turtle necks, blue jeans, soft shoes, and a mod sort of wide Indian belt; has a beard and gets in to see everyone about everything." Cogger felt that the needs of Cleveland's people and neighborhoods were urgent and pressing, but the leadership of the city seemed unable to look beyond downtown.

Two other early recruits were John Linner and Douglas Wright. They were newly minted graduates of the master's program in city and regional planning at the University of Iowa. Both were young, smart, and empathetic toward the human dimension in city planning, interested in the incidence of costs and benefits arising from public policy, and convinced of the need for and the realistic possibility of change. Both were excellent writers, an essential talent for a city planner. Ernie Bonner put them to work on housing, community development, and transportation issues. Together, Wright and Linner wrote the "Cleveland Housing Papers," a collection of studies that began the long process that ended in a change in the state law on tax delinquency, foreclosure, and land banking (Chapter 7). Later, when he was working on our annual capital improvement program, Wright's research into the capital needs of the Municipal Electric Light Plant led to our controversial proposal to expropriate the Cleveland Electric Illuminating Company (CEI), the local investor-owned utility in the Cleveland region, and use its production and distribution capacity to expand Muny's public power system (Chapter 12).

Unlike Bonner, Cogger, and me, neither Linner nor Wright believed in the need for a fundamental redistribution of money and power in the United States. They did agree, however, that imbalances and inequities existed, and they were eager to explore approaches to correcting these conditions. They also believed that certain common ideas in American urban public policy should be resisted because they were just plain dumb. Linner, for example, opposed a proposal for a new $1.2 billion long-distance rail system in the Cleveland region, not only because it took away from the transit needs of the transit-dependent, as Cogger and I believed, but also because it was stupid to squander transit dollars that should be spent in more cost-effective ways.

Later, John Linner wrote in response to one of my articles: "I think you place too much emphasis on egalitarian, redistributive stuff. . . . Making cities better and alleviating the suffering of the poor is not simply a matter of taking from some and giving to others. . . . Making cities better can also be viewed as making better use of the human and physical resources that are there. Perhaps this is posing the issue as one of efficiency rather than one of equity, but it's a point of view that does not ignore the problems of the poor."

Wright commented on the same article that "the most novel aspect of our whole operation in Cleveland was that we actually tried to do something concrete—fixing houses faster, improving transit service, getting the parks to someone who could do a better job with them."

In the next few years we added Ken Bounds, John Claypool, Barbara Clint, John Finke, Susan Hoffmann, Susan Kaeser, Earl Landau, Joanne Lazarz, Craig Miller, Mary Niebling, Ruth O'Leary, Susan Olson, Don Plaskett, Bill Resseger, Mindy Turbov, Bill Whitney, and John Wilbur to the planning staff—a truly outstanding group of planners. This nucleus of planners really helped shape the policies and programs of the commission, since I depended on them to review and respond to my ideas and to develop much of their own work programs as well.

Today, in 1990, most of these professional planners continue their involvement with planning at responsible levels. Janice Cogger is director of a neighborhood community development corporation in Cleveland; John Linner is director of economic development for the city of Toledo; Doug Wright is a consultant in San Francisco, after a stint as special advisor to the secretary of the Department of Transportation; Ken Bounds is with the mayor's office in Seattle; John Claypool is director of the Philadelphia First Corporation; Barbara Clint manages complex development projects for Cleveland nonprofit agencies; John Finke is western director for the National Development Council; Susan Hoffmann is teaching at a community college in Iowa; Susan Kaesar, Ruth O'Leary, and Susan Olson are working as planning consultants while raising their families; Earl Landau works in the Cuyahoga County Welfare Department; Joanne Lazarz is a planner with the Wisconsin Department of Transportation; Craig Miller is the law director for the city of Cleveland; Mary Niebling is with the Massachusetts Department of Development; Don Plaskett is a special assistant to Cleveland's mayor; Bill Resseger is special assistant to the director of the Department of Community Development in Cleveland; Mindy Turbov is project manager for a national housing developer; Bill Whitney is deputy director of the Ohio Community Development Division; and John Wilbur is coordinator of community affairs for the East Ohio Gas Company.

We did not have to advertise the positions as they opened up on the staff. Ernie and I simply got in touch with friends whose judgment we trusted at various universities and asked them to recommend students who might fit into the program we were developing. The system worked so well that in the ten years of my tenure as city planning director, a period in which I hired more than thirty city planners, I never had cause to regret a single appointment.

Those who applied for the jobs we offered were an interesting group. They were well-trained, talented, and, for the most part, personally unattached. They were not interested in high pay, which was fortunate, since most of the jobs paid salaries of $12,000 to $15,000 (in the early 1970s). And they were not interested in amenities, which was also fortunate, since Cleveland lacked the sunshine, surf, or flashing nightlife of New York, Boston, San Francisco, and other cities favored by the young and unattached. They were interested in working on issues that were relevant to human needs, within a context where their idealism was encouraged.

These planners confirmed in me the notion that city planning students were substantially more idealistic than students in, say, business or law schools. This should not be misunderstood; planning students, like other students, want jobs when they finish their schooling, and they want reasonable salaries and status. But many planning students also want to make things better in our society and are willing to address market failures in land use, the environment, and social justice in order to make things better. In a word, planning students want to do good as well as to do well. It is precisely this appetite for reform that is objected to by those who raise the flag against planning in our society. And it is precisely this taste for reform that those of us who teach or hire planners must try to protect and nurture.

It seemed that much of what I did for the next few years had to do with encouraging these bright young people to come to Cleveland, encouraging them to devote themselves to some portion of our work program, and protecting them from distractions and the larger, destructive political forces at work in the city.

Encouragement included interdepartmental praise and praise from the mayor when I could arrange it. Staff members were encouraged to talk to local reporters and become visible in the media. This is probably different from procedures in other planning agencies, where reporters are encouraged to talk only to the director. I had confidence, however, that my staff and I saw the world in the same way and would give reporters about the same perspective. It was also important, I thought, to give staff members the recognition they deserved as serious professionals. When outstanding studies or reports were completed, staff members were urged to publish articles in professional journals on the findings. Reports were also sent to relevant state and federal agencies, and on two occasions HUD secretary James Lynn sent messages of congratulation to the analysts. At the same time, I tried to protect the staff from "macing" (i.e., frequent demands for political contributions) and from straight-out political assignments, such as circulating leaflets for a campaign. I was not totally successful. When Bill Whitney and Susan Kaeser showed up from Wisconsin for their first day of work in 1973, I told them they would have to register as Republicans before they could be put on the payroll. This did not make me happy, and it made them even less so, but they swallowed hard and went off to Republican headquarters.

There were two areas where I felt I had to caution some of my staff: one was a matter of style, one a matter of perception. Frequently, planners with advanced degrees find that they are unique in the bureaucracy of central city government. Their educations may be substantially superior to those of most other civil servants, and most politicians as well. This was certainly the case in Cleveland in the 1970s, when Ph.D.s were virtually nonexistent and holders of master's degrees numbered fewer than 200 out of a work force of 11,000. Given their education, new recruits may be tempted to answer questions promptly, clearly, and in great detail. I think this is an error because it may convey signs of arrogance and disrespect for fellow civil servants and political leaders. This does not mean that better-educated planners should talk down to politicians and other civil servants; it means that they should try to temper their pace and style with respect for seniority and the legitimacy of the electoral process.

Fortunately, most of the new planners understood that, and in Ernie Bonner we had a superb technician who could, when the moment required, fall easily into the language of the street. When Ernie made a comprehensive presentation and a member of the audience asked a question that made it clear he hadn't understood a thing, Ernie's response was: "You've got it perfectly, only a little off," and then he would patiently explain it all over again. That was the style that seemed to work best.

Perception was also a problem for a few of the new planners. When Ralph J. Perk replaced Carl B. Stokes as mayor in 1971, some of the new people despaired. Perk, they said, was "Republican" and "conservative." On probing, they concluded that nobody was just a set of labels. I asked them to probe further, and they prepared a more encouraging capsule of the new mayor's background. Perk's thumbnail sketch showed him to be a Cleveland-raised high school graduate, a second-generation American of Czech ancestry, a self-employed iceman during the Great Depression who knew the discipline of poverty, a successful city and county politician who emphasized in his campaigns his concerns for the "little people." Perk was also the father of a large family and the long-time owner-occupant of a modest, wooden-frame house on E. 49th St. about four hundred yards from the noise, grime, and smells of Interstate 77 and the Industrial Flats. Although Perk was a "Republican," he had built his career on issues like saving Muny Light, low taxes, and opposition to industrial air pollution—issues that were not popular with the party leadership. In short, Perk might be (and proved to be) supportive of many of our arguments. We tried not to buy labels, but to know as much as possible about the backgrounds of the key people we had to deal with.

Although Mayors Stokes and Perk had similar poor and working-class backgrounds, our ability to survive the change from one administration to the other was probably aided by our work in "Operation Snow-Bird," an effort to become usefully visible to Perk early in his mayoralty. Snow removal is an important and annually recurring issue in Cleveland politics; mayors are frequently chastised for their lack of response to major snowfalls. Mayor Perk was inaugurated in the second week of November 1971, and I suggested to him before his first press conference that, if the snow removal issue came up, he should respond by saying that he would have a plan within the week. We had no plan at all, but Bonner and Wright were sure we could put one together in a hurry. Sure enough, the subject came up at the press conference, and Perk responded as we suggested. We got to work immediately.

The plan we prepared was done with the assistance of Joe Stamps, Commissioner of the Service Department, who had responsibility for snow removal. It was built around a simple probability model. As the prevailing pattern of winds brought snow closer and closer to the city, that information would be reported to local checkpoints, and more and more street-salting and snow-removal equipment would be activated. At a 90 percent probability of snow, the entire snow-removal fleet would be on duty.

We laid this concept out in four days and supported it with large-scale, simple graphics that we knew would photograph and televise well. Mayor Perk, well briefed, called his press conference and outlined the procedures in his snow-removal plan. The media were impressed. Perk had identified himself as a leader who was on top of the issues of the day and able to respond rapidly. He may have realized for the first time (since we were previously unknown to him) that his planners could be prompt and useful in more than zoning and land-use matters.

Some of the members of this new core staff grew very close to one another, and I grew to be personally fond of them, as well as professionally appreciative of their work. For many years, I would pick up three or four staff members in my city-assigned car—an old police cruiser with the shotgun rack still in place—

and we would discuss the issues of the day on our way to work. This "committee on wheels" was more productive of ideas than any other committee I can recall. When any of us gave a party, the others were sure to be there, along with a sprinkling of other agency personnel from City Hall. It was a time of hard work, almost total absorption in the job, and great camaraderie.

The camaraderie among the new staff members also had a down side that I tried to minimize but could not overcome. It was the isolation from the "old" staff, the staff I had inherited. We were conscious of the problem and worried by it and made efforts to bridge the gap. Once-a-week staff meetings included everyone; assignments in "new" studies and analyses were offered to "old" staff members; new recruits gave classes on the latest in mathematical and measuring techniques and the uses of census data. Nothing worked very well.

The efforts designed to draw the inherited staff into the evolving new work program proved to be disappointing. With the exception of Layton Washburn and Rosetta Boyd, both of whom proved to be marvelously flexible and extraordinarily valuable, the inherited staff was left to do pretty much what it had been doing before I arrived.

Although attitudes were generally cordial, there was some occasional resentment expressed by "older" staffers that the new group was at the center of the action while they were on the periphery. The division between "old" and "new" groups continued in muted fashion during my entire decade in Cleveland City Hall.

How did the recruited staff and director work together so well? After all, there are probably few planning agencies where directors and staff like each other to the point that they socialize together. I think the camaraderie was based on three factors. First, there was the exhilarating feeling of being a member of a small, committed group involved in a unique experience, mapping new ground in planning practice. Second, the open interaction among members of this group reinforced *esprit de corps*. Frequent meetings with wide-open participation encouraged everyone to believe that his or her ideas would be listened to and might be adopted; staff members were rarely ordered to undertake assignments that they disliked; they were not only allowed but encouraged to express openly their views on those things in public life that they found distasteful; people were treated as mature professionals, not merely junior bureaucrats.

Third, all the members of the group were new to Cleveland and lacked the strong, local friendships that normally accompany long residence in a place. Joined by similar backgrounds, interests, and values, we naturally turned toward each other as we began to develop our local social contacts.

3

Writing the Policy Planning Report

Like most city planners, I considered my most important professional assignment to be the preparation of a current General Land Use Plan. As I learned in graduate school, the preparation and publication of a general plan and the land-use regulations and capital improvement programs necessary to implement the plan were the most important products of the planning agency. Planners traditionally assumed that every piece of land in the city had intrinsic value, and that pressures for new development were strong and required regulation in the public interest. Public and private development decisions were powerfully influenced by the plan. When I arrived in Cleveland, the city's plan was twenty years old, and a new plan or an extensive updating of the old plan seemed in order.

But as Bonner, Cogger, Wright, and I familiarized ourselves with the city and its people, we began to think that the accomplishment of this traditional planning task would be irrelevant because (1) there was little demand for land or new development; (2) in most of the city's residential neighborhoods, property was being disinvested and abandoned; (3) only in downtown Cleveland was there interest in new construction, and that was only in the development of new public and private office space. The problems of the city seemed to hinge, not on land use or zoning, but on general municipal decline, public and private poverty, the many effects of racial discrimination, unemployment, crime, the declining quality of public institutions, and similar issues. These did not seem susceptible to treatment by the traditional tools of city planning: land-use planning, zoning, urban design, and capital improvement programming. But having perceived this did not tell us what to do.

We looked to each other for ideas and hoped for directions from our political and professional environment too.

We turned first to the City Planning Commission. The commission was made up of seven members, six appointed by the mayor with the consent of City Council, and one councilmember appointed by the Council president. Most commission members were civic leaders who served on a volunteer, part-time basis. The commission hired the director and provided general guidance to the staff. On inquiry, we found that the individual commission members had lots of ideas on high-priority work assignments, but nothing that made much sense to us. One commission member wanted the staff to rewrite the city's forty-year-old zoning ordinance, although that ordinance seemed to have little to do with the political and commercial basis on which City Council actually made zoning decisions. Another suggested studies of off-street parking and street furniture in the downtown area; a third thought that a comprehensive study aimed at straightening out Cleveland's winding Cuyahoga River (which divides the city's east and west sides) would help straighten out the city's many problems as well. The staff and I were not convinced that any of these efforts would prove particularly useful, and since the commission members were not insistent that their suggestions be followed, we considered but did not act on them.

The mayor's office gave us little direction. Mayor Stokes and his top aides had their hands full. Stokes was trying to get control of the Police Department, and compared with that effort, a work program for the planning agency wasn't even a blip on his radar screen. Before my arrival, he had used his planners very sparingly. He regarded them as did most Cleveland politicians—as technical functionaries half in and half out of city government who handled zoning and land-use matters exclusively. Few politicians in Cleveland perceived planners as useful specialists with powerful analytical techniques and a comprehensive overview. If they thought about it at all, they would have denied that planners held a more rational or comprehensive view of the city's needs or the public interest than they themselves had. The mayor and Council members could and did respond to individual issues that were presented to them by the planners, but they rarely gave their planners clear instructions during the early stages of an issue. Rather, they took a more prudent position; it was unwise for an elected official to say anything at all during the early life of an idea. This attitude frequently left planners with nowhere to look for leadership. It did, however, offer us great opportunities to educate the city's political leaders in the years to come.

We turned to the city charter and found it not particularly helpful. The charter directed the Planning Commission to prepare a long-range land-use plan, to publicize it, to advise the mayor and council on zoning changes, and to review capital improvement requests from other city agencies with respect to their possible impact on the land-use plan. But Cleveland's long-range land-use plan had been prepared in 1949. Like most such plans, it had called for modest growth, but it had been overwhelmed by the bitter reality of decline. Until the causes of decline could be addressed, a new master plan to control growth seemed inappropriate.

My new staff members and I had to turn to each other, the moral foundations of U.S. society and the planning profession, and the realities of life in Cleveland to guide our work. We agreed that we would not undertake a new traditional land-use plan. But if we were not to produce a new land-use plan for Cleveland to guide our work and the day-to-day decisions of the Planning Commission, what would guide our activities? What would be our new statement of purpose?

We decided that a new type of plan—a policies plan— might be the answer. The plan would be based on an overarching goal that would fit the needs of the city and its people. Since planning is about the future as well as the present—about ends as well as means—the picture of the future we would try to paint would be that of a more equitable society rather than a new arrangement of land uses. Our goal would provide direction to the City Planning Commission and ourselves and would also provide a rationale for all the objectives, policies, and programs we would support. We would make no pretense of having developed a full list of objectives or a comprehensive set of policies. When we had decided on a dominant goal, we would publish our ideas, the justification for them, and samples of our work, as a progress report. We would not wait until we had a written document in hand, nor would we defer action until all conceivable program options and interdependencies had been considered. Rather, we would try to pursue policy formulation, program development, and program implementation simultaneously and continuously, as the real world demanded, because public decision making rarely waits for the completion of detailed, "comprehensive" plans. It takes place as a continuous process. We wanted to be prepared to intervene with analyses and recommendations in a timely fashion when decisions were being made.

Bonner, Cogger, Wright, and I argued about whether to write anything down at all, at least in the form of a report or plan of some kind. (While Layton Washburn from the staff, Allen Fonoroff from the commission, and other interested parties contributed comments and ideas from time to time, the early discussions and drafts of the *Policy Planning Report* were undertaken by Bonner, Cogger, Wright, and me, with Cogger writing the final report.) The four of us shared a similar view of the world, after all, and of our responsibilities; we felt we needed no formal document to guide us in the execution of these responsibilities. Yet Bonner and I argued that a report should be written, not necessarily for us, but to guide local decision-makers and encourage other practicing planners elsewhere and possibly convince them that they, like us, could not only care about the problems confronting inner-city residents but do something about those problems. Cogger disagreed. "Those who already agree with the message," she said, "will read and applaud. Those who are pursuing other courses will ignore it." Ultimately, we decided that a report should be written, mostly for other planners who might be considering their own models of redistributive justice.

POINTS FOR DISCUSSION

The heated discussions around what came to be titled *The Cleveland Policy Planning Report* continued. They took place mostly in a large, attic-like space on the sixth floor of City Hall that we had cleaned up and renamed "The Penthouse." We worked among the huge air-return ducts that we had painted in bright colors only a few weeks before and the "sculpture gardens" we had designed and assembled. The meetings lasted a few hours each day for about six months, in snatches of time the participants could spare from their other tasks. At the same time, Cogger, for example, was working on a major format revision of the city's capital improvement program, and Wright was beginning a series of housing studies. We held these discussions under uncomfortable conditions. The buzzing of the overhead fluorescent lights was very distracting. We had nothing in the planning literature to use as a guide. But little by little, with Bonner and Wright smoking their pipes or fiddling with them and Cogger's knitting needles clacking away, progress was being made.

We explored philosophical and strategic questions, each with their own practical implications. We asked, for example, questions like these:

- City planning is often defined as a set of activities concerned with the use of land. How could we redefine it so that planning could be of maximum utility to the poor and working-class residents of the city whom we were anxious to serve?
- Neither the mayor, the Council, nor the City Planning Commission was asking for a new approach to city planning. What gave us the right to choose our own goals and objectives? Did our legitimacy flow from the planning profession, or its statement of proper ethical behavior? From the broader Judeo-Christian tradition? How could we justify aid to those in need?
- In wanting to serve the poor, how could we identify and work with our clients? Would they share our goals? Should we try to serve the broader, unorganized poor, or just organized neighborhood organizations as if they were surrogates for the poor?
- How could we arrange our efforts so we would not be seen as outside manipulators, unresponsive to community needs and desires?
- How could we broaden the short-term concerns of the average citizen to include the larger issues we thought fundamental to achieving real change in our society? Bonner, Cogger, and I thought, for instance, that income redistribution and devolution of power were good ideas but ones unlikely to appeal to the man in the street. In the same way, supporting a neighborhood organization in a fight against a freeway was one thing, but encouraging the organization to question the whole biased transportation planning process was quite another.
- Suppose our efforts to help Cleveland's poor and working-class population were successful beyond our wildest dreams; would that prompt other, better-off Cleveland residents to leave the city? Would it encourage potential investors in the city not to invest? Would that be good for the city or the poor?

Besides the philosophical and strategic aspects of the discussion, personal matters were discussed as well. So long as city planners have acted as advocates for real estate and other business interests, planners have enjoyed broad support. But we were speaking of advocating the interests of the poor and working people of the city. No matter how rational our position was, it was sure to be controversial. Would we be able to hold our jobs? Most of the new professionals who were joining the staff were very well trained and single or newly married with no children. They were traveling light, and if they lost their jobs in Cleveland, they would have little difficulty finding good jobs elsewhere. By contrast, I had a wife and three small children in school. Years before, my wife, Virginia, had agreed that I would give up my small travel, carpeting, and advertising businesses and go back to graduate school, and I had done so. I had deeply enjoyed my two years of graduate work at Cornell, but those years had been very difficult for her, making do for our family with practically no income. Now that I was director of city planning and earning a good salary, I was not about to take any big risks without her concurrence. I wanted her approval before I launched off on a new approach to my job that might be chancy as well as difficult. Virginia not only agreed but provided me with additional strength when things in City Hall got particularly intense. If she had been less willing to live under pressure-filled conditions, I might not have been able to stake out some of the controversial positions I adopted over the next ten years.

After six months of heated and often frustrating discussion among the four of us—frustrating because we could find no paths in planning practice or literature to follow—the framework of the *Policy Planning Report* became clear. During the formulation of our ideas, we stayed in close touch with the City Planning Commission, ever mindful that without the commission's support, we would be skating on thin ice with the day warming rapidly. Over the four years from the conception of the idea to the publication of the *Report*, there had been considerable turnover on the commission, with a total of fourteen members serving on the seven-member board. During that entire time, a solid majority of the commission was not only agreeable to what we were trying to do but enthusiastic about it.

Allen Fonoroff, a professor of planning at Case Western Reserve University and one of the commission members instrumental in bringing me to Cleveland, saw the logic of our approach and its broader applicability within the planning profession. His support was steady and unconditional. Robert D. Storey, a black attorney, saw in our work a humane commitment to the poor and working classes who lived in the city, as did Bishop William Cosgrove, who was closely identified with the Commission on Catholic Community Action of the Cleveland diocese. Wallace G. Teare, a distinguished local architect who had been designing important Cleveland buildings and public housing projects all his life, was intrigued with the intellectual logic of our reasoning. Members of the commission were always willing to meet and, within limits, join us in the discussion, asking many sharp questions along the way.

Interestingly enough, the commission chairman at the time of the actual publication of the *Policy Planning Report* was James B. Davis, charter member of the fight against the Clark Freeway (Chapter 5), Cleveland law director during the transit negotiations (Chapter 8), and the lawyer who filed the antitrust action against CEI (Chapter 12). (James B. Davis is not to be confused with James C. Davis of Squire, Sanders, & Dempsey and the Growth Association, who also appears in the cases that follow.) Davis was a self-proclaimed "right-wing Republican," a man of great rationality, honor, and personal probity and a man willing to take on foes as powerful as the private utility company. He was also Mayor Perk's long-time friend and personal lawyer. As a lawyer, he understood the lawyer–client relationship, and he believed that planners and other city officials should represent their city's resident population. Davis saw the planning commission staff as doing that and also serving as a unique policy and program development group with analytical skills that could provide useful information on alternative proposals quickly and accurately. To him, we were a great asset to the mayor's office. As he said in an interview with the authors in 1987, "The planning staff was one of the most skilled and useful outfits in City Hall. It could do lots of things quickly and well."

THE *CLEVELAND POLICY PLANNING REPORT*

The *Report* began to take shape as a series of papers written by each of us but ultimately pulled together by Janice Cogger. The argument for our *Report* began with our shared vision and goals:

- Individuals choose their own goals and the means to pursue those goals.
- Institutions are established to assist individuals in pursuit of their goals. In the process, institutions themselves establish goals—some of which are aimed at insuring their own survival.
- Nevertheless, those institutional goals which are self-serving must be clearly secondary to those which further the pursuit of individuals' goals.
- Individuals and institutions pursue their respective goals through decision and action. Decisions must be made from among those choices which the individual or institution perceives.
- Individuals are better off with more choices in any decision.
- Institutions serve individuals' goals most effectively when they provide a wider range of choices to individuals.
- In a context of limited resources, institutions should give priority attention to the task of promoting more choices for those individuals who have few, if any, choices.[1]

Thus, our logic directed the commission's efforts toward the accomplishment of one simply stated goal: equity requires that locally responsible government institutions give priority to the goal of promoting a wider range of choices for those Cleveland residents who have few.

Although Bonner, Cogger, Wright, and I felt that this statement reflected our purpose in a clear and concise way, we felt we had to elaborate it in the *Report*. Accordingly, we discussed five clarifying points.

First, we tried to make clear that the goal was to provide as wide a range of alternatives and opportunities as possible, leaving individuals free to define their own needs and priorities. We observed that government efforts to alleviate poverty often emphasized a "service strategy," which provided or subsidized the provision of particular goods and services. These often, unfortunately, failed to satisfy the needs of those whom they supposedly served. Low-income families had no choice but to accept benefits on the terms offered by the suppliers or forego all assistance. In the interest of maximizing choices, we

---

[1]Cleveland City Planning Commission, *Policy Planning Report* (Cleveland: CPC, 1975), p. 9.

made clear that we supported an expanded "income strategy." We would seek to provide individuals with the means and the opportunity to obtain those goods and services that they perceived as best fulfilling their needs.

Second, our goal called for a more equitable society, not for a more efficient political or economic system. We did *not* mind if policies serving the goal of equity also served the goal of efficiency; we *did* intend to underline our view that efficiency was not an end in itself, but a means to an end. The rationale for seeking more efficient collection and expenditure of public funds, for example, was to ensure maximum resources for the promotion of a more equitable society.

Third, the focus on institutions in our goal statement recognized the crucial role played by legal, political, economic, and social institutions in promoting and sustaining inequities. Changes in these institutions would need more than political rhetoric and good will; they would require actual alterations in the laws, customs, and practices of the institutions themselves. This would be difficult to do.

Fourth was a point upon which we placed the greatest emphasis. Our goal of achieving equity was to guide all of our efforts. It was to enable the commission and staff to identify those issues to which we would devote priority attention in our work program—issues involving equity. The goal would give clarity and power to the staff's analyses. In evaluating proposals that would come before the commission for review and comment, and in developing our own policy and program recommendations, the questions "Who pays?" and "Who benefits?" would be key elements in our analytical framework. In keeping with our goal, we would try to see that program benefits went to those most in need, and that those least able to pay would not bear a disproportionate share of the costs. When proposals submitted for our review indicated the opposite under analysis, we would redesign them, suggest alternatives, or oppose the proposals and lobby against them.

Finally, we recognized that our efforts to promote more choices for Cleveland residents who had few or none placed us in an advocacy position on behalf of people less favored by present conditions. They were obviously not the most powerful, nor often, would they be the most numerous. Our recommendations in their behalf would not be accepted in all cases. And our advocacy in their behalf was not intended to ignore or demean the interests of more favored individuals or groups. We did not intend to avoid conflicts of interests or ideas; they were to be understood, clearly articulated, and submitted to the relevant executive, legislative, or judicial body for resolution. Unlike most city planning agencies, we were clearly not just seeking consensus. We wanted to identify and clarify the often opposing interests of the more and the less favored and keep before decision-makers the probable consequences of inequitable decisions for the future of Cleveland. Under these circumstances, we knew it would be difficult to avoid conflict; we would have to be prepared to work through it. Ultimate consensus and the adoption of desirable policies would probably have to be forged out of conflict between various interests.

The planning agency's role would be to offer information, advice, and policy guidance to decision-makers, the press, and the public consistent with this framework. This would be true of the new policy studies and routine charter-delegated work of the staff.

Stating our position at long last was very satisfying to us. After six months of discussion, which seemed at times as if it would never end, we had a conceptual framework that justified the long meetings in the penthouse. By this time we had some examples of work that reflected the intent of our words. We also began to introduce our point of view to the documents of the city. For example, the *1972 Annual Report* states that

> city planning takes as its ultimate goal the challenge of promoting a more equitable allocation of society's benefits by helping to overcome obstacles to access and choice among those poorest and least powerful members of our society; and to accomplish this goal the commission functions as an agency for social and economic change.

Yet, while both our policy framework and our work program were shaping up, we knew that the bureaucratic and political environment of the city government was tightly constrained and unlikely to be easily receptive to our value-laden rhetoric. In anticipation of that day when we might have to defend ourselves, we sought strong arguments justifying our approach.

We justified the selection of our equity-oriented goal in three ways: by appeals to tradition, reason, and necessity. The commission, we stated, was not acting in an unusual or extraordinary way, but merely serving tradition by affirming what has been advocated consistently throughout history: that equity in the social, economic, and political relationships among people is a requisite condition for a just and lasting society. In support of our position we quoted selections from Plato and Jesus, Thomas Jefferson and Franklin D. Roosevelt and Cleveland's great reform mayor, Tom L. Johnson. We could just as easily have quoted all the Founding Fathers. I felt that these men— George Washington, Benjamin Franklin, James Madison, and the others—were genuine heroes whose clear and unambiguous message was one of freedom, liberty, and justice. Ours was not a bizarre position; it represented the deepest thinking and the strongest, most humane currents in the Judeo-Christian social, religious, and political discourse.

To justify our goal in contemporary terms, we applied the arguments of the American philosopher John Rawls, who argued that, in a just society, basic liberties were to be guaranteed for all individuals, and social and economic inequalities would be permitted only to the extent that such inequalities improved the lot of the least advantaged.

Necessity—the realities of life in Cleveland—also mandated our goal. We pointed to the many inequalities in income that separated the people of the central city from those of the suburbs, region, and nation, and wrote:

> In an environment characterized by deteriorating inner city neighborhoods and burgeoning suburban subdivisions, by vastly expanded mobility for those with automobiles and significantly diminished mobility for the transit-dependent, an environment characterized by massive inequalities in the distribution of income and power, there is no more appropriate goal which the commission could adopt than the goal of promoting greater equity.

SOME EARLY STUDIES

Some of the earliest studies executed by the staff under Bonner's direction (including many discussed in greater detail in the cases that follow) drew directly from our conceptual framework. They can be separated into two groups: studies and analyses of policies designed to promote changes in the level and distribution of income and power; and studies of policies designed to improve city residents' choices among the goods and services offered by the public and private sectors.

The first group included two major projects. First, we did

an early analysis of federal legislation on public assistance reform and made recommendations for changes to better serve our income redistribution objectives.[2] Second, we studied the feasibility of redeveloping a substantially vacant and vandalized industrial area for a black neighborhood economic development organization that was then without funds or staff.[3]

In the first effort our long-run objective was a redistribution of income through much needed reform in our federal public assistance program. The short-run objective was to place information, critical analysis, and alternative programs in the hands of Mayor Stokes, local business leaders, and various U.S. congressional representatives, who could, from their forums, hope to influence the decisions being made about this legislation at the national level. In the process we pointed out how income, investment, and jobs were interrelated. Our problem of declining and increasingly marginal retail centers, for example, would be much relieved through a just and adequate income maintenance program that would put up to $40 million a year of new money into neighborhood retail cash registers.

In the case of the economic feasibility analysis, our immediate objective was to transfer the power of planning professionals—our access to information, critical analytical skills, and institutional role—to a group of low-income black citizens who had neither the resources nor the professional skills to deal with a complex redevelopment scheme. The ultimate objective was to promote the redevelopment of land burdened by obsolete, vacant, and vandalized structures into industrial use in order to further the availability of jobs in the neighborhood and thus accomplish some redistribution of income. The outcome of the study was specific and realistic. If redevelopment was to take place, it would require major public and private demand-side subsidies; no feasible supply-side contribution toward the cost of acquiring the land or constructing new facilities could make an industrial redevelopment project pay in that depressed and abandoned east side area.

Low- and moderate-income housing studies were part of

---

[2]Cleveland City Planning Commission, "The Proposed Family Assistance Plan: A Critique, Some Suggested Modifications, and Their Impact on the City of Cleveland," August 1970.
[3]Cleveland City Planning Commission, "Redevelopment of the National Screw and Perfection Stove Site," March 1971.

our program to improve residents' choices in goods and services.[4] The basic problem, of course, is that while the poor cannot afford housing defined by our society as "standard," our society is not only unwilling to commit the substantial funds needed to house these families in public housing units, but is also unwilling to provide choices—in location or type— among those units it does construct.

So we developed a proposal for a new kind of housing subsidy, a housing allowance, which Mayor Stokes presented to the National League of Cities in 1971.[5] Our proposal was also the heart of an article we drafted for Mayor Stokes for a legal journal. Our findings, in company with the findings of similar studies being done by others at the time, made clear that a subsidy going directly to low- and moderate-income families, rather than to developers and owners of low-income housing units, would give households more of a choice and accomplish other important objectives as well. The staff argued for housing allowances in congressional testimony and through the mayor's office and our U.S. congressional delegation. In spite of the fact that housing allowances (or vouchers) have been strenuously attacked by many housing experts because they do not lead to an increase in supply in tight housing markets, I continue to believe that housing allowances are appropriate in markets suffering (like Cleveland) from insufficient effective demand.

While supporting the passage of housing allowance legislation, we also made clear our forceful support for present programs for low- and moderate-income housing throughout all suitable locations of the city and region (Chapter 6). Part of this concern was expressed in a new town proposal for 865 acres of city-owned land located east of Cleveland in an unincorporated area named Warrensville Township.[6] Submitted to HUD, the proposal called for an international design competition for the new town and the implementation of innovative

---

[4]Cleveland City Planning Commission, "The Cleveland Housing Papers," August 1970–May 1973; and see review in *Journal of the American Institute of Planners* 40 (July 1974): 290.

[5]"A Housing Allowance Program for Cleveland: Issues and Implications," May 1973.

[6]Cleveland City Planning Commission, "Warren's Ridge New Town: A Pre-Application Proposal," April 1971.

programs in health care, education, and general services, as well as the allocation of 2,800 of the 8,000 planned dwelling units for low- and moderate-income families.

Other studies, entirely local in focus, had to do with increasing transit and taxi service to poor neighborhoods and setting up new recreation facilities, using criteria of density, poverty, and juvenile delinquency to locate sites.[7]

THE IMPACT OF THE *POLICY PLANNING REPORT*

What effect did the *Report* have on the mayors we served, on planning practitioners, on the teaching of city planning, and on the city of Cleveland?

Mayor Stokes, under whose administration the *Report* was conceived, was no longer mayor by the time it was printed. Stokes supported the studies and analyses that the planning staff undertook. He used the status of his office to promote many of our recommendations. He also appreciated the stream of speeches and articles that flowed from his planners and that he used for a variety of local and national purposes. Our work fitted snugly with Stokes's objectives and strengthened the links between the mayor and his constituency.

The *Report* was actually printed in the administration of Stokes's successor, Mayor Ralph J. Perk. Interestingly enough, Perk, who was a conservative Republican, was as supportive of most of our proposals as Stokes had been. Perk was not very interested in details. When I presented him with a copy of the *Report* hot off the press, he leafed through it and scolded me because we had not included his picture. Nonetheless, in the Perk administration, against the background of a mayor less charismatic and liberal than Stokes, our own role as advocates became more visible, and we achieved many successes.

Mayor Dennis Kucinich, however, was a diligent student of the city planning operation. We had worked closely with him as councilman on many issues. He had read the *Report* and

---

[7]Cleveland City Planning Commission, "Toward Equitable Transportation Opportunities for Cleveland's Elderly and Poor," August 1972; "A Proposal for Fare Reduction for Off-Peak Transit Riders," August 1973.

had empathized with its approach. Many of the policies he espoused later as mayor might have been taken directly from the *Report*. Kucinich told an interviewer later that everything he knew about city planning he learned from the city planning staff.

What impact did the *Report* have on planning practitioners? The answer is not clear. We were asked to discuss the *Report* at conferences for years. Professional interest was great. Yet nowhere was the *Report* copied in detail as a model for other planning agencies. It may be that the *Report* and the ideas it presented were too great a departure from the accepted style of local planning. Perhaps so, yet I am confident that equity planning will come into more prominence in the years ahead.

If the *Report* had little apparent effect on practitioners, it did have an impact on the teaching of planning. Almost the entire first printing of the *Report* (500 copies) was requested by planning professors from colleges around the country, who, no doubt, were interested in presenting their students with an alternative model of redistributive planning practice. Even today, fifteen years after we wrote it, I am invited to colleges to discuss the *Report* and our general approach to planning. Students seem to be interested in and enthusiastic about our work. Perhaps in this respect our impact on the future practice of city planning is wider than we can ever know.

Finally, how did the *Report* affect the planning process in the city of Cleveland? For my staff and me, the *Report* worked beautifully for the entire ten years I spent in City Hall. We felt no need to overhaul it. Under the three mayors I served, the planning operation grew in importance, budget, and prestige. I believe we were more effective in influencing local decision making than most planning agencies. In the process, of course, we received our share of criticism, much of which came from fellow planners. We faced and responded to four main criticisms.

First, some held that our approach was too ideological. We replied that an ideological commitment to beautiful design, efficiency, or the value of real property lay behind every planning perspective. But planners often focus on professional techniques that obscure these ideological biases. By contrast, we tried to make our commitment explicit. Although decision-makers did not always agree with our position, they understood it and, more often than not, respected us for articulating it.

Second, some argued that proper policy formulation and program analysis demanded more expertise and time than we could muster, so our product did not merit serious consideration. But we knew that those who do not deal on a day-to-day basis with local government may overestimate the importance of highly sophisticated technical analysis. Given the time and resource constraints and the political parameters of local decision making, it was more appropriate to articulate issues, provide clearly organized supporting data, and recommend policies and programs in keeping with defined objectives.

Third, some held that our approach was too political and therefore too dangerous. In turn, we argued that involvement in policy and program formulation inevitably means involvement in politics. This did not *put* politics into planning: it has always been there. As our experience demonstrated, there were risks, but they were manageable. In light of the limited information available to local decision-makers and the shifting political coalitions characteristic of local government, planners with an informed, equity point of view could survive and prosper and even improve the quality of political decision making.

Fourth, some held that our approach was too broad, threatening to diminish the stature of city planners as professionals with definitive expertise in land-use matters. We responded that this was true—our practice did take us away from a concentration on land-use issues, but this did not compromise our identity; it extended it. The planning staff was not only consulted on zoning and land use matters but was viewed as a significant player in a variety of policy areas, including housing, transportation, and managerial effectiveness. Our stature did not diminish; it grew.

Beyond our own extensive and successful use of the *Report*, current planning efforts in Cleveland are now using many of the criteria found there. After noting the similarity of objectives, Bob Brown, director of the city's new general planning effort, wrote to a student in 1987:

> I do not mean to imply that all policies of the 1975 *Policy Planning Report* are mirrored in current policies and programs. However, I do believe that a commitment to neighborhoods and the needs of poor city residents continues to characterize the city's planning, redevelopment and revitalization efforts.

What of the future? There is little doubt that more and more American cities will come to have black and Hispanic mayors in the years ahead. These minority mayors will demand more consideration for the needs of their constituents from all city agencies. In this context, the "old style" of city planning directed primarily toward the interests of propertied groups simply won't do. City planners will have to learn how to incorporate more considerations of equity into their day-to-day operations. Some variation on the *Cleveland Policy Planning Report* might be a good place to start.

4

Euclid Beach

The Euclid Beach case began as a dispiriting defeat and ended ten years later as part of a victory that would delight the most zealous park enthusiast. It was also the first significant issue I had to deal with as director of the Cleveland City Planning Commission. It was on the agenda of a staff meeting held at 10 A.M. on my first day on the job, November 7, 1969.

The old Euclid Beach Amusement Park was a vestige of Cleveland's elegant past. It consisted of sixty-seven acres with a roller-coaster, a Ferris wheel, a dance pavilion, and a beautiful bathing beach along the shoreline of Lake Erie. People had come from all around the Cleveland area to spend a day or a weekend at Euclid Beach Park.

Its facilities, however, were available to blacks only on a limited basis. The history of Euclid Beach Park illustrates how racism restricted access to Cleveland area resources for many of Cleveland's citizens. Until after World War II, the park's management had a long history of racial discrimination. Blacks were excluded except on certain days during the season. In August 1946, an interracial group was denied entrance, with management citing its policy of keeping the races separate. Protests and demonstrations followed during August and September. Management claimed these were communist-inspired. On September 21, a scuffle during a demonstration led to the wounding of a black city police officer, and the park's season ended earlier than planned. When it reopened in 1947, the dance pavilion was operated as a private club.

By the mid-1960s, however, the park had lost popularity, and its owners had sold the land to private developers. They had demolished the rides and pavilions and leveled the land and were now before the City Planning Commission with plans to build a residential development of 3,480 apartments in eight

59

twenty-story towers. In order to do this, the developers needed a zoning change from a one-family-housing classification to the city's highest residential zoning category, which allowed for densities of up to 52 families an acre and building heights of up to 250 feet. Residential densities of this scale were very unusual in Cleveland and limited to a few downtown blocks.

The staff advised me that they had been studying the proposed zoning change for months, ever since the legislation had been referred to the City Planning Commission by City Council. When I asked for the results of their analysis, the staff responded, "City Council is in favor of the legislation and the mayor hasn't been asked, but he hasn't volunteered a preference." But what, I asked, did we, the zoning experts on the planning staff, think about the rezoning proposal? Planners, after all, claim to be the specialists best able to point out the relationships among different land uses. The staff, it seemed, had no opinion at all, since they had been without a director for the past three months. Staff members also conceded when pressed that they had no idea what the neighbors or environmentalists or good-government groups thought about the proposed development, since they had never attempted to elicit a response from these groups. What did our own 1949 General Land Use Plan say about ideal densities and other land uses in that area? Well, the plan was badly out of date and no one had consulted it, but now that it had been mentioned, it turned out that the plan called for the preservation of the entire lakefront in that area for park and beach purposes. The 1949 plan explained that the lakefront park would offer Cleveland's citizens more fresh air and outdoor recreational space and make the city generally more pleasant.

It was not an ideal analysis, but as was to become apparent in the weeks to come, the staff's functions had been reduced almost entirely to routine zoning administration and the presentation of occasional minor studies. On zoning matters, the staff typically followed the lead of the ward councilmember. On important policy matters, the planners were not asked for, nor did they offer, their counsel. Overwhelmingly, their work was routine and noncontroversial.

By contrast, I had spent five years in a planning agency in Pittsburgh that was a highly active and visible division of local government and an important source of new proposals, advice, and ideas for the city. I had gotten along well with John T. Mauro, Pittsburgh's planning director, and although I argued with him about many of the ideas he promoted, it was enjoyable to be part of an agency that was involved and useful, well known for its competence, and well respected. I was also impressed by Mauro's style of operation. Now that I was director of my own agency in Cleveland and working for one of America's first black mayors of a large city, I wanted to see how planning could be made more useful to Cleveland's poor and working-class residents. Every project review might offer opportunities to raise the issues I wanted to discuss. I knew some of those positions would be controversial, but that was the kind of agency I wanted to direct.

The contrast between two directors of the Pittsburgh Planning Commission—Calvin Hamilton, who left shortly before I arrived in that city, and John Mauro, his successor—had been instructive. I learned that there could be enormous differences between directors and that those differences could reshape the operations of the agency, apparently without anyone's commenting on it or (maybe) even being aware of it. Hamilton was a professional planner with an important and excellent reputation in the professional organizations of which he was a member; with the consultants whom he employed; with university faculty members who took classes to see and hear about Pittsburgh's mathematical state-of-the-art simulation model, paid for by HUD and evolving under Hamilton's leadership; and with the federal bureaucrats who funded Hamilton's community renewal program. By contrast, Mauro had no planning credentials at all but was very well known in the city of Pittsburgh, where he had been a reporter for a local daily newspaper, a public relations man for the Golden Triangle Association (a downtown business group), a local Democratic party wheelhorse, and Mayor Joseph M. Barr's urban renewal coordinator.

Under Hamilton, the Pittsburgh City Planning Commission had great status with an audience outside the city. But to the home audience, including city residents and Pittsburgh's mayor and City Council, the Planning Commission and its simulation model were virtually invisible. John Mauro changed all that. Under his direction, the planning commission became one of the most visible and influential of all city agencies.

Mauro himself played a key role in keeping the headquarters of U.S. Steel in Pittsburgh, locating the new Three Rivers Stadium, and redeveloping the city's lower northside.

I argued with Mauro a lot because I thought he paid too much attention to the needs of the establishment and the local Democratic party, but I learned some valuable lessons while watching him operate. For instance:

- Before any hearing before the Planning Commission, especially an important hearing, write out the facts of the case and the reasons for your recommendations; and write them as if you expected to see them on page one of the newspaper the next morning.
- Be friendly and open with reporters. Don't try to snow them. Write your own press releases on controversial actions. Make sure the media understand the rationale for your action. Try to make the reporters like and respect you; they can make you and your operation look terrific or terrible.
- There is an Establishment with a capital E. It consists of the old, rich families and the managers of the city's leading banks and corporations. On most matters it knows what it wants, but only in the most general terms. You can bargain with it and sometimes, within limits, win major concessions for the public.
- Try to make your office look good physically. Hire smart people and send them around town to represent the planning agency to the relevant committees, and the word will get around that you've got a serious shop that is determined to be a part of the serious decision-making process and has to be included and respected.
- Don't limit your approach; "planning" can be defined very broadly. In Pittsburgh, under Mauro, planning came to represent deal-making and public-entrepreneurship functions that were far removed from the letter of the Planning Commission's charter. In Pittsburgh, for example, Mauro had me doing neighborhood planning and redevelopment with several black and working-class neighborhoods. I was also lead planner on a "great high school" program for the Pittsburgh board of education. Nobody had done either of these things before.

A few days after the staff meeting to consider the Euclid Beach proposal, I drove with Layton Washburn, who had been on the commission staff since 1938, out to the Euclid Beach site. It was located at the far northeastern extremity of the city and was flanked by residential properties on one side and Villa Angela, a girl's parochial high school, on the other. Wildwood Park, a city lakefront park, was only a quarter of a mile to the east, and it was easy to imagine a magnificent public park and beach running along the lakefront at this point for two or three miles. Washburn and I thought it would be a good idea to do what we could to help develop such a park in the public interest. We were encouraged in that direction by a planning doctrine, which I thought plausible, that had it that public beaches, parks, and open spaces were valuable to a community and that their provision was a public good that would be universally applauded. Planning doctrine considered such parks especially valuable in high-density residential areas similar to what was being proposed and in sensitive locations such as waterfronts. Euclid Beach qualified on all points. The presence of parks, our training said, promised beauty, recreation, and rising property values. Parks promoted the common good by being both socially desirable and protective of property values. We felt that the public would be broadly supportive if we pressed for concessions from the developers on this issue.

The strategy we developed would attempt to negotiate a quiet settlement in which we would give the developers the zoning they wanted if they would dedicate the beach to the city. If we failed to negotiate such a quiet settlement, we would recommend that the Planning Commission disapprove the rezoning and try to sustain the disapproval with City Council. Then the developers might be more willing to deal.

Accordingly, a few days later we called the developers in for a site plan review. They arrived with the councilman who represented the ward. Washburn, John Wilkes, and I pointed out that the plan had a lot of problems. For example, the densities proposed in the developer's site plan were completely out of keeping with the prevailing densities and character of the neighborhood. The present zoning called for a maximum density of five houses per acre and a height limit of 30 feet; the zoning requested by the developer allowed for fifty-two units per acre and a 250-foot height limit. We also pointed out that the densities proposed in the plan would require about $1 million in public capital improvements, including a major relief sewer and road widenings, and that the site plan promised no amenities whatever, not for the public at large and not for the developers' tenants, just eight twenty-story towers in a sea of surface parking. Under the circumstances, we concluded, it was very unlikely that the Planning Commission would be able to support the proposed rezoning legislation.

Instead, we proposed a compromise. The planning staff would recommend the proposed zoning on three conditions: first, the developers would agree to share the costs of the required capital improvements for sewers and roads; second, the developers would agree to reduce the density, building five rather than eight towers and building a parking structure to reduce surface-level parking; and, third, the developers would agree to dedicate the beach portion of the parcel in perpetuity to the city for public beach purposes. It seemed to us that this kind of compromise was in the best interest of everyone. We sat back to await the developers' counter-proposal.

In Euclid Beach, as in most of the cases that follow, the strategies we developed over the years were negotiating strategies, designed not to stop development but to trade, to give in order to get. We sought not merely to make deals, but to pursue our equity agenda. In all of these cases we were being asked to "give"—zoning adjustments, consent agreements, subsidies, and so on—so why not hope to get the best we could for the city in return? Most of the lawyers we dealt with in these negotiations seemed to see and understand our bargaining goal as simply getting the best deal possible for our clients, the people of the city, a position their own training had prepared them to appreciate. Of course, some positions, such as the sale of the Municipal Electric Light Plant, were simply nonnegotiable.

It should be clear that no politician, city official, or group of private citizens asked us to take this position on Euclid Beach or on most of the other matters we were to consider over the next ten years. The planning staff defined the parameters of the issues. We discussed our Euclid Beach position in advance with the chairman of the commission and he approved, but the chair rarely had negative comments and never once in ten years asked us to revise a proposed staff recommendation. We also privately discussed the issue with Mayor Stokes, stressing the importance of a new lakefront park to the city and to the progressive vision he was trying to project in his administration. He was encouraging, so I assumed we had his support. (I do not know what we would have done had Stokes said no. I had no wish to contradict or embarrass him and even less to lose my new job.) Eddie Baugh, director of the Parks and Recreation Department, liked our position and promised to testify in favor of the deal before the Planning Commission and City Council. Washburn and I went together to consult with Baugh and his staff, not only because he respected Washburn's judgment, but because he had long-time friends and associates in the Parks Department, whereas I was an untested newcomer.

We also talked to the ward councilman. He was not interested in our offer; he supported the developers' rezoning legislation as it stood. But the councilman seemed less hostile to our proposal and our threats of disapproval than exasperated by our failure to act quickly on the legislation. "Do anything you want," he said, "just get it back down to Council, where we can take care of it." The developers were completely uninterested in any negotiations and rejected our compromise out of hand. The organized groups in the immediate neighborhood that we consulted prior to the hearings were generally hostile both to the proposed new development and the rezoning and also to the idea of a new public beach, preferring that nothing whatever be done. Most of them were small organizations made up of nearby property-owners who seemed primarily interested in protecting their real estate values. It was clear in our discussions that the neighbors, who were all white, were concerned about the race of those who might come to use the new beach or the new housing; they preferred to see the land undeveloped.

Ultimately, Washburn and I decided to go ahead with our strategy and recommend that the Planning Commission disapprove the rezoning legislation unless the developers agreed to the compromise we outlined. In the hearing before the commission, the developers and the councilman argued for the rezoning without any prior concessions, but the commission followed the recommendations of its staff and disapproved the zoning legislation.

I felt good about the commission's support, but I was not without concern over our "victory." I knew from my training and from my experience in Ithaca and Pittsburgh that planners operate in a political environment and that it is important to gain and hold the confidence of political and business leaders. If you alienate enough powerful people, you jeopardize your recommendations, the reputation of the planning agency, and your job. At the same time, it seemed to me that we had the responsibility to represent the best interests of the people of Cleveland as we saw them. We went about doing that in a cordial but nondeferential way, without compromising the facts of a case or our professional integrity. A good way to do this was to project an air of professional and technical competence and an apolitical, conservative, even skeptical public stance. The stance was built by always speaking soberly, using numbers when we had them to describe and quantify the issue, and wearing conservative suits and ties.

I felt we also needed a consistent approach to the items on the planning commission's bi-weekly agenda. Accordingly, we worked out a standard reporting format for issue review, analysis, and recommendation. This written document clearly set out the facts of each case under review, the staff's evaluation and discussion, a recommended course of action for the commission, and the reasons for the recommendation. The format was simple, straightforward, and consistent. It provided a clear history of the issue for incorporation into the official commission minutes as well as a convenient handout to newspaper and television reporters. The report did not emphasize any conflicts that arose within staff discussions. If views conflicted, and they frequently did, we tried to iron them out within our staff discussions and present a unified position to the world. We tried to avoid qualifying statements or uncertainty, preferring instead simple and straightforward themes. We used this new format for the first time on the Euclid Beach issue:

ZONING

Ordinance No. 815–69 (Prince) to change the Use, Area, and Height Districts of lands between Lake Shore Boulevard, N.E., and the Shore Line of Lake Eric, and between East 156 Street and approximately one thousand seven hundred eighteen (1,718) feet easterly. (Map Change No. 1153—Sheet No. 7.) *Motion 11-18-69:* Motion by Mrs. Panehal, seconded by Mr. Fonoroff, that Ordinance No. 815–69 be disapproved.

Proposal:

This ordinance proposes to change the zoning of lands between Lake Shore Boulevard and the shore line of Lake Erie and between East 156 Street and approximately 1,718 feet easterly from a One-Family Use District to a Local Retail "F" Area and a "5" Height District, which permits the maximum gross floor area of residential buildings to equal two times the land area and the maximum height to be 250 feet.

The area in question contains approximately 67 acres and is the site of the now defunct Euclid Beach Park, which was a quasi-public amusement park for many years.

The proposed multi-family development consists of eight 20-story apartment buildings containing 3,480 suites of which 2,088 will be one bedroom and 1,392 two bedroom units and will occupy the entire site. This is a density of 52 families per acre. 3,480 parking spaces will be provided as follows: 2,610 above grade and 870 below grade.

Evaluation:

After reviewing the site plans for the proposed development, and as a result of public hearings and meetings with interested parties, the staff submits the following:

1. The area is desirable for apartment development because of its size, nearby retail business, its proximity to similar and compatible uses, the convenience of public transportation, as well as freeway accessibility without infiltrating the residential areas. Existing school facilities in the area are adequate.
2. There is a serious question as to the high density of the proposed development, the need for additional off-street parking and more open space.
3. The General Plan of Cleveland (1949) recommends the use of the lakefront in this area for public park purposes for which reservations should be made.
4. A satisfactory traffic flow can be provided for proposed development by relocating the driveways and other interior modifications as recommended by the report of the Division of Traffic Engineering and Parking.
5. The sewer system will have to be upgraded in this area in accordance with the recommendations of the report of the Clean Water Task Force, which represents an expenditure of between $700,000 and $1,000,000.

City Planning Staff Recommendation:

The City Planning Commission recommends disapproval of Ordinance No. 815-69.

Reason for City Planning Staff Recommendation:

1. The proposal includes private control of the entire acreage and does *not* provide for public control of the area fronting on Lake Erie. This is in conflict with the often-stated policy of the Planning Commission to preserve existing recreation and park lands and to expand these holdings wherever suitable in the broadest defense of the public interest.
2. The proposal is in conflict with the General Plan of the City of Cleveland which proposed the lakefront be held in the public domain.
3. The proposal raises questions of unsuitably high residential densities on the site.
4. The proposal would call for an expenditure of up to $1 million on sewer improvements necessary to benefit the development.

Yeas: Klein, Panehal, Storey, Fonoroff, and Dobrea.
Nays: Blaha.

Motion passed.

The commission's public hearing on Euclid Beach was covered by the *Press* and the *Plain Dealer,* Cleveland's two daily newspapers, and local television stations. It offered us our first opportunity to meet reporters and begin to develop good relations with them. It was the beginning of a close, respectful, and in some ways symbiotic relationship. We would provide the reporters with data, or an insider's view of a given situation, or an explanation of how one urban phenomenon related to another. They in turn would provide us with a broad forum for issues we wanted to place on the public agenda and with a growing measure of credibility.

My respect for the power of the press may have come from my undergraduate training in journalism and from John T. Mauro. Mauro's speed and success in raising the status and visibility of his agency were based on his long association with the press, the downtown establishment, and the local Democratic party. That could equally well have made him an easy target, had it not been for the way he handled the media. Mauro wrote his own agency press releases; he was cordial and open with reporters; and, most importantly, he made sure that the reporter covering an issue understood it in depth—no matter how long it took. When I asked him about this practice, after one interminable session with a reporter who simply couldn't get it right, Mauro said: "You can have the best ideas in the world; you can do the most careful analysis of an issue; you can write it up in the most brilliant style possible; but if you don't get it in the papers, no one will know it has been done. And if no one knows about it, you might as well not have done it." I didn't believe all of that, but I did believe that planners need to keep the support of the newspapers and the good-government organizations that are inclined to support local city planning.

I must confess that I genuinely liked most reporters. I was always available to them and returned their calls and answered their questions as honestly and thoroughly as I could. When they wanted inside material that it might be dangerous to release, I often leaked it anyway, asking them to keep my comments off the record. They always protected my confidentiality. Occasionally, I would talk with reporters about something I'd seen that suggested a unique angle on a story, and I think they appreciated this. For example, the Downtown Cleveland Corporation once invited in some Transcendental Meditation people to help local boosters think positively about Cleveland's downtown. I told columnist Dick Feagler about it, and it turned up in a funny column. I also think the reporters appreciated our honesty and respected the information my staff developed.

We were especially anxious to deserve the respect of one particular journalist, Roldo Bartimole, who published *Point of View*, a biweekly political newsletter with a tiny circulation. Roldo was the Cleveland version of I. F. Stone: a brilliant investigative reporter who wrote with honesty, accuracy, and wit about the seamier side of local politics and the cozy, often corrupt, relationship between politicians and businessmen. We wanted Roldo's support.

I did not believe that the power, influence, and effectiveness of a planning agency were fully set out by the enabling legislation that created it and established its authority. They arose more from demonstrated competence and a reputation not only for defining problems and articulating goals, but for solving those problems and achieving those goals. A good many of my ideas on this topic were drawn from John Mauro's expansionist style of operation and from courses on government I had taken at Cornell with Alan A. Altshuler and A. M. Hillhouse. "Power and Administration," an article by Norton Long, was also an important source of ideas.[1] Beyond that, we wanted to do more useful and interesting things than the city charter specified.

The vote by the Planning Commission endorsing our Euclid Beach position was easy; now came the hard part—sustaining our position with City Council, where a two-thirds majority, or 22 votes of 33, was needed to override recommendations by the Planning Commission. Eddie Baugh, the Parks director, was glad to join our lobbying effort. We also lobbied individual Council members before the scheduled Council committee hearings, placing particular lobbying emphasis on the black councilmembers because we believed we had Mayor Stokes's support on the issue and they would be likely to follow his lead. Our message emphasized the importance of the lakefront park to the long-term attractiveness and livability of Cleveland. Members of Council seemed mildly interested, but none of them committed themselves to our support.

Council brought the matter up within two weeks. In the

[1]Norton E. Long, "Power and Administration," *Public Administration Review* 9 (Autumn 1949): 257–64.

interim, we had managed to get a representative from the Sierra Club to agree to testify for our position, but he, Baugh, and I were the only ones who spoke against the rezoning legislation as it was written and in favor of the Planning Commission's position. Neighborhood groups and nearby property owners testified against our proposed compromise. Their testimony was full of concern over the possibility that the users of the park might also be criminals. Racial fears, it seemed to me, were at work again. Although Mayor Stokes took no public position, I was confident that I had at least 14 of the 33 votes (mostly from black councilmembers) and would be able to sustain the Planning Commission's rejection of the zoning change. It was not to be. When Council called the roll, the commission's ruling was overridden by a vote of 31 to 2, and it was rumored that our two supporting votes were from councilmembers who had gotten confused and didn't understand what item they were voting on.

I was devastated. Planning doctrine and instinct both suggested that we were on the side of the angels on this issue. Who could be against more public parkland and beaches? Why had we taken such a beating? Could we expect the same treatment in future zoning issues?

I sought some clues from the political environment, and the reasons for our defeat became immediately obvious. Cleveland's City Council is elected on a ward basis; in 1969 there were thirty-three wards. (Recall that Cleveland voters reduced the number of wards and city councilpersons to twenty-one in 1982.) No member of Council was encouraged to have a citywide perspective. Most of them were inclined to believe that their constituents were hostile to policy innovations, and preferred their representatives in City Hall simply to go along with the wishes expressed by whatever constituents were interested in any given issue. Accordingly, councilmembers were far less interested in "leadership" than they were in not alienating any of their constituents. Some councilpersons were also given to seeing the practice of politics as a form of commerce and were not above trading zoning favors for campaign contributions.

Most importantly, the nature of ward-based politics put each councilmember in direct control of the zoning in his or her ward. A tradition of backscratching was all-controlling. When rezoning proposals occurred, each councilperson would support the zoning preferences of the others. In that way a solid block of Council could be expected to override any Planning Commission ruling that was in conflict with the ward councilmember's wishes, and each councilperson was in all-but-absolute control of the zoning in his or her ward. That was why the councilman in Euclid Beach didn't care what the planners did; he simply wanted the legislation acted on and returned to Council, where tradition and collegiality would dispose of it in his favor.

What did this suggest for future zoning controversies? It suggested that, at least for the foreseeable future, Council would continue to handle zoning matters in the same way. For the planning staff, the lesson was clear: continue to advise Council on zoning matters because the charter demands it and Council expects it. Don't devote too much time to the activity, and don't be too disappointed when you fail to make a difference in the outcome. But continue to raise the relevant, equity-laden questions about the future of the city whenever the chance arises. And continue not just to raise the questions when possible but to show the equity consequences of proposed projects as well.

Following Council's rezoning of Euclid Beach, the original developers capitalized the new zoning into the price of the land and sold it to a second developer. That developer ignored the original site plan submitted to the Planning Commission and, by 1989, had built three high-rise apartment buildings and a number of three-story apartment buildings, a nursing facility, and a Pizza Hut restaurant.

There is a pleasant postscript to this story that brings us full circle. In 1981, Layton Washburn's vision of a public park at Euclid Beach prevailed. Thanks to his planning and persistence, legal assistance provided by the Trust for Public Land, and $1.3 million provided by the state of Ohio and four Cleveland-area foundations, the city bought the beach that we had demanded for free in 1969 as a concession for the rezoning. The land purchased has now been added to the Cleveland Lakefront State Park. (A more complete description of the park may be found in Chapter 10.) This addition was joined to Wildwood Park to the east, and the two- or three-mile beach along Lake Erie that Washburn and I envisioned in 1969 is now a reality.

5

Regional Issues and the Clark Freeway

City planners have for the most part been believers in the necessity of regional planning and the possibility of regional solutions. I certainly was before coming to Cleveland. Afterward, I was still a believer in regional planning, but more worried about its potential for abuse.

In December 1969, Sid Spector, one of the mayor's executive assistants, asked me to represent Stokes at a NOACA board meeting to be held the next morning. I was pleased to go. An assignment like that meant visibility, and visibility meant the possibility of influence for planning. NOACA was the Northeast Ohio Areawide Coordinating Agency, formed in 1968 to satisfy federal requirements for areawide review of federal grants-in-aid applications (known in local government as the A-95 Clearinghouse Review function). Although the agency, under the federal rules, had to comment on all areawide grant requests as well as recommend and perform various regional studies, the city had taken little interest in its operations. The casual, off-hand request for me to attend the meeting as Mayor Stokes's alternate was a typical afterthought. The mayor practically never attended these meetings himself, and no one else may have been available. I was given no agenda; I was just told that when I-290 or the Clark Freeway issue came up, I was to "vote for further study."[1]

Although Stokes attended only one meeting in 1968, and Cleveland had only one seat on NOACA's forty-nine-person board, the mayor had formally agreed to the agency's formation and to its membership structure. By July 1969 Cleveland's one

---

[1]"I-290" and "Clark Freeway" refer to the same route and are used interchangeably in this chapter.

seat had been raised to three, but the city, with 25 percent of the region's population, still had only 6 percent of the votes. It seemed hardly to matter, though, as NOACA's activities were almost invisible from Cleveland City Hall. That was before December 1969; afterward, NOACA no longer lacked visibility.

The board was to convene at 9 A.M. The night before, however, I received and accepted an invitation to join at an 8 A.M. breakfast a group of eastern suburbanites who had been involved in anti-highway controversies for years. The cities of Shaker Heights and Cleveland Heights had set up transportation advisory committees in 1965. Their purpose was to disseminate information on the proposed Lee and Clark freeways, to rally popular opinion and lead the fight against the freeways, which threatened both communities, and to collect funds to support their efforts. The members of the group who attended the breakfast included William A. Lowry, William B. (Brad) Norris, James B. Davis, and Richard S. Stoddart. We were joined by William Gaskill, the city manager of the city of East Cleveland. Bill Lowry was a lawyer for the medium-sized law firm of Hahn, Loeser, Freedheim, Dean & Wellman; Brad Norris was the corporation legal counsel for the Carling Brewing Company; Jim Davis was a lawyer in his own practice; Dick Stoddart was a lawyer with Shaker Savings & Loan Company. All were Republicans except Lowry, who was an active Democrat. The first three lived in Shaker Heights; Stoddart was a Cleveland Heights councilman.

The members of this group were later to become an extremely useful support network for each other. One of them may have been essential to surviving the transition from Mayor Stokes to Mayor Perk. James B. Davis, avid anti-highway advocate, was also Ralph Perk's personal attorney. When Perk became mayor, Davis became a tremendously supportive chairman of the Planning Commission. Later he served as city law director during the Cleveland Transit System–Regional Transit Authority negotiations (Chapter 8).

Lowry helped us prepare the "Route Alternative for Reserved I-290 Funds" report. Later, he helped us prepare a legal case (which was ultimately won) that charged the state with discriminating against Cleveland through its regulations demanding that the city pay a 5 percent share of project costs for all interstate highways. The settlement, which took place long after I had left City Hall, was worth millions to the city.

Norris, who rejoined the law firm of Hahn, Loeser later in the 1970s, helped prepare and ultimately litigated the CEI– Muny Light restraint-of-trade suit in federal court. He also helped in the CTS–RTA negotiations and was one of the original members of the RTA board of trustees.

Stoddart was also involved in the RTA negotiations. Gaskill, a public administrator, later became utilities director for Mayor Stokes and county administrator for Cuyahoga County in the mid-1970s. He was very cooperative and cordial in all our dealings. All these men (Lowry died in 1985) are good friends to this day.

Members of this group were forceful and clear about their opposition to I-290. They had been fighting it and most of the network of highways proposed by the state Highway Department and the county engineer for the east side of Cuyahoga County since 1964. They were convinced that the construction of this highway network would spell the end for their pleasant communities—and they were right. For example, the east– west Clark Freeway and the north–south Lee Freeway were to intersect in the heart of the Shaker Lakes park district, where a four-level stack seventy feet high was to be constructed in a sixty-five-acre interchange. Devastation, desecration, and disaster were the only words to describe such a proposal.

This anti-freeway group was up against powerful opposition in the federal Bureau of Public Roads, the state Highway Department, and the County Engineer's Office. But they were not without ingenuity and resources of their own. For example, learning of the proposed right-of-way for I-290, they influenced their local government to build a nature conservancy squarely in the middle of the route alignment. Any attempts to remove the nature conservancy would enlist every conservation agency at every level of government as an ally in their struggle against the highway.

The group wanted to know the city of Cleveland's position on I-290. I couldn't tell them much. As a new hire (this was my second month on the job), I did not have much information about the origin, history, or details of the issue. I did know that the proposed route was to go from East 55th Street in the city to terminate at I-271 on the county's eastern border, and that on its way it would pass through densely populated, mostly black, low-income neighborhoods and then cut through industrial zones and some higher-income white neighborhoods on its

way east, out of the city (Map 2). I did tell my breakfast compan-
ions that I was prepared to demand "further study" if and when
the I-290 route came to a vote. They were pleased because they
knew that a favorable vote by NOACA on I-290 would undo all
the groundwork laid by their committees. We left our meeting
understanding that for our own perhaps different reasons, we
were all on the same side of this issue. It was reassuring for me
to know that, if I needed them, I had some allies who had been
involved with the issue in a thoughtful way for many years and
who could command resources.

The main item before the NOACA board was a discussion
of a recently issued NOACA report, *A Framework for Action*,
and the approval of a corridor for I-290 on the east side of
Cuyahoga County. After some spirited discussion, in which I
took little part, Cuyahoga County Commissioner Frank Gorman
proposed that more studies be conducted on two possible corridors before designating either as I-290. I stood with the
"ayes," but we lost 23 to 10. Then Albert S. Porter, Cuyahoga
County engineer for twenty-nine years and Democratic county
chairman for six, moved to designate the southern corridor as
I-290. This passed, over our bitter opposition, 27 to 5.

I was stunned! Here I was, proudly representing the mayor
of the central city that would bear most of the costs of disloca-
tion and the other burdens of highway construction, being
almost casually overwhelmed by a regional group, some of
whose members boasted that they had no idea of where the
route was.

The NOACA board was angry at Stokes, partially because
he never came to meetings, but, I believed, partially because he
was glamorous, handsome, an international figure (which they
were not), and black. I was very proud to be Stokes's representative and shocked to be treated with such disdain on the I-290
issue. I felt that this treatment was in a sense racially based and
directed personally against me as Stokes's alternate.

I returned from the NOACA meeting to tell Stokes what
happened, but he already knew. Newspaper reporters had
called, told him of the vote, and asked what he was going to do.
He had stalled them, and now asked me what I thought was
appropriate. It seemed to me, I said, that we ought to press
NOACA to rescind its decision. This would be in line with our
stated position in favor of further study. The tactics and strategies would be evolved as the situation developed, but, at a

MAP 2. Cleveland and Eastern Suburbs with Proposed Clark Freeway and Alternative Alignment

--- Clark Alignment (I-290)
••• Alternative Route
—— Existing Interstate Highways I-480 and I-271

minimum, we ought to get the decision reversed, and soon. With only three Cleveland votes on a forty-nine-person board, we were virtually powerless to prevent similar actions in the future. Stokes nodded, then asked one of his secretaries to call the other cabinet members. Those who were available joined us for lunch at the Hollenden House. The topic before the group was NOACA.

Most of the cabinet members had no opinion on NOACA; they had no contacts and no dealings with the agency. A few members of the group pointed out that attempting to have NOACA rescind the I-290 decision was probably going to be hopeless: the board's vote of 27 to 5 was overwhelming; we had little leverage with board members that we hadn't already used; some members of the Cleveland business community were in favor of the I-290 highway; and the federal government would back up its substantial investment in regional agencies like NOACA. John C. Little, the Mayor's executive assistant, and I argued the contrary. Little pointed out the political aspects: that NOACA was a new, fragile institution; that the great (though unquantified) loss to the city in jobs, taxes, and housing would damage the administration and the city; and that on any battle with NOACA, support from City Council was probably there. (I learned then that NOACA was virtually the only issue on which the Stokes administration and City Council could agree.) For my part, I argued the role of the professional: that federal highway policy was more and more insistent on "coordination" and "cooperation" since the 1962 Highway Act, and that the trend of urban highway construction lay in the direction of increased flexibility and democratic responsiveness, both implying more room for negotiation. In fact, I said, drawing on comments by my former Cornell professor Alan Altshuler at a recent planning conference, the California Department of Transportation was applying its own new rule that no resident displaced from the route of the Century Freeway in Watts was to be left worse off as a result, either financially or with respect to quality of housing. I took that to mean that the California Department of Transportation was prepared to build housing and subsidize rents if it had to. Stokes was immediately interested in this. All of these factors suggested much more room for negotiations than might be apparent.

This meeting helped answer a question that had been troubling me: if you are not a mayor's old friend, trusted political advisor, or important and powerful contributor, how can you get his attention? The answer was clear: with information. In this case, the highly specialized Century Freeway decision rule, presented in a way that was understandable and relevant to policy, not only commanded Stokes's attention but opened up many unconsidered policy options.

I was surprised that no other cabinet member joined forcefully in the discussion. Later I learned that no one in City Hall was officially "responsible" either for the Interstate Highway System as it affected Cleveland or for relationships with the regional agency. Incredible as it sounds, a policy vacuum existed on the transportation issue, with the mayor's advice coming from a Cleveland Transportation Advisory Committee made up of outsiders to City Hall in whom Stokes had little confidence. In such a situation, city planners had a great opportunity not only to plan but to make policy as well.

This policy vacuum was only one of many that existed in Cleveland City Hall. Relationships (in more than a "liaison" sense) with the county, state, and regional agencies were equally neglected. Internal analysis focused on program improvement was also lacking in the line agencies. The local "Urban Observatory," a program using university professors to solve city problems, was drifting. It occurred to me that every time a new policy or program initiative came down from the federal or state government to local government, local government had to struggle with questions of proper administration. Many of these initiatives offered openings to planners if they were interested and could find some free time or slack in their own system.

We concluded the lunch discussion without an indication from the mayor as to how he was leaning. I returned to my office and called a meeting of the planners who had been assigned to NOACA or to transportation matters in general. What did we know about I-290? Had we done any critical route analyses? Had we looked at alternative routes from the perspective of costs to the city? No, nothing along these lines had been done. I could find nothing to suggest that the Cleveland City Planning Commission had been anything but supportive of all NOACA's highway plans. We had made no effort to define the proposed freeway as a problem—a project that would destroy neighborhoods, reduce the supply of affordable housing available to Cleveland's low-income population, and deepen racial isolation and the city's fiscal problems. No one had raised those issues within the staff. Since no one had asked the staff to look at the highway from these "problem" perspectives, they hadn't. They looked at it in terms of highway engineering criteria—as an "improvement" to the regional traffic flow.

I assigned someone to develop estimates of costs to the city, including the local share of project costs, loss of jobs, loss of housing, and loss of tax income. We used the numbers we generated in all our future presentations, and, rough as they were, they were never challenged. In fact, other agencies began using them as if they were "official." The fact that the route alignment drove straight through several low-income black neighborhoods was apparent. Whether the route was simply the outcome of engineers' serving origin–destination lines or least-cost criteria, or whether white politicians were aiming to clear blacks from their districts, was not clear. What *was* clear was the devastating impact I-290 would have on the supply of low-income housing available to blacks.

This early meeting suggested that the in-house staff I had inherited was not going to be of much use in developing transportation policies focused on equity or the needs of the city. I would have to find that kind of staffing elsewhere.

In the next day or two, Stokes called me into a meeting that also included "Buddy" James, the law director. We discussed what should be done about NOACA. One option was simply to withdraw from the agency and try to destroy it. We all agreed that if the city simply withdrew, we would surely take a beating in the press for quitting in the face of one adverse decision. We did not want to take that criticism unless we absolutely had to. We also could not forecast the reaction of the federal agencies on whose good will and support we depended to an abrupt, unilateral decision like withdrawal. Even if we did withdraw, however, we would still have to have all our grants-in-aid requests reviewed by an A-95 clearinghouse. The only such agency likely to step in in the absence of NOACA was the state Department of Development, and no one knew what that agency was like. We concluded that we would probably have more success if we stayed within NOACA, worked within the organization to have the I-290 decision rescinded, made an effort to increase the city's representation on the board, and tried to use the agency to move toward the letter of federal regulations, which spoke the language of equity in housing, equal employment opportunity, and citizen participation.

Following these initial discussions, Mayor Stokes decided to stay in the agency and try to reshape its policies. The next week the city of Cleveland filed a suit in federal court claiming its right to proportional representation on the NOACA board under the one-man, one-vote rule. Pending the outcome of its suit, the city announced that it would no longer pay its dues to the organization. This put NOACA's budget in jeopardy because the organization needed dues from local government in order to draw its federal matching funds.

In day-to-day dealings on the NOACA issue, I became the point-man. When asked questions by the media about the NOACA suit I always tried to separate the board, its director, and its "unfortunate," "regrettable," or "shortsighted" decision (never its "stupid" or "racially motivated" decision) from the NOACA staff. The board had in mid-1969 elected from among its most rural members an executive director who pledged to limit NOACA's growth and keep staff activities to a minimum; it was already isolated from the agency's planning staff. We wanted to deepen that division and use the NOACA planning staff for our own purposes—in effect, to supplement our own staff at City Hall. That was not as difficult as it may sound. Many members of the NOACA staff had already quietly indicated that they were on the city's side in the controversy. For strictly professional planning reasons, they thought that the city was correct in resisting the NOACA board's decision. They had already prepared and recommended other courses of action that the board had rejected. Many were idealistic and liberal professional planners; I wanted them as allies.

We also privately pointed out, as often as we could, that the city was not interested in struggle for struggle's sake, but simply wanted the I-290 decision rescinded. If that was done, I made clear the likelihood that the city would withdraw its suit, pay its dues, and resume the status quo ante at NOACA. We wanted to negotiate: that is, reach some mutually agreeable accord after some discussion. That meant all parties to the dispute would have to be able and willing to exchange ideas, objectives, and meanings. The city obviously never had the power to force all the other parties to do what we wanted. With those members of the NOACA board who were convinced that the city's leadership was trying to overturn the social order and who would bitterly attack the city, I would sometimes point to the top of my head, and observe, "Look. I don't have any horns. Let's talk like reasonable people."

I thought it was time to call on our network of allies, and I began a series of meetings with Bill Lowry of the Shaker Heights Transportation Advisory Committee. Lowry, a careful student of transportation issues in Cuyahoga County, pointed out that simply saying no to the NOACA-approved I-290 route alignment was probably not an optimal position for the city. For one thing, Cleveland City Council had approved the general concept of the regional highway system years earlier. For another, the Cleveland Planning Commission had cooperated with and approved every single area highway study going back to 1944. Moreover, about $100 million had been reserved by the federal government to build the Clark Freeway. Given the multiplier effect on the local economy, Lowry pointed out that it might be a good idea to try to spend the money on a highway somewhere in our area that would not have a destructive impact on Cleveland and its people. Lowry, Washburn, and I carefully reviewed the various consultant studies of the entire proposed regional highway system and identified such a highway link, one that extensively used railroad rights-of-way. It was part of an approved highway called the Bedford Freeway. The problem was that the highway alignment would need a good deal of design modification, and no one on the planning staff at the time or on the city's engineering staff had the expertise or the time to do the modifications needed.

I decided to see if I couldn't set up my own little consulting group. I took the problem to one of the principals at Dalton, Dalton, & Little (DD&L), the region's largest planning, architecture, and engineering consulting firm, but a firm that had not gotten much highway consulting business from the county engineer. Would they be interested in helping me modify the design of the Bedford Freeway? I told them that if they agreed, their work would have to be pro bono, and that I would strictly protect their confidence. I also told them that if we stalled the present route alignment, other routes would have to be studied, and they might participate in that new business. Two days later, much to my surprise, they put two engineers at my disposal. To the DD&L engineers I added a highway planner from the NOACA staff who was supportive of our position and wanted to help (in the utmost secrecy, of course).

I have found through the years and on many different issues that it is often possible to get excellent professional assistance from staff members of outside agencies who are angry about or disappointed by their own agency's decisions. If you are visible and publicly identified with a position these professionals favor, they may be very helpful, but always on a *sub rosa* basis, because to be identified in this work might cost them their jobs.

I went to DD&L because I knew I needed engineering help with the new highway alignment, and I knew I could not get the help in City Hall. Preparing legislation and going out to bid for the help was too time-consuming: the time for decisions was imminent, and I was not sure I could get any legislation calling for consultant work past City Council. As it turned out, DD&L provided expert help quickly. (They were eventually hired in the late 1970s to do the study that ultimately emerged from our 1970 proposal.) By February 1970, working with our shadow consultants, we had an alternative to the approved I-290 route, a route we selected to limit the taking of housing, parks, jobs, and tax rateables in the city. Instead of dislocating 875 homes, 110 businesses, and acres of city parkland, as the original alignment would have done, our proposal would cost the city only 164 homes, 30 businesses, and no park acreage.

We published the proposal in March 1970, only four months after the conflict emerged. Bonner, Washburn, and I had written the proposal; Bill Lowry had reviewed it and added comments of a generally legal nature; and the excellent map-work and graphics had been done by the *sub rosa* and ad hoc engineering group I had put together. The study, entitled "Proposed Route Alignment for Reserved I-290 Funds," was couched in conciliatory, cooperative language. It was not based on original research or on a totally new alignment. But it did make use of data analysis and discussions with neighborhood groups in the right-of-way and with Councilman Jack Russell and Council President Jim Stanton, and it used origin and destination materials and land-use forecasts. It minimized takings of land for the right-of-way within Cleveland, turned the highway away from Shaker Heights and Cleveland Heights (which was Lowry's prime objective, of course), and spent the $100 million in reserved highway funds in Cuyahoga County.

It was also thoroughly ignored by the state Highway Department when I presented it a few weeks later in Columbus to an audience that included Phil Richeley, state highway director; Tony Garofoli, Cleveland councilman; and Tony Russo, state representative for the area.

It was not ignored, however, by the media. I had given Don Silver, who covered transportation issues for the *Cleveland Press,* an advance copy, and Silver had played it as a front-page story with a diagram of the proposed new route. All three Cleveland television stations carried the story as we made the presentation to the Planning Commission. The report further expanded the growing reputation of our office as a place where important public work was going on and where reporters might find interesting stories buttressed by facts and a consistent, logical point of view.

The alternative route proposal also served strong public notice that there was a serious disagreement among technicians, the kind of substantive disagreement that encourages politicians to negotiate policy. Up to this time, the highway engineers had utterly dominated the controversy. They believed and wanted others to believe that their traffic trip and cost data were authoritative and impartial; that their route selection was unbiased and optimal; that any change would add confusion, delay, and cost. They also believed that making concessions to the demands of any group would encourage other groups to make their own demands and that ultimately their impartial, scientific criteria would be compromised by ad hoc political attacks. But our alternative route proposal was not a political attack; it was an attack on their rational methods by the rational methods of other technicians. Thus, politicians would have to decide the technical conflict.

Our proposal also served to keep the issue hot and before the public. To modify well-established local policy, persistent challenges must be made on many levels. These challenges both give allies an opportunity to publicly reaffirm their support and place pressure on other public officials for support. Such pressure led to a pledge in April 1970 by Governor James A. Rhodes, then locked in a primary fight for a seat in the U.S. Senate, that he would never force a highway on a community that did not want it.

Finally, the alternative route proposal gave the City Planning Commission an opportunity to modify its *Transportation Plan,* which it did in May 1970. The alternative route was now "official"; future efforts to change it would have to deal with that fact and allow opponents to litigate the issue. Any official challenge to I-290 would buy time for anti-highway groups.

The Cleveland–NOACA dispute went to Washington in May 1970. It included complaints by the NOACA board of mistreatment by HUD. Stokes, who had been very supportive of the highway positions we had helped evolve, invited me to join him as his staff for the meeting. Although the mayor was invited to join a NOACA board delegation to Samuel Jackson, HUD's assistant secretary for metropolitan planning and development, Stokes and I visited Secretary Jackson alone. Jackson, who was the highest-ranking black person in the Nixon administration, was cordial and receptive to our position, especially with regard to the impact of the highway on jobs and low-income housing. Jackson was able to restore good will between the NOACA board and HUD, but reminded the NOACA representatives that Cleveland's demands for greater representation had resulted directly from the board's choice of a freeway location. He insisted that the board should ensure that there was adequate housing for people displaced by regional facilities—essentially the argument Stokes and I had urged on the secretary.

Up to this time, we had only implied that the need for relocation housing and the related needs of low-income families were part of the basis for our opposition to the I-290 decision. It now seemed appropriate to make these points explicit. I knew of no better way to do this than at a NOACA board meeting. It seemed to us that if a regional agency existed and HUD regulations stressed regional cooperation and problem solving, then NOACA could be a vehicle for attacking a variety of social problems, many of which were concentrated in the central city. Indeed, agencies such as NOACA should not limit themselves to functional, engineering-type issues; those issues are not the ones that vex our society. A major goal of regional agencies, we felt, should be social equity. Accordingly, in August 1970 we drafted and introduced for NOACA board approval two resolutions: one encouraging local communities in the region to take positive steps to provide moderate- and low-income housing; the second urging all communities to enact equal opportunity employment laws. In a statement before the board, I reminded its members that they had often criticized

Cleveland for its lack of regional statesmanship and regional cooperation in opposing I-290. I called attention to the need of Cleveland's poor for more housing choices in the region and suggested that the city might be willing to consider the highway in the interests of regional cooperation if we could receive realistic assurances that our displaced poor could be relocated, if they so chose, in new public housing located in the rest of the region. The board finally approved the equal employment resolution after heated debate at several meetings, but made no effort to encourage local governments to implement it. The housing resolution died in committee. I expected nothing more, but the strategic point had been made again.

The city's bargaining position was restructured in remarks made at an American Institute of Planners and U.S. Department of Transportation seminar in November 1970. This seminar was chosen because I had been asked to summarize the papers delivered by Don Hyde, formerly head of the Cleveland Transit System, and Albert Porter, the Cuyahoga County Engineer, who was the strongest proponent of the I-290 freeway. My summary laid out the bargaining idea in greater detail as it applied to another freeway controversy that was beginning to emerge. After putting forward, and rejecting, the economic and social costs if the proposed freeway was built under given rules of compensation, I said:

> But talking room exists if the state highway department, or some more comprehensive transportation/development agency, could (1) absorb the entire project cost, (2) rebuild the lost housing in the city on a unit-for-unit basis, and (3) compensate the city for its loss of property and income tax revenues. The city, then, would be in line with the ground-rule that it would not be left worse off than before the highway.

After two years of disagreements and negotiations, the dispute moved to a climax. With Cleveland persisting in its suit and refusing to pay its dues and the federal government threatening to withdraw funds, the NOACA board agreed in January 1971 to a reorganization plan that would give Cleveland eight members on a fifty-two-person board. Cleveland refused to accept the scheme because the scheme made specific provision for the membership of the Cuyahoga County engineer, ensuring, in our view, that pro-I-290 interests would continue to dominate agency activities. The board then voted to deprive

Cleveland of all voting rights. In June 1971, with some urging from Mayor Stokes and Law Director James, HUD withdrew its certification of NOACA as the A-95 review agency for the area. NOACA became the first and only agency in the nation to have its HUD certification withdrawn, an act that threatened its budget and its existence.

About this time, after three and a half years in office, Stokes announced that he would not seek a third two-year term as Cleveland's mayor. In November 1971 the voters of Cleveland elected Ralph J. Perk, the Republican county auditor. One of Perk's campaign pledges was to end the "bickering" between Cleveland and NOACA and to "join with the suburban municipalities to cooperatively guide the region's future." He promised to rejoin NOACA, pay Cleveland's dues, and withdraw the city's lawsuit. Following his inauguration, Perk moved to do just that, but not before having a long discussion with James B. Davis, his personal lawyer and a charter member of the anti-freeway coalition, and myself. With much fanfare, Perk attended a NOACA board meeting and spoke to the board of the need for regional harmony and unity. Much more quietly, however, the new mayor insisted on the same conditions as Stokes for restoring regional harmony: an improvement in the city's numerical representation on the board and the rescinding of the I-290 decision. The board members were impressed, I think, by Perk's willingness to come out and talk to them, especially after Stokes's reluctance to do so. And it soon came to pass that in the winter of 1972, HUD recertified NOACA after the agency raised city representation to eleven members of a fifty-six-person board and also agreed to an affirmative equal employment program, accepted a regional housing element as part of its work program, and rescinded the I-290 resolution.

Perk decided to continue to use me as his representative on the NOACA board and, so far as I can recall, never attended another NOACA board meeting in his six years as mayor.

As of this writing, the Clark Freeway has not been built. The alternate route proposed in 1970 by the Planning Commission was also not built. The $100 million reserved for the Clark Freeway, however, was ultimately used in Cuyahoga County for transit under a law permitting transfers among transportation modes at local option.

NOACA has reassumed its innocuous, placid, almost invisible existence, simply executing consensus studies and rubber-stamping the wishes of its constituent members on all grants-in-aid. The municipalities that make up NOACA continue as before to act as communities of limited liability, accepting no responsibility whatever for the problems of the region.

6

Low- and Moderate-
Income Housing

Early in 1970, Irv Kriegsfeld, director of the Cuyahoga Metropolitan Housing Authority (CMHA), brought proposals for 1,200 new public housing units to the City Planning Commission for its comments, as required under Ohio law. I scheduled the proposals for an immediate hearing. And all hell broke loose.

Two of the most serious problems in Cleveland involved housing. The first was the overwhelming concentration of the region's low-income public housing within the city, and within the worst neighborhoods of the city. Without the dispersion of new public housing units into better city neighborhoods and into the rest of Cuyahoga County, my staff and I reasoned, the minority disadvantaged would be increasingly isolated in the backwaters of the city and lose opportunities for the new decentralizing services and jobs. Their continued concentration in the city would be bad for them and bad for the city as an institution.

The second problem, which was revealed by housing research conducted by Janice Cogger, John Linner, Doug Wright, and Ruth O'Leary, was the systematic redlining of many of Cleveland's residential neighborhoods by private banks and savings and loan companies. Redlining meant that decline in these neighborhoods was a self-fulfilling prophecy, since owners seeking funds for the sale or rehabilitation of their properties would be denied the necessary credit.

We decided to try to eliminate or ameliorate both problems. In the first case, the city planning staff prepared a "fair share" proposal to decentralize new public housing construction into the sixty other jurisdictions of Cuyahoga County. In the second, our efforts to end redlining took us through two years of negotiations with twenty-two of Cleveland's commercial banks and savings and loans (S & Ls) and ultimately to the inauguration of a lending program called CASH, which was begun in 1977 and is still being operated in 1990.

THE FAIR SHARE PLAN

The "Fair Share Plan for Public Housing in Cuyahoga County" was the full title of the proposal we prepared and made public in 1970. It was an outgrowth of the fact that in Cleveland, as in many other American cities, public housing had been built where it was politically feasible: in black neighborhoods and in undesirable mixed-use areas. Although the CMHA had authority to build public housing in all sixty municipalities of the county but one, public housing existed in fact only in three jurisdictions: Cleveland, East Cleveland, and Oakwood. Of 12,000 public housing units owned and operated by CMHA in 1972, 11,700 were located in Cleveland. The county's other municipalities had declined to accept any public housing by the simple expedient of refusing to sign a cooperation agreement under which they would agree to provide full municipal services while accepting a payment by CMHA in lieu of full property taxes. Without a cooperation agreement, CMHA could not build in these jurisdictions.

Our fair share plan arose as part of an attempt by CMHA, then under the capable direction of Irving Kriegsfeld, to break out of the agency's traditional pattern of locating in all-black neighborhoods of the central city. Toward that end, Kriegsfeld was preparing to build 1,200 new units of public housing in the relatively more affluent neighborhoods of the city's far east and west sides.

Kriegsfeld's emergence as CMHA director had been preceded by a great deal of national and local pressure. In 1966, representatives of the U.S. Civil Rights Commission visiting Cleveland had been extremely critical of CMHA's practice of building only where ward councilmembers approved—in effect giving veto power over site selection to Council—and of racial segregation in CMHA's projects. After passage of the Housing Act of 1968, HUD ordered public housing authorities to select sites for new construction and to purchase housing on the open market for use by low-income tenants only within the guidelines of the new Housing Act and the Civil Rights Act. In Cleveland, HUD mandated that CMHA produce new units only on a one-for-one basis: a unit could be produced in a black neighborhood only after one had been produced in a white neighborhood. HUD and local pressure had also forced Ernie Bohn, long-time CMHA director, to resign. Kriegsfeld was Bohn's replacement.

I liked Irv Kriegsfeld. He was smart, tough, and an aggressive advocate for low-income housing. I had the feeling that he would do everything he could to follow HUD directives, expand CMHA's program, and make it work for the tenants and the city.

My staff met with Kriegsfeld to talk about his proposed program and what the planning staff might do to help. Ohio state law mandates that the public housing agency submit its plans to the City Planning Commission for the commission's advice. Our reviews of the plans could be gentle and positive. But what could we do beyond that? We all knew that any effort to develop new public housing in nontraditional neighborhoods of the city would be tremendously controversial. Perhaps we could help CMHA by taking some of the heat? We asked if the planning staff could do a study demonstrating that, under the right set of conditions, the construction of new public housing would not have a negative impact on surrounding real estate values. We had in mind replicating an independent university study that showed no decline in property values as a result of racial integration. Kriegsfeld agreed that this would be a good idea, but it would take too long to be useful for the present situation. What if, we suggested, the city planning staff proposed that new public housing not only be decentralized within the city, but also introduced into the county on a fair share basis? Kriegsfeld's eyes lit up, and we knew we had a deal.

We were delighted to be able to help CMHA in this way, in part because we had intended to have the staff produce a fair share plan in any event. Fair share seemed to be one answer to the problems that I had come to believe (and still believe) lay at the root of central city distress in many cities throughout the United States: racial discrimination and concentrations of poverty. The fact that Irv Kriegsfeld agreed with my views made helping CMHA that much more satisfying.

Racial discrimination, we thought, was why the median

income of blacks was only 60 percent that of whites and why blacks remained intensely segregated both within metropolitan areas and within central cities. While the segregation of other ethnic groups had diminished over time, black segregation remained at a high level or had even increased in some areas. Racial discrimination and residential segregation involved heavy costs for black families as well as the city of Cleveland and all of American society. Blacks paid in the humiliation they often faced when seeking housing outside the ghetto; in higher costs for housing, insurance, and mortgage financing; in the loss of jobs in a suburbanizing job market; and in the need to accept the poorer public facilities and services available in the central city. Cleveland paid for racial segregation in the currency of social conflict and crime and in the weakness of demand for investment in ghetto areas. In this sense, the environment of the ghetto compromised the city's ability to redevelop itself. And American society as a whole paid for racial discrimination and segregation in the loss of international prestige, as other nations noted the gap between our egalitarian rhetoric and reality; in prison costs and welfare support payments; in the high costs of school busing to achieve constitutional protection for students; and in the expense of constructing more and more transportation arteries to connect with ever more distant suburbs.

All of this was unfair, we agreed, and should be opposed by city planners and other public administrators as well as by the public at large.

Kriegsfeld and I also agreed that the way the land development process worked in our metropolitan areas disadvantaged central cities like Cleveland. While artificially raising the price of housing on the fringe and thus screening out lower-income groups, the process assured the better-off members of our society fine neighborhoods, schools, and services and burdened the central city with pockets of concentrated poverty containing many households with high welfare dependency rates, low economic capabilities, and major social problems.

Cogger, Linner, Wright, and all of the planning staff working on housing agreed that this metropolitan development pattern was unfair as well as discriminatory. We wanted to help improve the ability of CMHA to serve its tenants as well as help provide more housing choices for poor Cleveland families who might want to live in the suburbs or in better parts of our own city. But we were under no illusions. We understood clearly that challenging the status quo with regard to the location of public housing would be extraordinarily controversial. We also knew that our position might threaten the traditional image of the City Planning Commission as a dispassionate observer, above the fray. This might well cost the commission the loss of its image of objective detachment. It might also cost us our jobs. In addition, we realized that we were defining the clients for our work very narrowly: most people in Cleveland and in the county would probably prefer the present arrangements. That is, after all, why these conditions persisted. Yet the public we chose to serve in this case was weak, was most in need, and certainly needed our advocacy more than the other groups. Helping this group would put us in the mainstream of our social and religious traditions as well as within the code of professional ethics of the American Planning Association. Finally, we figured that if things got tough, Mayor Stokes would support us. All things considered, we thought the timing would probably never be better. So Kriegsfeld and we agreed to be as supportive of one another as we could as we tried to decentralize public housing out of the traditional neighborhoods of Cleveland and into the county.

In February 1970, after long discussions with the planning staff and private discussions with Planning Commission members who had reservations but promised their support, Kriegsfeld brought in his package of 1,200 new public housing units. Ohio law did not specify that the commission's approval was essential or that the project could not go forward over the commission's objection. What was essential was the public hearing itself. We scheduled the proposals for an immediate hearing in an atmosphere of bitter controversy.

Controversy was most intense around three items: a proposal to build about 350 family units on undeveloped land in the all-white southwest corner of the city, a section called "Old Brooklyn"; a proposal to build a complex (to be known as Lorain Square), consisting of a high-rise for the elderly and 24 family units in 12 duplexes in an all-white west side area that just happened to be the home ward of Jim Stanton, the powerful president of City Council; and a proposal for 280 units in Lee–Seville on the southeast side of the city, where the site was surrounded by the single, detached homes of middle-class blacks.

We held the hearing for the first proposal in the Planning Commission's conference room on the fifth floor of City Hall, with presentations from Kriegsfeld, Mayor Stokes, and HUD representatives from Chicago and Washington. Outside City Hall, hundreds of pickets protested against the proposal. Their complaint was environmental, they said; the neighborhood sewers and schools "couldn't take" the new families. The room was jammed when meeting time arrived, and when the pickets, led by their councilman, tried to get into the room, a great crush ensued. The police had to be called to keep the crowd from breaking down the glass doors. The hearing was held with the councilman and his livid constituents shouting at Stokes and the HUD representatives from the back of the room while the planning staff commented, as calmly as possible under the circumstances, on lay-out and design, simply trying to fulfill the hearing requirement of the state law and thereby help build the housing.

The next hearing was even tougher. We had scheduled the commission's hearing for the last two proposals together and had announced it two weeks in advance in the *Plain Dealer*, hoping to get as much public comment as possible. The day after the newspaper announcement, I was in a cabinet meeting in Mayor Stokes's office when the receptionist called me out of the meeting. There in the waiting room, with his fists balled, was a tense, glowering Jim Stanton, all six feet four inches of him, looking angry and menacing.

Stanton was a tough young politician who had been described as "an expert in political assassination" and a "belly puncher."[1] He had served in City Council for ten years. In 1963 he had successfully engineered a coup against the previous long-time president of City Council and had taken over the leadership of Council himself. Because of the fragmentation of Cleveland into thirty-three wards and the need for anyone who wanted favors from the city to be able to deal with a single person who could speak for and deliver the votes, the position of Council president was one of enormous power. Stanton enjoyed this power and used it forcefully. Later in 1970, Stanton was elected to the U.S. House of Representatives, where he served three terms. He ran unsuccessfully against Howard Met-

---

[1]Edward P. Whelan, "Can Jim Stanton Muscle His Way Into the Senate?" *Cleveland Magazine*, February 1976, pp. 49–60.

zenbaum for the Democratic senatorial nomination in 1976 and after his defeat moved to Washington, D.C., as a businessman. In 1989, with the support of former House Speaker Tip O'Neill, Stanton ran for the post of Democratic National Chairman.

Right now he was growling angrily at me. "Cancel those public housing hearings," he said, "or I'll cut your budget, cut your staff, and cut your balls off!"

I was momentarily stunned. Stanton not only had all the political power he needed to back up his threat, but he was physically an impressive and intimidating figure as well. I had no doubt that he could do almost everything he threatened to do to me. But if I canceled the hearings we would not satisfy the requirements of the state law, and the proposed housing would be delayed or go unbuilt. There was no way I could dodge Stanton on the issue.

I took refuge behind the reputation for ethical behavior and technical disinterest that is part of the tradition of the planning profession. I launched into a speech about the responsibility of planners to interject comprehensive rationality into the decision-making process: how planners served the public at large and the Council, as well as the mayor; how the dispassionate judgment of the planner was a necessary foil to the momentary passions of politics; how the hearings were an essential aspect of citizen participation; how the public had a right to know all the details of the proposal; how we were only trying to serve the whole public through the broadest interpretation of the public interest. Before I was well launched, Stanton beat a retreat, concluding, no doubt, that I was either completely crazy or too stupid to appreciate what he could do to me and my staff. The hearings went forward as planned. Stanton's pressure was more than offset by quiet praise and support from Mayor Stokes, who, it was plain, was taking a great deal of interest in the public housing proposals.

The hearing announcement stirred up so much local passion that it was clear that the City Planning Commission's conference room would be too small to hold the multitudes expected. So we rescheduled the meeting for Council's large and elaborate chambers. I took one other precaution: confident that the room, huge as it was, would be filled to overflowing with vociferous opponents of the proposals, I rented two buses with money out of my own pocket and made them available to the tenants of three CMHA towers for the elderly. I reasoned that these older folks, who were, after all, beneficiaries of CMHA's low-rent program, would provide support for Kriegsfeld's program and offset the anticipated hostility of the rest of the audience. It seemed to me that if these tenants were paying fifty dollars a month for a modern one-bedroom apartment with utilities included, they should be somewhat fond of their landlord.

The actual meeting fulfilled most expectations. The crowd was so huge it spilled out of the open doors of Council chambers. Predictably, it was made up of fearful, angry, and hostile people.

Both Stanton and Stokes took the opportunity to make speeches addressing their respective constituencies. The event was, like so many others in Cleveland politics, pure theater, filled with good guys and bad guys, stirring declamations and audience participation. Stokes went first. He spoke of the need for our society to be more caring and compassionate for those among us—the aged, the sick, the poor—who needed help. He mentioned his own youth and how he and his brother, Congressman Louis Stokes, had been raised in a public housing project by his loving widowed mother. He concluded with the type of peroration that is heard occasionally in black churches, where the minister repeats a theme of harmony, love, and peace and the congregation responds with rising intensity. For Stokes, it was a vintage performance, which got scattered, grudging applause even out of the mostly hostile audience.

Stanton's short speech, which followed, evoked the fears of the audience that their freedoms were being eroded by faceless bureaucrats in Washington, and by unnamed people he called "super planners" and "social engineers" who were imposing a set of unreasonable demands and an alien system on the America we all knew and loved. When he was through, the audience—including the two busloads of older folks I had brought down and paid for—rose as one person, cheering, whistling, and applauding. I briefly played with the idea of letting the old folks walk home.

After all of these theatrics, Kriegsfeld patiently explained the two development proposals for his projects while the planning staff, using maps and talking the language of urban design and architecture, made suggestions directed toward improving the site plan, the elevation, and exterior details. Despite the high temperatures in the chambers, our comments were cool, detached, technical, and professional, and we met the requirements of the state law without appearing to be partisan. For his part Stanton never retaliated against the planning staff, possibly because he viewed us as mere technicians.

How would other planning agencies have handled this issue? Knowing that new public housing construction in "non-traditional" neighborhoods is bound to be politically unpopular and intensely controversial, I suspect that most planning agencies would have declined to become involved in the matter, even to the point of delaying or refusing to schedule the public hearings. Delaying the hearings would have been simple to do and simple to rationalize: surrounding property owners would have to be notified; councilmembers would have to be spoken to; proper clearances would have to be obtained from members of the City Planning Commission. As the hearings were delayed and publicized, the opposition would grow and have time to initiate counter-strategies. In the end, the hearings would never have taken place, and the projects, having failed to meet state requirements, would never have been built.

For our part, the pressure bothered us, but we wanted to build the housing and to help the agency that had the responsibility to do so more than we wanted to avoid the pressure. Our goal of providing "more choices for those who have few, if any," clearly spelled out the only response we could reasonably make. The pressure came with the territory. On issues such as this, planners may win some and lose some. What matters is that they persist in representing equity-oriented objectives and in bringing before the community the equity consequences of certain decisions.

Ultimately, about two-thirds of all the units CMHA proposed in this package were built, but not without great cost. First, City Council, stung by CMHA's unwillingness to confine its development activity to traditional wards, refused for a period to sign a new cooperation agreement that called for 3,700 new units of public housing. Without the agreement, CMHA lacked authority for any new construction beyond that in the development package we had just approved. The city's failure to ensure the continuation of its low-income housing program led HUD, at the deliberate instigation of the Stokes administration, to refuse to certify the city's Workable Program, a document necessary for obtaining most federal funds. This lack of certification, in turn, led HUD to cut off funds for its urban renewal, model cities, demolition, and neighborhood development programs. Council was distressed. As the mayor well knew, councilmembers wanted to spend this money. With HUD's help in the form of this kind of pressure, Council agreed to another cooperation agreement with CHMA within three months.

More importantly, pressure from persons disaffected by Kriegsfeld's aggressive program began to affect the stability of the CHMA board. At the time of the Planning Commission hearings, Kriegsfeld enjoyed a narrow 3–2 majority, but in December 1970 one of his supporters resigned. In January 1971, the Board of County Commissioners appointed attorney Robert Sweeney, a former congressman, to the open slot. At his first meeting, Sweeney provided the swing vote to fire Kriegsfeld.

Ironically, our fair share plan, which was intended to deflect some of the pressure away from CMHA, was of no use for that purpose. The hearings and approvals had moved much faster than we had anticipated, and the plan was not ready till months later. Moreover, in publishing our "Fair Share Plan for Public Housing in Cuyahoga County," we realized that neither the city of Cleveland nor CMHA had the power to impose any negotiations or any solutions on the independent municipalities in the county. We wanted to open the issue for discussion on the regional agenda, where we felt it belonged. And, after all, fair share proposals had been approved by Ohio's Miami Valley Regional Planning Organization and were being proposed by other planning agencies throughout the country.

Our plan, which was developed by Layton Washburn and myself, was quite simple. It allocated public housing units to each municipality in Cuyahoga County on an equitable basis. In the model we used, each community in the county was arbitrarily assigned a number of public housing units equal to 2 percent of the total number of housing units in that community in 1960. We then compared that 2 percent figure with the number of families living in that community in 1960 who were "eligible" for public housing by virtue of low income (under $4,000 a year). The formula we developed generated a total of 7,778 new low-rent housing units, including 3,700 units for the city of Cleveland. Other cities in the county were proportionately assigned fewer units: Parma got 431; Lakewood got 364; Hunting Valley (where, honest to God, they still ride to hounds) got 3. In no case, as we took great pains to point out in the report and to the media, did the number of units allocated for any community by this method exceed its "need" as measured by the 1960 number of "eligible" families in each community. We stressed the modest effort each community would have to make (some communities were assigned under ten units each) to reach these goals and assured everyone that, if the plan was developed as we proposed, no community would be over-whelmed with public housing.

We proposed fair share for three reasons. First, as already noted, we wanted to help the Kriegsfeld city proposals; second, we wanted to demonstrate that every one of the sixty munici-palities in Cuyahoga County was in need of some low-income housing to serve its own low-income families; and, third, we wanted to underscore the fact that if all shared equally, the impact on any one community would be slight. It was well understood by everyone that the city lacked the power to im-pose any such plan on other municipalities. Fair share was proposed only as a basis to begin reasonable discussion.

Instead of reasonable discussion, the plan drew storms of protest from mayors and councilmembers all over Cuyahoga County. Communities whose fair share assignment involved as few as two or four units complained bitterly about this "assault on home rule."

For myself, it was a revelation of the depth of hostility to the poor, and specifically to the black poor. In the early morn-ing after the plan had appeared on the front pages of the *Plain Dealer,* our home phone rang. My wife, Virginia, answered it. A voice rasped out, "Tell your husband to keep the niggers out of the suburbs or we'll crucify him." Virginia, with the presence of mind born of good breeding, responded, "Who shall I say is calling?"

Needless to say, our fair share plan generated great interest but little support. Our efforts to encourage some serious con-siderations of this or other distribution plans for low-rent hous-ing through public hearings at the county commissioner level and at the CMHA board met with indifference, and ultimately the plan died a quiet death.

Yet the problem has not gone away. In Cleveland and in many other large cities in our country, racial discrimination and segregation continue, and public housing is in trouble. The program is not only being starved for federal funds, but is under attack on sociological, architectural, and economic grounds—often by former allies. The fault, it seems to me, is not with public housing or the tenants, but with the simplistic assumption of policy-makers that housing alone could substantially reduce the many, tangled problems of the poor. In addition to housing, we need to address racial discrimination, improved education and other services, and create jobs.

The demand for public housing in many cities (in 1984 New York City had 150,000 public housing units, a waiting list of 175,000, and a 4 percent annual turnover rate) suggests that the provision of public housing remains a viable strategy for public policy making. More funding and better management will surely help. Whatever the precise shape of the solution, the need for clean, adequate, unsegregated, and nonstigmatized housing for the poor obviously remains.

THE CASH PROGRAM: AN ATTEMPT TO END "REDLINING" IN CLEVELAND'S NEIGHBORHOODS

The Cleveland Action to Support Housing program (CASH) was an effort, led by the city planning staff, to attack another of the city's housing problems. All our analyses made clear that city policy should promote housing rehabilitation in addition to CHMA-assisted new construction. Our objective was to encourage new public and private investment in the city's housing stock. The public funds available were clearly inadequate to the task: we estimated that 7,000 units in the city were suitable for rehabilitation at a total cost of over $1 billion; in 1978 the city put $6 million into housing rehabilitation. The question was therefore how best to encourage the city's commercial banks and S & Ls to reinvest in Cleveland. The fact that virtually no loans were being made for housing sales or rehabilitation in certain neighborhoods was well documented.

The staff, working with neighborhood organizations that were just beginning to focus on redlining as an issue, considered many options. These ranged from pressuring local lenders with threats of redlining complaints or other possible actions under the Community Reinvestment Act (CRA) to softer, more conciliatory approaches. We finally rejected the harder line because we doubted that Mayor Perk would support the city's filing a complaint under CRA. We needed to work out an agreement with the lenders so that they would willingly engage in neighborhood lending.

Staff members Janice Cogger and Ruth O'Leary argued that the best way to maximize private investment was to leverage our public monies with private dollars by reducing the lenders' exposure or risk. The idea was to use our public monies to underwrite any part of a rehab loan that was "unbankable." For example, if a loan applicant needed $10,000 to bring his house up to code standard, and was only "bankable" for $6,000, the participating lender would make the "bankable" loan and the city, using funds from the Community Development Block Grant (CDBG) program, would make a deferred loan for the "unbankable" $4,000. We would ask the lenders to modify their underwriting criteria slightly so that more borrowers would be bankable, and we would try to get them to lend at slightly below market rates. On the other hand, we would comfort the lenders by spreading what little risk there was over a big pool of participants and also by setting up CASH as a nonprofit corporation on whose board they would (by design) have four of the five seats.

CASH would establish a loan-review committee to evaluate all loan applications. When an application met the criteria, each participating bank or S&L would make the loan as its turn came up in the rotation. In that way, each lender would share equally in the "risk" (of which there was virtually none), and the borrower would be assured of the needed money.

This seemed like a reasonable approach, and we asked Mayor Perk if we could set up and head a new committee to propose such a lending program and get the support of the lenders. He agreed, and I launched into negotiations with twenty-two of the city's commercial banks and S&Ls. Ruth O'Leary served as staff through much of the negotiation that followed. The difficulty of these negotiations surprised me, even though I knew the reputations for lending conservatism of the city's lenders. Even with the modest, low-risk program we proposed, it took fully thirty meetings over a two-year period before an agreement could be reached. In the course of the negotiations, we had to give up on our efforts to get the lenders to modify their underwriting criteria, and also to provide loans at lower than market interest rates. They were simply unwilling to do either. It often seemed that the only friend we had on the other side of the table was Ed Wagner, a vice president of Cardinal Federal Savings & Loan, who had been active in underwriting mortgages in Ohio City, a Cleveland neighborhood where a modest bit of gentrification had taken place, and who was interested in encouraging other lenders to join his S&L in the city's neighborhoods. Otherwise, it was a highly unresponsive group.

At the eleventh hour, after thirty meetings and the agreement of all the other lenders around the table, Brock Weir, chairman and chief executive officer of Cleveland Trust Bank (now Ameritrust), threatened to withdraw. Weir resented having Cleveland Trust, one of the largest banks in the United States, lumped into a lending pool with the S&Ls. He also resented having to accept a loan assigned by the CASH loan review committee. "No one," he said, "was going to tell Cleveland Trust when to make a loan." Fearing that if Weir withdrew, all of the other participants would also refuse to participate, Community Development Director Ruth Miller and I paid a visit to him and persuaded him to go along.[2] After thirty meetings over two years, we were on the threshold of setting up and exploring the promise of this leveraging program—if only we could get Council to cooperate.

The long CASH negotiations came to an end just about the time Dennis Kucinich replaced Ralph J. Perk as mayor of Cleveland. In November 1977 Kucinich appointed me director of the Community Development Department, where I would have more direct say over the city's CDBG funds (subject, of course, to the wishes of Council and the mayor).

The primary programmatic vehicle for housing rehabilitation at this time was the CDBG-funded Three Percent Loan Program. Under this program, any qualified applicant could receive a rehab loan of up to $20,000 at an interest rate of 3 percent with a term of up to twenty years. I immediately assigned Ruth O'Leary, whom I had brought over to the Community Development Department from planning, to do an evaluation of the Three Percent Loan Program: evidence that the program was having little impact on the rehab needs of the city

---

[2]One year later, in the Kucinich administration, Weir was the only one of the six local commercial banks holding the city's notes who refused to accept the city's proposal to refinance the notes. The other five banks then also withdrew their earlier support. Cleveland went into default.

would incline the mayor and council to endorse the CASH concept. O'Leary's study showed, as we expected, that CDBG spending on housing was so thinly spread through the city that it had virtually no visible effect. In addition, we learned that the majority of low-interest loans were being made to middle-class residents, who were using the money to remodel kitchens and bathrooms and to put up aluminum siding. In light of the data provided by the study, we proposed to scrap the city's Three Percent Loan Program, the major rehab program operating in almost all the city's wards, and replace it with CASH, operating in a concentrated way in five target areas. We, in fact, intended to concentrate CASH still further, through smaller target areas selected jointly by my staff and neighborhood-based development corporations. There, all houses would be inspected for code violations, and homeowners willing to fix up their homes could get CASH loans plus new sidewalks, trees, and street lamps if needed. By concentrating our improvement dollars in focused areas and by using the neighborhood organizations to help execute the program, we hoped to turn around the negative investment trends in these areas and see visible improvements. For once, the city would be spending its money and the private money we leveraged in a targeted plan.

Unfortunately, Council at first refused to endorse CASH. The Three Percent program was politically popular, even though O'Leary's study showed that many wards eligible for the program had no loans at all and gained no substantive benefits. That argument did not work; for a councilmember, it was more important to say, "I got the Three Percent Loan Program for my ward," than to think carefully about the effects of the program. Mayor Kucinich complicated matters by regarding the CASH program as a "bureaucratic waste of time." I finally obtained the mayor's support (but never captured his enthusiasm) simply by insisting on the program as something I absolutely had to have for a successful Community Development program.

Council finally came into line when I got Ken McGovern, assistant director of University Circle, Inc., to join me in a visit to Richard Tullis, chairman of the Harris Corporation. At our request, Tullis called George Forbes and asked him to pass CASH. The Council president listened to Tullis. As a result of the mayor's decision to go along with something I really wanted that he was indifferent to, and the corporate community's willingness to ask George Forbes for a favor, CASH was passed by Council in February 1978. At the same time, Council also continued the Three Percent Loan Program, which made political sense to councilmembers but little programmatic sense to anybody else.

Considering everything, I was pleased with the outcome. At last the city had a program that would concentrate its housing expenditures and so would be much more visible than past programs. CASH also promised to leverage private dollars, an absolute necessity if we were to make a dent in our housing problems. And the program was aimed at low- and moderate-income people. We had gotten less than we aimed for, but it was at least a beginning.

Unfortunately, the CASH program didn't work very well. The original concept was based on the idea of leveraging many private dollars for investment, with fewer public dollars, in neighborhood housing. We reduced the risk for the private lenders by having the city underwrite "unbankable" loans and by setting up a large pool of lenders. The lenders, in return, should have participated enthusiastically. We had hoped that CASH would not only end redlining but would leverage three or four private dollars for each CDBG dollar we put into the program. In fact, HUD's second annual report on the CDBG stated, with regard to similar programs in other cities, that $2.40 of private money was being leveraged for each dollar of CDBG funds. But as the 1978 CASH Annual Report made clear, the leverage ratio in Cleveland was inverse: only 23 cents of private investment was made in Cleveland for every public dollar. The private lenders' contribution to resolving Cleveland's housing crisis through CASH was minuscule: it amounted to only $12,000 and two loans per institution in 1978.

Ruth O'Leary, Bill Resseger, and John Linner (as the most involved staff people at this time) considered ways of increasing the leverage ratio. There were a number of actions we could take: we could establish a loan-guarantee fund to take all the risk out of lending to an "unbankable" applicant; we could draw down all the CASH funds in advance from each year's CDBG and deposit them at low or no interest with participating lenders who would agree to double or triple the size of our deposit in loans; or we could threaten the lenders by challenging their operations under the CRA. But as we discussed the options, the Kucinich administration came under attack. It was the beginning of a prolonged siege culminating in a 1978 attempt to recall the mayor, which Kucinich barely turned back by 278 votes.

Shortly thereafter, in August 1978, I was removed by the mayor as Community Development director and sent back to the planning director's job. Mayor Kucinich, it seemed, had tired of our strategy for the use of the CDBG, especially our emphasis on a close relationship with the neighborhood-based organizations. Instead, he had decided that from then on CDBG funds were to be used in traditional political ways—to reward friends and punish enemies. If a neighborhood group refused to follow the mayor's lead, the mayor refused to support their projects and on occasion raised up competing, surrogate groups through which to channel neighborhood benefits. Instead of helping him politically, Kucinich's CDBG strategy brought him into conflict with his own natural base of support and added to his problems. Under constant attack by the newspapers, television stations, and City Council, and losing support in many Cleveland neighborhoods, Kucinich was swept out of the mayor's office a year later.

And what of the CASH program? Today, in 1990, CASH is still operating, but under a new format. Loans are made by one of twenty participating lenders at a 6 percent interest rate. The city then draws down one-half of the face value of the loan from the CDBG and deposits that amount with the lender. The private–public leveraging ratio is now two for one. However, the present program does not have the targeting feature that was key to the original program, and for all the city now knows, formerly redlined neighborhoods are still being denied credit.

CASH also provided some impetus for a more aggressive city policy on the placement of its own deposits. With the passage of the Bank on Cleveland Ordinance in 1987, the city announced its intention to place its deposits with the bank or banks that can show the most proactive neighborhood lending program. Perhaps some future modification of the CASH program will better encourage what we intended: a three-way partnership among the city, its community-based development organizations, and its banks to improve the flow of credit and the rehabilitation of neighborhood housing.

7

Tax Delinquency and Land Banking

We didn't start out to change the state law regarding property ownership in Ohio, but that's where we ended up.

It began with our determination to address the issue of low-income housing in Cleveland. We made this a high priority in our work program for a number of reasons. First, low-income housing was a problem of obvious importance; one needed only to walk or drive around Cleveland to see major concentrations of dilapidated housing and rotting neighborhoods. Second, it seemed clear to my staff and me that all of our national and local housing policies and programs had accomplished relatively little for those who actually needed decent housing the most—the poor. Others—developers, builders, lenders, construction workers—may have benefited from these programs, but quite obviously large numbers of poor people in Cleveland were still living in poor housing. Third, housing was a familiar area for my planners, and planning agencies were expected to be repositories of housing data, analyses, and recommendations. This, unlike a few other issues in which we came to be involved, was an area of expertise and investigation in which we obviously belonged.

There appeared to be general agreement among the mayor, City Council, and most city officials as to what the low-income housing problem was: there was a scarcity of such housing in the city. The assumed remedy was direct and uncomplicated: to build more subsidized housing where such construction was politically feasible, that is to say, in the city's black neighborhoods.

My staff and I were not convinced. If conventional wisdom was correct, why were rents in Cleveland so low? And why were abandonment, vandalism, and demolition so widespread—particularly on the black east side? We decided to undertake a research effort aimed at casting more light on the issue by answering three basic questions: (1) what was the nature of the low-income housing problem in Cleveland? (2) what was the nature and effectiveness of the public response to the problem? (3) what changes in public programs and policies would be needed to achieve a more effective response?

These studies, executed by Doug Wright and John Linner, under Ernie Bonner's direction, began in early 1972 and were completed in the fall of 1973. The findings argued forcefully that the conventional wisdom was incorrect and that an alternative definition of the housing problem was more applicable to the situation in Cleveland. The problem was not a scarcity of low-income housing units in the city. Because of sweeping population declines and generally low income among the remaining families, a surplus of low-income units—most of them of substandard quality—had been created. The central problem was not a lack of housing but a lack of income.

The housing studies included a brief analysis of tax delinquency and abandonment of property. We found about two thousand vacant and vandalized housing units in Cleveland, and we estimated that the rate of residential abandonment was three units a day. We concluded that because of low income, large numbers of Cleveland households simply could not afford standard housing. In addition, public housing built in politically acceptable locations had the perverse effect of further depressing an already depressed housing market. Along with other studies taking place about the same time, we found that owners of marginal residential properties in Cleveland were not getting enough revenues to maintain their buildings properly. We also found that in some Cleveland neighborhoods, property tax delinquency was a significant and growing problem, and that there was a high correlation among deterioration, tax delinquency, and abandonment. The market for real estate in these neighborhoods had virtually collapsed. Many property owners had lost interest in their holdings and had simply stopped spending money on them. Ultimately, these owners and their tenants walked away from the property; the property was burned or otherwise vandalized; and the city was left with an uncollectable demolition lien and the cost of cleaning, trimming, and otherwise maintaining a vacant lot. None of these costs were likely to be recoverable. Our investigation made clear that local regulations and state law regarding the prompt foreclosure of abandoned, tax-delinquent properties were not working. The city incurred major costs for these properties, yet the titles generally remained with the tax-delinquent owner. These lots would be extraordinarily difficult to redevelop so long as they remained subject to these procedures.

As a result of the analysis, we came to believe that our attention and the attention of other city officials should focus on saving the existing housing stock from deterioration and abandonment, on making foreclosure faster and more certain, and on compensating the city for costs related to tax delinquency and abandonment.

Our housing studies concluded with two policy recommendations for federal, state, and local government. First, we recommended that an adequately funded housing allowance program be made the cornerstone of federal policy in housing. We believed that such a program would provide assistance to *all* qualified families for the rental of standard housing and would address poverty, the heart of the problem. Second, we recommended that state laws and local procedures be changed to allow the city to demolish abandoned structures more quickly, and to recover demolition and maintenance tax liens. As part of this proposal, we also recommended that the city be allowed to take title to tax-delinquent and abandoned properties and land-bank them, acting as trustee for the other two taxing bodies, the Cleveland school board and Cuyahoga County. We made our recommendations to the City Planning Commission, sent copies of our study and recommendations to all the relevant agencies we could think of, and then considered what we might do next.

Many planners in a similar situation might be tempted to stop at this point and avoid pursuing matters any further. Such planners seem to think that once their studies are complete, their regressions run, likely solutions identified, and recommendations made, their responsibilities are over: what lies beyond the planning commission exceeds their charter-mandated responsibility or their technical expertise. They may also consider further activity to be counterproductive or politically dangerous. But if planners do not take their recommendations beyond their commissions, who else is there in local government to pursue or implement them? One might respond by saying that it is the responsibility of elected politicians to

implement such recommendations, but politicians rarely innovate; they react to the initiatives, pressures, and innovations of
others. Political policy making does not move in anything like a
straight line from proposal to objective. Instead, it moves crab-
wise (when it moves at all) with an eye carefully cocked to the
breadth of support and the avoidance of controversy. In fact,
there is no other agency in local government with the time
or perhaps the interest to move planners' recommendations
along. If planners care about the future (and the very concept
of planning implies that they do), they must be prepared to
do more than merely present their findings and recommendations to their commissions. They must do more. *Whether* they
choose to do more and *what* they choose to do may, more than
anything else, serve to distinguish one planning agency from
others.

With respect to our proposal for a national housing allowance program, we wrote a position paper for Mayor Perk.
Oddly enough, it was quite similar to the policy paper we had
drafted earlier for Mayor Stokes. As the Republican mayor of
one of the largest cities in the country, Perk was a favorite of
President Nixon. Perk was planning to run for the Senate in
1974 (a race ultimately won by John Glenn), and he seemed
pleased to have his planners help develop his housing position, especially since it seemed to fit so well with the Nixon
position on housing vouchers. We also publicized our findings
with Cleveland-area congressional representatives and with
HUD secretary James Lynn's staff in Washington. John Linner
and Doug Wright, the two planning staffers most responsible
for the "Cleveland Housing Papers," also wrote an article on the
proposal for *Planning* magazine.

We were under no illusion that our research would make
the difference in refocusing national housing policy on housing allowances for the poor. But we preferred to believe and to
hope that important shifts in national policy could be effected
by such research, publicity, and political support. Our well-
researched stand in support of a Nixon initiative probably
helped substantiate our reputation as technically competent
and apolitical "professionals."

Our second recommendation led us to a major success: a
change in state law to allow the city and county to speed up the
foreclosure process for tax-delinquent properties and to allow
the city to land-bank those properties that were unsold at sher-

iff's sales. We felt that this was an extremely high-priority issue, first because ultimate redevelopment of these delinquent and abandoned parcels would be impossible without clear titles, and second because we felt that public ownership was essential for immediate control and interim reuse.

As it turned out, our efforts were a textbook case of planning research, policy development, and implementation.

We began by concluding from our studies that the state law had to be changed. Then we tried to estimate what it would take to change it. We thought it would be appropriate to try to provide leadership on this issue because we probably understood the issue better than any other city agency and had the time to devote to it as well. To change the state law, we decided, we would need the support of the grassroots neighborhood development groups, the city administration and City Council, the state legislature and governor, the county auditor, sheriff, and prosecutor, the school board, the county commissioners, and the business community. A new state law had to be supported by close to total consensus. Given the "veto-group" politics in Cuyahoga County, objections to our proposals from any one of these groups could have scuttled the whole idea. We knew that few proposals emerge as law from the American legislative process unless the vast majority of articulate, interested groups favor some version of them. We also knew that we had to obtain support from politicians who would probably be anxious to avoid controversy until some consensus had developed. In this case, we were proposing to change state law with respect to the ownership of real property in Ohio, a conservative state. Virtual unanimity seemed required, but we were not sure we could achieve it, since we were probably seen as adversaries by at least a few influential people in Cleveland.

Strangely enough, though, this did not concern us deeply. If one of the participants should try to hold up the bill, we thought we could get other powerful actors to overcome this resistance. We expected participants to act in their own self-interest, and we were confident that our proposed law was desirable on all counts, with many potential winners and few losers. For example, both developers and neighborhood groups would want to have access to city-owned parcels with cleared titles for their development plans, especially when the alternative was property in the hands of indifferent multiple heirs of estates. These parcels were usually loaded with liens far beyond their market value. The city would benefit from a law that shortened the foreclosure period either by forcing delinquent owners to pay their taxes or by taking title to land against which the city had legitimate liens. The city, through a land-banking process, might also be able to assemble enough land at no cost to make large-scale redevelopments possible in the future rather than trying to buy individual parcels from many owners when the time came. The county was interested in forcing tax-delinquent owners to pay up. And the other taxing bodies might get some future revenue, instead of foregoing any hope of any tax revenue as at present. Best of all, a change in the law would cost the city nothing. The only losers we could identify, and the only potential source of opposition, would be some speculators and scattered holders of marginal properties hoping to sell their buildings before losing their land through foreclosure. If they surfaced at all, we thought, their views would not be given serious consideration by the legislature.

It occurred to us early on to try to get a sense of how the business community would respond to our efforts to change state law. I decided to test out the prospects with Joe Pigott, the executive director of University Circle, Inc. (UCI). UCI was a nonprofit agency that managed the properties and development plans of Case Western Reserve University, hospitals, museums, and other great cultural institutions in Cleveland's University Circle area on the east side. Its board was a who's-who of the Cleveland elite, with strong connections at all levels of government. Quite frequently, UCI needed land for its development plans. Pigott and I had been friendly adversaries on a number of development proposals, but we could talk about issues honestly. If I could engage Pigott's support, I might also be able to recruit some of the power and influence his agency represented.

I felt I could talk constructively with Pigott despite our occasionally adversarial relationship. For one thing, as city planning director I was a member of the UCI board of trustees. I was, in principle at least, one of Pigott's bosses. The planning staff had also worked cooperatively with UCI on a number of proposals that we agreed were appropriate, such as the rehabilitation and conversion for residential use of the Commodore Hotel and Fenway Hall. Although Pigott and I had disagreed on certain issues, such as the UCI's proposal to demolish parts of residential streets like Hessler Road and East

115th Street, I had never attacked him personally, nor had he personally attacked me. We also respected and genuinely liked each other. But even if none of this had been the case, and we disliked and distrusted each other, I still would have gone to Pigott and asked for his help because the change in law we proposed was not only good for the city, it was good for his institution—UCI.

I was not disappointed; Pigott immediately saw the possibilities of the change in state law I was suggesting and was enthusiastic about it. He asked me to take the idea to one of UCI's lawyers, Jack Dowd, and test his reaction. Dowd was a partner in the prestigious law firm of Squire, Sanders, and Dempsey, often called Ohio's "shadow government" because of its members' extensive work on state and municipal bond issues. I knew Dowd from frequent contacts in City Hall and from his legal work for the Planning Commission on the "Warren's Ridge" new town proposal, floated in 1971. Dowd had done the section dealing with state and local legal impediments to the new town and how to overcome them with new legislation.

Dowd supported our political analysis of the situation and thought we might be able to get the consensus and support we needed from the state legislature if we could do a more detailed study to provide the statistical and descriptive back-up to justify such a change in the law. This would cost money that I did not have in my budget.

Our next stop, as it frequently was when we needed money and wanted support for a good project that was not in the budget, was the powerful Cleveland Foundation, the country's oldest community foundation and one of its largest. The Cleveland Foundation, which gave away about $15 million a year in the 1970s, had supported many of our initiatives. Its director, Homer C. Wadsworth, was a genial and intelligent man who rarely backed away from controversial issues. As a result, the foundation's support was given to practically every innovative activity in the community. We met with Wadsworth and laid out our proposal. At the end of our meeting, Wadsworth simply asked us to prepare a formal proposal for his board's consideration.

We drafted and submitted one that called for a grant of $50,000. Half of that amount would support a study of tax-delinquency laws in other states that we might use as a model. The other $25,000 was for a law firm to help draft the legislation. The grant was made at the foundation's next quarterly meeting. We then hired a consultant (Real Estate Research Corporation), assigned Susan Olson of our staff to work with the consultant, and launched our detailed research program. Olson's research was ultimately published as a book.[1] Craig S. Miller, our in-house attorney, was charged with shepherding the bill through the Ohio General Assembly.

Olson and Miller turned out to be excellent choices. Olson was a planner who had done eye-opening analyses of the impact of Cleveland's urban renewal projects on the market for downtown office space. Her studies were the first to make clear that the market for office space in downtown Cleveland was not growing, but shifting. By building many new office buildings, we were simply emptying older ones. Miller was the lawyer I had added to the planning staff because I was dissatisfied with the legal services the commission was getting from the city's Law Department. He had done excellent work on the Tower City case (see Chapter 12) and was very effective, along with John Gotherman, director of the Ohio Municipal League, in moving the tax-delinquency bill into law in Columbus.

Olson's detailed research found that tax delinquency was not a problem in all Cleveland neighborhoods. Most of the delinquent parcels were located in decaying inner-city areas, where crime, blight, and poverty were common. A combination of social and environmental factors made these parcels virtually worthless. Owners were abandoning their property because they felt it no longer had any economic value. As their interest in the property waned, they stopped paying taxes on it.

This had created a serious problem for the city. It was receiving tax revenue from fewer and fewer parcels. Yet the city had to protect the health and safety of residents who lived near these delinquent and often abandoned properties. We observed that abandoned buildings posed a serious threat to their neighbors: they caught fire and harbored criminals, and children might be injured while playing in them. Owners who abandoned buildings seldom were interested in paying to have them demolished, although this was their legal responsibility. If an owner refused to demolish a dangerous building, the city had to do so. And if he refused to keep a vacant lot free of junk

---

[1]Susan Olson and M. Leanne Lachman, *Tax Delinquency in the Inner City* (Lexington, Mass.: D. C. Heath, 1976).

and litter, that responsibility also fell upon the city. We stressed that in a time of fiscal austerity, Cleveland was spending more than $1.5 million annually to discharge duties such as demolition and lot clean-up that were legally the responsibility of private owners. Of course, the city could and did add these costs to the owner's tax bill in the form of a lien, but this accomplished nothing, since the owner had already stopped paying taxes anyway. The liens were, for the most part, completely unrecovered. Cities can incur expenditures on private property, but if owners decide their property has zero or negative value, which is frequently the case in abandonment, the city will have a difficult time collecting.

In Cleveland's most deteriorated neighborhoods, more than 25 percent of all the parcels were tax-delinquent in 1974. Many of them had little value and no immediate prospect for reuse. Forty percent of all the delinquent parcels in Cleveland were vacant lots, and another 8 percent had only vacant buildings. Delinquent taxes usually exceeded the property's value. Hence, the owners were not likely to redeem them.

We agreed that Ohio had laws to deal with these situations. Under Ohio law, when owners failed to pay their taxes, counties could foreclose on the delinquent properties and sell them to recover the money owed to the local taxing bodies. However, the foreclosure procedure was simply inadequate to deal with the problem we faced. It had been written during the Great Depression and was designed to aid landowners who were down on their luck but who would repurchase their property when times got better.

First, the procedure was too slow. Although the law allowed property to be sold within three years of the time it became tax-delinquent, the process actually took much longer. All parties who had an interest in the property were made parties to the suit, although it was often impossible to locate all of them. If a parcel was transferred to a new owner midway through foreclosure, the entire procedure would have to start all over again. In Cuyahoga County, it took an average of nine years to bring a delinquent parcel to a sheriff's sale. Some parcels we examined were still rattling around in the administrative machinery twelve years after their first missed tax payment.

Second, we found that the procedure was too expensive. Including title searches, appraisals, advertising fees, and other items, the cost of selling a parcel in Cuyahoga County averaged $400, and this did not include the salaries of the county employees who administered the foreclosure procedure.

Third, the process recovered little in the way of back taxes. In fact, administrative costs often exceeded the sale price. For example, our research showed that between 1969 and 1972, 437 Cleveland parcels were sold at forfeiture sales. One-third of these parcels brought less than $50 each; only 5 percent of them sold for as much as $500. Figuring the average cost of selling a parcel at $400, the public spent about $175,000 bringing these 437 properties to sale. The buyers paid a total of $72,000. Therefore, the public lost over $100,000 simply by foreclosing on them. And, of course, this said nothing about the $375,000 in delinquent taxes that were never recovered. By selling delinquent land at these prices, we concluded that the city was simply throwing good money after bad.

Finally, we found that the procedure did not return these properties to tax-producing status. Our studies revealed that half the Cleveland parcels that were sold for taxes from 1967 to 1972 were back on the delinquent rolls within two years after sale. It was clear that most of these parcels had been purchased by speculators who did not pay their taxes unless they sold the property.

To illustrate the futility of our system at that time, we cited the example of one parcel located in a declining area in Cleveland. This particular property became delinquent in 1963. It was offered at sheriff's sales, but no bidders could be found. Consequently, it was forfeited to the state. By this time, it had accumulated a total of $2,350 in delinquent taxes, and the public had already spent several thousand dollars simply bringing it through the foreclosure process. In 1972, this parcel was purchased by a speculator for $100, and he allowed it to become delinquent again in 1973. At the time of our study, this owner owed $687 in back taxes. We anticipated that some time in the future we would have to repeat the whole procedure, probably with similar results. To describe such a process as "rational" seemed to mock the meaning of the word.

We concluded our analysis by noting that the present system of laws, procedures, foreclosure, and sale-at-any price did nothing to remedy the problem. Instead, we proposed that the foreclosure procedure be simplified and streamlined to reduce delays and eliminate unnecessary expense. The method used at that time was too unwieldly to deal with the sheer number of parcels that were becoming delinquent. In our proposed new law, introduced as House Bill 1327, we would deal with these properties by notifying the last listed owner at his or her tax mailing address, with notice by publication to all lien-holders. This alone, however, was not enough. There would still be thousands of vacant lots and empty buildings that would bring little revenue at tax sales. These parcels had no immediate prospects for redevelopment and only attracted speculators who allowed them to become delinquent again. It seemed to us that a municipal land bank was the only solution, and that was what we proposed.

The municipal land bank idea was not new; it had been a feature of other cities' attempts to control tax delinquencies. Missouri law, for example, had created the Land Reutilization Authority in St. Louis. To a certain extent, our own approach followed the St. Louis model.

The new law that we proposed provided that whenever a vacant lot or abandoned building could not be sold for the sum of the delinquent taxes, special assessments, and administrative costs attached to it, the local municipality would assume ownership in trust for all the taxing bodies. An agency such as Cleveland's Community Development Department would hold and manage this land until it could be sold for some productive use. The proceeds of the sale would then be distributed among all of the taxing jurisdictions that held liens against the property, after the city reimbursed itself for the cost of acquisition and maintenance. It was our hope that this could spur large-scale redevelopment of decaying inner-city neighborhoods without the city's having to acquire land through costly eminent domain proceedings. And, we were careful to stress, this would *not* mean displacing people from their homes, because only vacant property could be taken by the land bank we proposed.

We observed that this approach would have several advantages over the one operating at the time. It would not require counties to spend time and money reoffering parcels that have little value, and this alone would result in considerable savings to the public. Second, we would not be locked into a cycle of selling delinquent properties only to watch them become delinquent again. Furthermore, if these parcels were to become more valuable, the public would reap the benefits rather than speculators who did not pay their taxes or maintain their property. Most importantly, this proposal could help us put vacant inner-city land back into some productive use. Rather than lying fallow and abandoned, this land could (at least in theory) provide jobs, homes, and taxes to a city that desperately needed them.

As HB 1327 moved through the legislature, we worried a bit. I testified before the House Local Government Committee, as did Jack Dowd, Craig Miller, and John Gotherman.

There were a number of familiar figures from Cuyahoga County, such as Ed Feighan, an old friend, and Harry Lehman, the representative from my own district, on the Local Government Committee. They proved not to be very helpful. Although they were cordial enough and ultimately voted for the bill, they had been offended by Mayor Perk's strategy for managing the legislation. Rather than select a member of the Cuyahoga County delegation to act as floor manager, the mayor, for reasons known only to himself, had chosen a legislator from Barberton, an Akron suburb. Members of the Cuyahoga County delegation resented this and chose to sit on their hands rather than actively work for HB 1327. Nonetheless, the sharp, hostile, in-depth questions that often suggest major opposition did not surface at the committee hearing. I felt relieved; if that opposition existed, it would have surfaced here.

We accommodated mild opposition from a few banks and S&Ls. My staff and I had taken care to enlist support from Cleveland's newspapers, the Growth Association, the rest of Cleveland's business community, and the Ohio Association of County Auditors, led at that time by George V. Voinovich, Cleveland's mayor from 1979 to 1989. Officials from Dayton, Youngstown, and other Ohio cities that suffered from the same problems testified for the bill. Miller and Gotherman answered questions as they arose: thanks to Olson's research, they had data on all the vital issues relevant to the legislation at their fingertips. Their work in committee, on the floor, and in the back halls, coupled as it was with Olson's excellent study, was outstanding and essential to the passage of the bill.

HB 1327 passed with only a few, minor amendments at the end of the same session in which we had introduced it. Governor James A. Rhodes signed it into law in June 1976, about four years after we had started the process.

Would we have started this whole process if we had known

that it would take four years to complete? Certainly. Government often moves slowly. Our studies and the other actions we took to support and justify the legislation could probably not have been done in less time unless we had assigned many more staff members to the project. To do that, we would have had to strip them from other important assignments.

When Doug Wright and John Linner finished outlining the scope of the tax-delinquency problems, we could have written reports, presented them to the City Planning Commission, and gone on to something else. In that event, it is doubtful that anyone would have done anything further at all. Having outlined the problem, however, it was clearly up to us to go beyond the commission and try to accomplish the needed change in state law. If we were serious about the ends of our work, here and elsewhere, we had to involve ourselves in the means of change, however messy and time-consuming.

By early 1990, following a rather shaky start-up period, the city has taken title to approximately twenty-five hundred parcels of tax-delinquent abandoned land. Acquisition has gone more slowly than anticipated because of lack of interest in the County Prosecutor's Office. Another ten thousand parcels have missed tax payments for three years or more, have been certified delinquent, and await foreclosure. Some of the acquired parcels have been sold to adjacent property owners; others have been contributed to Lexington Village, a major housing development on Cleveland's east side. What will be done with the other parcels is unclear. Presently there does not seem to be any large-scale demand for this land, and little can be gained from selling these parcels now. Holding them for large-scale future use will take strategy, wisdom, and political courage.

As I look back on our work on these two housing issues, three aspects of the staff's work seem most important. First, the planning staff redefined the local housing problem, emphasizing rehabilitation of the existing supply rather than the provision of new housing units. The staff also pointed to the heart of the housing problem in Cleveland as inadequate income on the part of Cleveland families rather than insufficient supply. With good analytical work, we helped others think about the complex housing problem in a new, manageable, and goal-oriented way.

Second, the perseverance of the planning staff was central to changing the state law governing the foreclosure of tax-delinquent properties and their land-banking. The changed law provides the promise of an enormously useful tool for the future redevelopment of these abandoned properties. Instead of having to engage in a drawn-out, expensive process of assembling parcels from many owners and clearing the titles, the foreclosed properties will be assembled cheaply and expeditiously, with any clouds on their titles cleared against the day when the land becomes "ripe" again and redevelopment is possible. Although the planners' role was key, it was played out in concert with many other actors from all over the state of Ohio. Some may have faced Cleveland's planners as adversaries at one time or another; nonetheless, all were willing to cooperate with them on this issue.

Third, this issue illustrates not only the length of time necessary to change urban policy but the unevenness of the process. The case began in 1970 when Bonner, Wright, Linner, and I decided to study housing abandonment and what happens to the tax-delinquent abandoned land. The results were then picked up by Olson and Miller, who were not even on the staff when the original research was begun. Meanwhile, Bonner and Wright had left for new positions in Portland. Olson's detailed study became a book and was crucial to Miller's efforts to move the bill through the Ohio General Assembly. Linner described the process in an article so that other planners could build on our experience. People outside the planning agency, like Joe Pigott of UCI and especially John Gotherman of the Ohio Municipal League, unexpectedly helped; people expected to help, like Ohio Representatives Ed Feighan and Harry Lehman, did not. The issue moved into different phases; the staff changed; the one resource that remained constant was persistence.

The passage of the new law, of course, is not the end. Its potential may still be squandered. A future administration may decide to sell off the properties in the land bank for short-term financial or political gain. Or the law's procedures at some time in the future may generate enough political opposition to nullify its potential. Indeed, in the early 1980s, portions of the law were found to be unconstitutional, although its basic structure remains in force.

But the opposite may be true as well. The city may use its land-banked properties wisely. Other Ohio cities may benefit from the law and the procedures it makes possible. New laws may be passed that build on and improve the original law, such as House Bill 603, passed in 1988. New developments may be made feasible at lower costs using land-banked parcels. In fact, the now-completed first phase of the Lexington Village residential development benefited from the land bank's contribution of several parcels, as well as the expertise of Mindy Turbov, a former Planning Commission staffer. This 183-unit development was located on the almost completely abandoned site of the 1966 Hough riots. It needed heavy subsidies to get under way. If the city had had to find each owner-of-record for all the tax-delinquent parcels in the site and negotiate a purchase price for each, the project might not have been built at all.

So the uncertainty of future redevelopment and the political hazards of holding land in public ownership should not discourage planners and cities from trying. Ultimately, all or most of the land now abandoned by owners as worthless will probably be redeveloped, even if at much lower densities than in the past. If the public is to define the shape, timing, and purpose of this redevelopment, public ownership is essential, and planners can play a key role in providing such ownership.

8

Regional Transit and a Committed Planning Presence

So many actors shape public policy in the United States that it is often difficult to know who is responsible for which outcome. Not so in the case of Cleveland's regional transit system. Here, Cleveland's planners played a key role in establishing the terms and conditions for setting up the regional system and for protecting the interests of Cleveland's transit-dependent population (those who depend entirely on public transit for their mobility). This chapter covers the protracted negotiations and the other events leading over a five-year period to the creation of Cleveland's regional transit system.

Ours is a private automotive society. In the twelve years following the end of World War II, the number of automobiles in use in the United States more than doubled to over 50 million, and the figures have continued to rise steadily. In spite of the energy crisis and the rapid inflation in the prices of motor vehicles, gasoline, and maintenance, the number of motor vehicles in use has accelerated. From 1950 to 1975 the proportion of American households owning two or more cars rose from 7 to 33 percent, and the percentage of adult Americans licensed to drive increased from 43 to 83 percent.

Although most Americans enjoy the freedom of movement conferred by automobiles, those without access to automobiles have found their mobility reduced in both relative and absolute terms. Indeed, the rise of the private automotive so-

A modified version of this chapter, entitled "Urban Transportation Equity in Cleveland," by Norman Krumholz and Janice Cogger appears in Barry Checkoway and Carl V. Patton (eds.), *The Metropolitan Midwest* (Chicago: University of Illinois Press, 1985).

ciety has contributed to the decline of the public mass transit systems. Once most people were driving, public transit ridership dropped, fares increased, and service declined. For the transit-dependent rider, each passing year brought fewer destination options, longer waits, and higher costs. The Cleveland Transit System (CTS) ran 14.9 million fewer vehicle-miles per year in 1974 than in 1960, and at almost triple the fare. In addition, the scattered patterns of new development in metropolitan areas make many destinations virtually inaccessible to those without a car.

This might be a relatively unimportant problem except for the fact that the transit-dependent—the poor, the elderly, the young, the sick, and the infirm—make up a substantial group in most central cities. In Cleveland an estimated 32 percent of all households did not own a car in 1970; of the 46,000 Cleveland families with annual incomes under $5,000 a year, 46 percent owned no car; 48 percent of all households headed by persons over 65 had no car. In a very real sense these transit-dependent households have been injured by the private automotive society. It follows that they deserve some redress through transportation measures directed specifically at their welfare.

For most city planners, however, the issues arising from transit dependency have not been paramount. Planners have traditionally defined urban transportation problems in terms of automobile access and traffic congestion. During the 1950s and early 1960s, planners and highway engineers united to call for the expansion of arterial systems and highways. As highway construction met increasing opposition in urban areas and as concern over energy, air pollution, and environmental issues became widespread, planners shifted their emphasis from the automobile to mass transit. Implicit in this turn to mass transit was a commitment to make transit service more accessible and attractive to those with automobiles—not necessarily to those who were transit-dependent.

The Cleveland City Planning Commission staff had a different planning orientation. Our goal of promoting a wider range of choices for those Cleveland residents who had few choices or none at all led us to define Cleveland's highest transit priority as the restoration of some of the mobility lost by the poor and elderly when the nation (and the city) turned to automobiles. Our aim was not to seek general support for transit subsidies to be used for purposes unrelated to equity or even to transportation, but instead to deliberately improve the equity of the distribution of transit subsidies and alleviate extreme transit deprivation. The case study of the struggle follows.

THE FIVE-COUNTY TRANSIT STUDY
AND PLAN

In 1969 officials of the Urban Mass Transit Administration (UMTA) of the U.S. Department of Transportation advised Cleveland officials that for CTS to qualify for the federal funds it desired, a regional transit plan would be required. Cleveland owned the CTS, which carried over 85 percent of the transit trips made within Cuyahoga County and which also extended into two adjoining counties. At the time, however, CTS was operating exclusively from fare-box revenues and was rapidly approaching financial disaster.

When CTS pointed out that because of its three-county service area it was already a regional transit system and would be pleased to prepare the required plan itself, UMTA informed the agency that a broader, regional planning framework was necessary. City and county officials then prepared a joint application for planning funds, which UMTA again rejected as too narrow in scope. Prodded by UMTA, CTS finally agreed to join a five-county planning effort directed by a twenty-two-member transit task force operating under NOACA, the regional planning agency. This was awkward, since the city was at that time suing NOACA in federal court to win additional representation on the NOACA board. Nonetheless, the price of obtaining access to federal transit funds was clearly participation in the broader planning effort, and it was a price CTS was prepared to pay.

What followed was a two-year, $750,000, five-county study for which UMTA provided two-thirds of the funds, leaving $250,000 as the local share. Cuyahoga County furnished $100,000, and because of the city's chronic fiscal crisis, the Growth Association provided $150,000. It seems likely that the Growth Association volunteered to provide the city's share because members of the Cleveland business community viewed the transit issue as significant.

I participated in this planning effort from its inception, as the transit task force representative first for Mayor Stokes and then for Mayor Perk. As a member of the task force's executive and consultant-screening committees, I stated our goals simply and frequently: to increase the mobility of the transit-dependent population and to bring greater equity to the allocation of transit subsidies. The task force agreed with the first goal and declared that one of the study's two overriding objectives was "to provide mobility to those persons in the area . . . who do not have reasonable access to alternative forms of transportation—the transit-dependent population." These views prevailed in the selection of a prime contractor that appeared from both its presentation and its reputation to be sensitive to socioeconomic considerations. These views also influenced the designation of a system design subcontractor with a similar reputation for a study of the transit-dependent population and ensured the earmarking of adequate funds for that study.

But these victories were only partial. The prime contractor's team and the project management set about responding to political pressures from the executive committee. These technicians essentially modified the work done by the system design subcontractor on the needs of the transit-dependent. The final plan met some of our objectives but placed major emphasis not on improved equity but on a massive rail construction program.

City planning staff members Janice Cogger and Himanshu Patel prepared a critique of the draft plan that focused on both the five-year and the ten-year transit development programs. The five-year program focused upon fare reductions, service coordination and expansion, capital improvements to upgrade existing service, and Community Responsive Transit (CRT). The ten-year program called for the investment of $1.6 billion for rail development. The underlying rationale for this proposal appeared to combine civic pride and political trade-offs. If Atlanta, Baltimore, Washington, Buffalo, and San Francisco were to have new rail systems or extensions, then Cleveland must also have new rails—especially since 80 percent of the costs would be borne by the federal government.

City planning staff members had minor reservations about the short-term program. We were concerned because the fare structure contained apparent inequities and the funding for CRT within Cleveland was sharply below the level recommended by the consultants. By and large, however, we decided the short-term program met our equity objectives. But we were opposed to the entire rail expansion program, since it was contrary to our goals of providing mobility for the transit-dependent and improving equity in the allocation of transit subsidies.

We carefully documented our objections. We tended to believe that most sophisticated quantitative analyses were elegant techniques that were partially designed to obscure the value biases of their creators. Fortunately, Patel was a Ph.D. in engineering and operations research and was not easily awed by the quantitative mystique. Working with him, we discovered that by asking the obvious questions, by identifying assumptions and tracing their quantification, and by ferreting out the differences between what numbers were claimed to prove and what they actually indicated, we could effectively criticize the consultants' "sophisticated" analyses.

We knew from the outset that the cost–benefit analysis was vulnerable. We were present at the meeting when it was first presented to the executive committee of the task force. A lawyer representing Ohio's largest bond counsel, who was the Growth Association's representative at this time, was disturbed to find that the benefit–cost ratio was only slightly in excess of 1.00. With our tongues sunk deep in our cheeks and a skepticism based on experience, Cogger and I proposed that something around 1.624 might be more acceptable to the task force and more salable to the public. Two weeks later, without making a single change in the plan, the consultants dutifully returned with a benefit–cost ratio of 1.71.

We found the "level of service" model, which was intended to provide a basis to compare and evaluate alternative transit proposals and which underpinned all of the patronage projections, to be equally meaningless. Although methodologies were state-of-the-art at the time, work opportunity data were obsolete, differences in the proximity of residential zones to various employment centers were inadequately spelled out, and the list of regional educational, cultural, and social centers reflected elite tastes. How many of our people would want to go to the Cleveland Playhouse or the proposed Salvador Dali Museum of Surrealistic Art? The critical employment data were not only ten years out of date but had been imperfectly collected in the first place. There were methodological problems as well as data problems—for example, trip preferences were weighed only in terms of destinations and not in terms of origins. In our minds, these errors tended to invalidate the entire study.

It seemed obvious to us that much of the consultants' technical work was nothing more than window dressing designed to justify the prior preferences of task force members. Observations at meetings confirmed this as the case. Lake County Commissioner Mike Coffey, who was also president of NOACA and a task force member, demanded that a proposed rail extension originally meant to terminate in a close-in eastern suburb of Cleveland continue eighteen miles farther through very low-density development to a city in Lake County; this was done. Mayor John Petruska of suburban Parma, also a NOACA and task force member, demanded a rail extension toward his city but stopping at its boundary (to avoid displacing any of his constituents); this was done too. Only our planning staff raised questions about the technical justification for either proposal.

The consultants did even more than comply with the wishes of the policy-makers; they frequently anticipated them. The five-county transit planning process offered several examples of what one analyst has termed "the premature imposition of constraints."[1] For instance, when the consultants began to develop proposals for major transit corridor improvements, they realized that because of Cleveland's freeway pattern, the west side might be adequately served by busways while the east side might require rail improvements. Sensing that the politicians who represented west side constituencies would find such a proposal unacceptable (because bus travel is "lower-class" than rail travel), the consultants recommended rail development for all corridors. In the case of the southeast corridor, they stated that the costs of the busway and rapid transit alternatives were not greatly different. A more careful examination revealed that this difference amounted to $43.2 million!

The CRT proposal provides another example of the premature imposition of constraints. The system design subcontractor analyzed the needs of the transit-dependent and recommended that CRT be subsidized at $5 per capita within Cleveland and at $3 per capita throughout the rest of the region.

---

[1] John Kain, "How to Improve Urban Transportation at Practically No Cost," *Public Policy* 20 (1972): 335–58.

But although this firm included that recommendation in its preliminary reports, the subcontractor never presented it to the task force. Instead, the task force staff recommended that CRT be funded at the $3 level throughout the region, including Cleveland. We ourselves analyzed this proposal and concluded that whoever developed the technical justification for the recommendation confused round trips with rides, because there was a 100 percent discrepancy between the stated assumptions on ridership and the implied assumptions in the revenue projection.

Our critique of the ten-year transit development program discussed all of these points in detail. Our official position on the five-county plan reflected the criticisms raised in that evaluation. We discussed our position in detail at well-publicized Planning Commission meetings and released our critique to the media in a short press release.[2] I spoke against it at public NOACA board meetings, where I picked up an unexpected ally, County Engineer Albert Porter, the "villain" of the Clark Freeway fight. We also sent our critique to UMTA officials in Washington. Several months later the secretary of transportation advised NOACA that no federal funds would be made available for rail development in the Cleveland area until an exhaustive analysis of less capital-intensive alternatives had been undertaken. The city planning staff had a party to celebrate our victory.

ESTABLISHING THE REGIONAL TRANSIT AUTHORITY

One assumption underlying Cleveland's transit planning process was that a regional transit authority, with the ability to generate local tax support and capture state and federal subsidies, would be formed to carry out the five-county transit plan. Early in 1974 the Growth Association wrote and the Ohio General Assembly passed legislation that provided for the formation of such an authority in Cuyahoga County. Early negotiations between the city and the county over the composition

---

[2]Cleveland City Planning Commission, "Position on the Five-County Transit Study," press release, April 1974. Also see "Staff Report on the Ten-Year Transit Development Program," July 1974.

of the authority's board broke down repeatedly. City Council President George Forbes used the meetings to demand that Cleveland be given absolute control of the RTA board. The county commissioners played out their own political agendas. Cleveland's Mayor Perk, who was making a run for the U.S. Senate, issued press release after press release extolling his leadership on the transit issue.

While all this was going on, the Cleveland Transit System's financial crisis was worsening. The CTS was the only major transit system in the nation financed exclusively from fare-box revenues. Thanks to cash reserves accumulated during the early 1960s and a loan from Cleveland in 1969, CTS had managed to limp along with periodic fare increases and service reductions. However, by November 1974 CTS had reached its limits. CTS management announced that cash reserves would soon be exhausted and the system would be able to provide only peak-hour service at approximately a dollar a ride. The availability of federal subsidies promised to postpone this deadline by a few months and thus make it coincide with the city's November 1975 elections. The political pressure was on, for no local official wanted his opponent to blame him for cutting transit service and raising fares. "Crisis" was moving the agenda ahead. As it often does in city government, a situation read as a crisis by key political decision-makers provides the impetus and opportunity for change. The similar role of an act of God, Hurricane Agnes, is discussed in Chapter 10.

In December 1974, fifteen days before the legislative deadline, Cleveland officials began the serious business of forming a regional transit authority. There were two major issues: the composition of the transit board and the conditions governing the transfer of CTS to the regional authority. The type of tax to be levied was not an issue. Although the state enabling legislation drafted by the Growth Association provided three choices—sales tax, property tax, or a combination of the two—there was no political support for the last two options.

The first issue was handled at meetings that included the mayor, the City Council president, the county commissioners, and representatives of some suburban jurisdictions. The formula decided upon was that the city would appoint four city residents; the suburban mayors and managers would appoint three suburban residents; and the county commissioner would appoint three members, at least one of whom must be a city resident. While area elected officials placed great emphasis on this phase of the negotiations, we ourselves had learned from experience that it makes very little difference who appoints whom when policy decisions that could benefit the deprived sectors of our society are being made. City representatives, whether they actually live in the city or not—and usually they do not—are just as likely as anyone else to ignore the interests of poor and working-class residents and to use their power instead to do favors for their friends and feather their own nests. Since the appointees are mostly middle-class, as are the bureaucrats administering the service, perhaps it is not surprising that it is mostly middle-class interests that are served.

The second issue was more vexing for city representatives. They had little notion of what to demand in return for the transfer of CTS to the regional authority. While some City Council members favored a cash settlement, the county commissioners were adamant that the city should receive no more than the $11 million it had loaned CTS in 1969, thus writing off to zero a system with a book value approaching $80 million. The question of cash compensation was settled quickly; the county commissioners won. The commissioners were equally adamant that the city should retain no special powers over the regional system's decision-making process. The idea that the city should have the right to veto certain types of decisions was also quickly dismissed. It was clear that the city of Cleveland should demand fare and service guarantees, but the politicians were unclear about what those guarantees should be.

At the first key meeting where these issues were to be discussed, there was an additional problem: the planning staff had not been invited to attend. There we were, the most knowledgeable group on transit issues in the city, with more than four years of intensive experience, not being asked to the first important negotiating session. We were outraged! First, we considered a mass resignation in protest. We rejected that because our objectives would have been lost forever. Instead, we decided to force our way into the negotiations. I walked into that first memorable negotiating session in the mayor's office with two staff members and sat down. When the issue came up, in front of forty or fifty participants, we confidently laid out the city's position, complete with flip-charts and handouts. The mayor loved it; he had no idea we hadn't been invited. Since no one knew we had not been invited, everyone assumed that we in fact represented the mayor. From that day forward until the deal was consummated, we spoke for the city on the issue. As we discovered later, our not being invited was not a piece of dark and subtle political chicanery, but simply a secretarial oversight.

We based our general strategy in the negotiations on findings from a number of transit-related studies conducted by the City Planning Commission in the early 1970s, as well as on our analysis of the transit development plan. We knew that the transit-dependent relied heavily on public transportation for nonwork purposes and thus traveled largely at off-peak hours. We knew that because of their location, they were already relatively well served for travel to downtown locations by the existing radial configuration of the system, but that they needed generally more diverse destinations and a system that was attuned to their health and social needs. We knew that physical infirmity might make it impossible for many transit-dependent individuals to use a fixed-route system even if they lived only a few blocks from a regular stop.

We also knew that the city's poor relied on buses rather than rapid transit or commuter railroads for an overwhelming number of their trips, and that per-trip subsidies were generally much more generous to commuter railroads and rapid transit than to buses. In fact, we had concluded that because of flat fares and regulatory policies that favor users farthest from the central business district, the main beneficiaries of the present transit subsidies were the more affluent riders.

Our package, which was based on these findings and on our principles, was easily understandable, if not original. We resurrected much of the short-term program of the five-county plan, modified it to better serve our strategic objectives, and translated it into terms that the decision-makers could understand. We believed that the Community Responsive Transit element of the plan offered the greatest potential benefits to the transit-dependent population, and we recommended that the city demand a substantial commitment to CRT as one of its highest priorities, that the elderly ride free twenty-four hours a day, that off-peak fares be substantially lower than peak fares, and that funds earmarked for rail system expansion be diverted to improve bus service.

Ours was the only detailed proposal brought to the bargaining table. Until it was presented, the only guarantees that had been discussed had stated that "50 to 60 percent of the service improvements should be located within the city of Cleveland" and that "the base fare should initially be established at 25 cents." Our proposal spelled out the specific service improvements that Cleveland should demand and pointed to the need to define more than the 'base" fare, for longer than "initially."

On December 31, 1974, the last day possible under the state enabling act, legislation was passed that established the RTA. Although the only guarantees included in the legislation were those that dealt with 50 to 60 percent of the service improvements and the initial base fare, provision was made for a more detailed delineation of the city's guarantees in a subsequent memorandum of understanding. The legislation also included a provision that we drafted and slipped in at the last moment forbidding the RTA to construct, engineer, plan, or otherwise contemplate a downtown distribution system during its first five years in operation. We had drafted this provision and included it in the legislation because we knew that the downtown distribution system was key to an expanded rail system and hoped that the provision might slow RTA down. The city leadership came into conflict with this provision a short time later with its support for the Downtown People Mover (see Chapter 9).

NEGOTIATING THE TERMS OF TRANSFER

Almost five months of bargaining followed. At issue were the guarantees to be contained in the memorandum of understanding. The controversy continued to pose flexibility for the RTA against firm guarantees for the city. Those allied on the side of unlimited flexibility included the county commissioners, the suburban representatives, the Growth Association, NOACA staff, and, ironically, the management of the CTS. Thwarted in their initial effort to transfer CTS to the RTA without any guarantees at all, this coalition fought to ensure that the fare and service guarantees for city residents be kept as meaningless as possible.

Why did this coalition come together? What were their interests? The county commissioners and suburban politicians apparently wanted the major share of service and improvements to go to suburban areas, because almost two-thirds of the total county population was located outside the city. They justified this by observing that county residents would pay the lion's share of sales tax revenues. NOACA, the regional planning agency, supported the interests of a majority of its board, which was heavily dominated by out-of-city and out-of-county representatives. The Growth Association, representing major corporations, law firms, and property owners in downtown Cleveland, supported fixed rail systems as a means to stimulate regional economic growth, raise downtown property values, and make downtown more accessible. Major law firms were interested in the expensive bond issues required for construction because they provide fees for the bond counsel who attests to the legality of the bonds as well as other, general legal business. RTA management was devoted to rail lines, we came to believe, because of the cost and prestige associated with such systems, because RTA wanted to maximize investment in the existing rail system, and because an unstinting devotion to rapid trains is apparently written in stone in the American Transit Association guidebook for general managers. All in all, these interests made up a formidable brick and mortar lobby.

There are, of course, many other reasons why a transit system might prefer broad, general, and unencumbered subsidies rather than earmarked subsidies directed toward the transit-dependent. Broad transit subsidies can be used to benefit a wide range of people besides transit patrons. For example, a well-subsidized transit agency can improve the relative accessibility of downtown, thus benefiting downtown property owners and businesses through higher rents, land prices, and sales volumes. It can raise salaries for transit management, who are, incidentally, already among the highest paid of all public employees, and for other employees who are also very well paid. It can provide lucrative contracts for consultants, planners, lawyers, contractors, and others. It can open up land not otherwise accessible and thus benefit property owners and developers. Finally, general transit subsidies can also be used to benefit high-income transit riders without having to bother too much about the less vocal transit-dependent or low-income riders.

The city's advocates were divided over the sub-issue of whether to place priority upon fare guarantees or service guarantees. Early in the negotiations Council leadership committed itself totally, and almost exclusively, to a twenty-five-cent fare.

Since the fare structure proposed in the five-county plan and supported by the anti-city-planning forces (a twenty-five-cent base plus both express and peak-hour surcharges) would cost the transit-dependent little more than a twenty-five-cent flat fare and would provide funds for substantially more service, we too supported this particular point. We decided to focus our efforts on obtaining strong service guarantees, and particularly the CRT guarantees. The only modification in the fare structure that we were prepared to fight for was reduced fares for the elderly. Our ally in this was James B. Davis, former Planning Commission chairman and former ally in the Clark Freeway fight, who was now law director of the city.

An important element of the negotiations was a series of technical meetings at which representatives from the city, county, NOACA, the Growth Association, and CTS met to discuss economic feasibility. The first few meetings were intended to establish a common vocabulary and to ascertain current CTS costs and ridership, past county sales tax receipts, federal operating subsidies available to the Cleveland urbanized area, and other economic matters. After that the agenda was a matter of technical bargaining.

This was not an assembly of unbiased technicians. Each representative had a definite interest to serve. We wanted to justify strong service guarantees for the city; the other participants wanted to justify no guarantees. The technical representatives from all other jurisdictions accused us of estimating revenues high and costs low; we accused them of the reverse. The key to the game was instant sensitivity analysis. When they offered us a million additional riders in return for reducing the increase on operating costs by 1 percent, we rejected the offer. We proposed instead that we leave the ridership figure alone and reduce the rate of increase on operating costs by 2 percent. Efforts to reach consensus generally stopped at the point where our yielding a few more dollars would cost us our case, and their yielding a few more would give it to us.

These meetings served two functions: they established a framework for other facets of the negotiations, and they discredited "our transit experts at CTS" in the eyes of Cleveland's law director. These meetings reaffirmed that in discussions of this sort there are many possible answers to complex problems, and that expertise is not sacrosanct but tends to serve the piper that is paying for the tune. Davis's new understanding of "expert" testimony was crucial to our obtaining his sustained support so that we would have free rein to fight.

Negotiations of a different kind took place at the Thursday policy meetings, where technical experts presented their cases to elected officials. Although these meetings accomplished some education of officials, they served primarily to keep the transit issue in the news. One of the more memorable meetings opened with a Cleveland councilman stating his pro-city interests while most of the suburban officials nodded contemptuously. As the meeting progressed, some officials suggested that the elderly might better maintain their dignity if they were to "pay their way." We argued that if the elderly were given free fares by the system but wanted to pay, no one would stop them. Opposition forces characterized trips to day care centers, neighborhood shopping facilities, and doctors' offices as "frills," but rail extensions to low-density ex-urbs were "essential." Revealed in all this was the tendency of politicians and technical functionaries to mistake their private interests for Truth. Cleveland's councilmembers, each of whom is elected on a ward basis, have been well educated by the media about their "provincialism" and lack of "statesmanship." On the other hand, suburban officials who directly serve the needs of their constituents are not "provincial" but engaged in the "democratic political process." Businessmen who pass taxes and costs off to others while maximizing their own profit and convenience are just "doing business," a form of behavior that is, of course, above reproach.

Throughout the negotiations there were bids and counterbids. Under the direction of the Cleveland Planning Commission, the Law Department developed a memorandum of understanding based upon the fare guarantees that we had proposed. Councilmembers rejected it, calling the proposed peak-hour surcharge a "rush-hour rip-off." It made great headlines but little sense for many Council constituents. County representatives took this opportunity to propose a twenty-five-cent fare for two years. Councilmembers demanded that this fare be guaranteed for four years. And so the bargaining went.

The Senior Citizens Coalition recruited some of its members to attend every public hearing on transit and had significant impact on the final outcome. The seniors, whose director was a friend of Janice Cogger and Joanne Lazarz named Margie Knipe, had developed joint strategies with the planning staff on several issues. This was one of those issues. Though efforts to charge standard fares to the elderly continued for some time, the opposition reluctantly granted free fares for the elderly at off-peak hours (twenty hours per day) and half-fares at peak hours.

Cleveland officials had never developed effective strategies to deal with citizen participation. While the City Planning Commission had not been known for its efforts to encourage citizen input in the planning process, we had found ways to facilitate it in the political process. The planning staff had, for example, worked closely for years with the Senior Citizens Coalition on housing and transit issues, and we had been responsible for putting together the city's first Dial-a-Bus project for the elderly (see Chapter 11). Over the years a symbiotic relationship had developed; the senior coalition had learned to trust us, and we had learned to use their organizational power to achieve common objectives. Calls to the Senior Citizens Coalition to inform them of transit meetings, to lay out the issues, to advise them on strategy, and to coordinate their transportation to meetings were undoubtedly worth more in Cleveland than invitations to Planning Commission meetings and discussions of general, unfocused objectives.

The Thursday policy meetings also reached agreement on such service guarantees as those that covered headways (the frequency of service) and route spacing (the distance between bus routes). By the final stages of the negotiations, only two issues remained: fares and CRT.

A last-ditch technical meeting was called by James C. Davis, the president of the Growth Association and managing partner of Squire, Sanders, & Dempsey. Davis was a formidable person: determined to speak his mind, determined to have his way, determined to bend those who opposed him. Although the stated purpose of this meeting was to develop consensus among the technicians on anticipated costs and revenues, the not-so-hidden agenda was to whip Cleveland's planners into line behind a proposal for a three-year fare guarantee and no CRT. When we refused to give up CRT, he ordered us to get out of the meeting. We complied, wondering at that moment if we had lost the whole game, not only on transit but in other equity areas as well. We could not have chosen a more powerful adversary, for Squire, Sanders, & Dempsey and Jones, Day, Reavis and Pogue, another local legal powerhouse, are often said to constitute a fourth branch of government in Cleveland.

That evening, Mayor Perk called me at home. He urged me to "make a deal," lest a failure be hung around his neck like an albatross in the upcoming election. I reassured him. "Just give me a few more days of negotiation," I said, "and I will make you look like an angel." As it turned out, this was correct. The ax did not fall. If anything, the Growth Association president had strengthened our alliance with the law director, who saw such heavy-handed tactics as unnecessarily abusive of his own negotiating team. The final round of negotiations began and ended during two days of Council meetings in May, when the stage was set for agreement on a three-year, twenty-five-cent fare guarantee. The only issue that remained was CRT, and our allies were few.

The representatives of the Senior Citizens' Coalition were still in the audience. Having benefited from a Dial-a-Bus program funded by a federal demonstration grant that we had helped to obtain, the elderly had no doubts about the value of CRT. We had also convinced some members of Council to fight for CRT, but we had not yet succeeded in convincing Council leadership. Only Councilman Dennis J. Kucinich, who later would serve one stormy term as mayor, understood the issues, shared our point of view, and fought for our objectives. His support was an important part of the final, generally positive agreement.

On the evening between the first and second days of meetings, our morale was low. The game was almost over, and we had no aces in the hole. We visited Jim B. Davis for a last-minute strategy discussion, and he confided, "It's not a wonder that you haven't won; it's a wonder that there is still a fight."

The next morning an editorial appeared in the *Plain Dealer*, the largest newspaper in Ohio, advising the city to give up on CRT. A similar editorial appeared in the afternoon *Press*. Clearly, the powers aligned against CRT were powerful enough to call forth the thunder, let alone editorials.

Until this final day we had demanded that the city's CRT guarantee be expressed in terms of an annual per capita subsidy. The opposition argued that the funds available for service improvements might be less than we projected, that fulfilling the CRT guarantee might cause more than 50 to 60 percent of the service improvements to be located within the city, and that the suburbs might be denied their fair share of increased service. On the final day, in a meeting in Jim Davis's office attended by Davis, myself, Cogger, and County Commissioner Seth Taft, we reluctantly changed our strategy. We agreed to take our chances and express the CRT guarantees as a percentage of the city's 50 to 60 percent share of service improvements. By noon an agreement had been reached. Our opponent's forces agreed to a CRT guarantee; we agreed to a radical reduction in the level of the guarantee. We felt that we had no other choice. That afternoon the City Council ratified the agreement at a meeting in the Council president's office. The meeting was open to the press and open to the technicians; it was closed only (by order of the Council president) to the two dozen people sitting in the Council committee room to monitor the meeting for the Senior Citizens Coalition.

We declared the CRT decision a victory. We had achieved several fairly significant service guarantees: the elderly would ride at substantially reduced fares, and although the commitment to CRT was not enough, it did represent a new departure. It was a step in the right direction. In the final agreement Cleveland was guaranteed that a twenty-five-cent fare would be maintained for at least three years; that senior citizens and the handicapped would ride free during nonpeak periods (twenty hours daily) and pay only half-fare at peak; that service frequencies and route coverage within the city would be improved; and that CRT would be initiated.

Today, in 1990, CRT is still in place. Ironically, now that CRT has been tried and has developed a strong constituency, RTA's ads boast devotion to the service. CRT has been expanded from the city to the entire county and provides free-fare, door-to-door, intra-neighborhood service to the elderly and handicapped. Its 1980 budget was $2.3 million, about 2 percent of the RTA operating budget. Fares for general ridership were held at twenty-five cents for three years as promised, then raised to fifty cents, then to eighty-five cents, where they remain at this writing. Fares for the elderly and handicapped have held firm. The RTA elderly and handicapped fare policy enables the elderly and handicapped to ride the fixed-route system for one-half of the regular adult fare during weekday rush hours and at no fare during all other hours. Service improvements within the city have also been maintained.

Did our transit-dependent clients win? Absolutely! We did not win everything we set out to accomplish. Nevertheless, transit-dependent riders gained far more than they would have had we not been in the fight.

9

The Downtown People Mover

Most planners believe that public goals should be set only by the elected officials they serve. But what should planners do when they are convinced that the mayor and council are supporting a project that is wasteful, destructive, and perhaps corrupt? To whom should they look for guidance: their political superiors, the ethical canons of their profession, the broader public welfare, or their own inner sense of duty? I believe their judgments must be shaped in large part by the general requirements of a well-informed planning process. In this case, that of the Downtown People Mover, that meant opposing the project and their mayor's wishes, a decision whose ethical ramifications still trouble me to this day.

In Cleveland, the idea of building a downtown distribution loop for public transit goes back to the 1920s. Some thirty years later, in 1954, Cuyahoga County voters approved a $35 million bond issue to build a downtown subway running from Public Square to Playhouse Square. This proposal was killed by the county commissioners. Under pressure from County Engineer Albert Porter, who wanted to emphasize highways instead of transit, they voted not to issue the bonds. It was also opposed, it is said, by Public Square merchants, who were not eager to have their customers "distributed" to other locations. The concept, however, lived on.

In the 1960s and 1970s, the Urban Mass Transit Administration (UMTA) of the federal Department of Transportation funded a number of research studies to develop and test new forms of public transit technology. One of the designs that emerged from research by Westinghouse, Otis Elevator, Budd, and other corporations called for small, unmanned, automated transit cars running on their own elevated rights of way. UMTA thought the concept had merit and, having developed the technology, now began to look for places to test and sell it. By the mid-1970s, UMTA was testing one such system in Morgantown, West Virginia, and was looking for other, larger cities interested in trying out this technology as a means of relieving urban downtown congestion. In April 1976, UMTA issued a request for proposals and announced that $220 million would be given to cities willing to participate in the project. Cleveland was one of the cities to respond with a proposal.

The Cleveland proposal was jointly prepared by two local engineering and architectural firms. One firm had been ingenuously described by the *Plain Dealer* as Mayor Perk's "favorite." The firm's principal had, according to *Cleveland Magazine*, married into the five-and-dime S. S. Kresge clan, and had designed more than four hundred K-Mart buildings for the parent firm, S. S. Kresge Company. He was also a member of the executive committee of the county Republican party and a partner in a number of business ventures with the Republican party chairman. Before Perk took office, the firm had received no work at all from Cleveland City Hall; from 1972 to 1976, said *Cleveland Magazine*, it was awarded over $150 million in architectural design contracts by the administration.[1]

Cleveland's proposal for a Downtown People Mover (DPM) called for building a 2.2-mile elevated structure over which automated and unmanned transit vehicles would travel in a one-way loop. The tight loop would begin and end at Public Square and would cover the heart of Cleveland's downtown. Most of the money to build it (80 percent) would come from the federal Department of Transportation; 20 percent would come from local sources. Early estimates placed the cost of planning and construction at $52 million. The mayor, his "favorite architect," the Downtown Cleveland Corporation, an arm of the Growth Association, and the Regional Transit Authority (RTA) were enthusiastic boosters, claiming that the DPM would end congestion, stimulate development, and generally save downtown. After a few months of intense lobbying by these interests, UMTA announced in December 1976 that Cleveland had been picked as one of the cities to participate in the multi-million-dollar demonstration. Cynics observed that the grant for the

---

[1]Diane Tittle, "Is This Any Way to Move People?" *Cleveland Magazine*, April 1977, pp. 74–81.

DPM was President Gerald Ford's last gift to Republican Ralph Perk.

The mayor's support for the DPM posed a severe dilemma for the planning staff. We had just completed the intensive negotiations leading to the establishment of RTA in 1974. We had accomplished much analysis, issued a number of public position papers, and taken some vocal positions, all in opposition to new or extended rail systems. All our analysis suggested that a more elaborate and effective downtown transit distribution system would have two drawbacks from the point of view of equity planning. First, any benefits it provided to downtown property owners, developers, employers, and employees would be secured at substantial cost to the entire transit system. Second, it would provide a rationale for expansions and extensions of the RTA fixed-rail system to other corridors in the Cleveland region. Both outcomes, our analyses made clear, were contrary to the transit needs of the 87 percent of RTA's riders who rode the bus, not the train, and the transit-dependent population of the city whose interests we were determined to serve.

We had other problems with the DPM. Although 80 percent of the $52 million capital cost would be contributed by UMTA, the local share for the demonstration system would come from RTA, out of the fares and service improvements of present riders, including the transit-dependent rider. Our analysis also showed that the DPM, if built, would run major operating deficits and that other transit services might have to be cut in order to cure these deficits. Our fears were not lessened when early estimates by RTA indicated that it would cost about $1.6 million a year to operate the DPM, which was to be available to riders free of cost.

The one-way loop proposed for the DPM produced a level of service to many destinations that was substantially *slower* than the city's existing loop-bus system. The "testing" aspect of the DPM demonstration was also a concern. "The Downtown People Mover Project," UMTA literature explained, "is intended to provide an operating, fully automated . . . system that cities can evaluate. . . . *If* such systems could be proven to be reliable, safe and economic, they *could* serve as a revitalizing force for our urban centers" (my italics). But what if the DPM proved *not* to be reliable, safe, and economic? Downtown Cleveland would be stuck with a concrete albatross.

The DPM also had a number of other failings. Aesthetically, we joined many other independent design critics who thought it would disfigure the downtown area. In New York City, the Third Avenue Elevated system had blighted whole districts. When the El was torn down, the districts boomed. We thought an elevated structure with all its shadows might have a similar blighting impact on downtown Cleveland, while destroying such architectural and historic gems as the original Cleveland Trust building at East 9th Street and Euclid Avenue. We also thought the estimated development costs were probably low. In Morgantown, West Virginia, what started as a $13 million, three-mile-long DPM shuttle, a gift, it was said, from President Richard Nixon to powerful West Virginia congressman Harley Staggers, turned into a $50 million cost overrun, an absurd amount of money to spend to move a few of West Virginia University's 10,000 students and faculty members each day. There was also the question of the technology—would it work? In Morgantown, the DPM did not provide dependable service; every time it got cold, the system froze up. Cleveland was colder than Morgantown. Indeed, the Morgantown DPM had proved to be such a fiasco that UMTA was considering dynamiting it at the same time the agency was awarding DPM planning contracts to other cities.

We were also frankly outraged that the mayor and RTA would propose to build a DPM, since such a project was a violation of the clause we had carefully written into the memorandum of understanding setting up RTA just a few months before. The clause, which aimed at restraining RTA expenditures relative to its rail system, stated that the transit agency must not spend any funds on the construction of a downtown distribution system during its first five years but should limit its expenditures to fare reductions and bus service improvements. When I complained about this apparent violation to Dave Goss, RTA's assistant general manager, he assured me that RTA was technically not in violation, because the city—not RTA—had applied for the DPM grant, and RTA would only contribute its 20 percent share if the memorandum of agreement was changed.

Nonetheless, Mayor Perk, City Council, and RTA were clearly leading the charge in support of the DPM. Perk was my boss. He had, mostly at my request, given me and the city planning staff unusually important responsibilities. I liked and respected him, as I did all the mayors for whom I had worked.

He was also the chief elected official in the city I was sworn to serve. The fact that he was elected gave him, it seemed to me, the strongest claim to legitimacy in policy formulation.

At the same time, it appeared to us that the mayor's position carried more negatives than positives. To begin with, the DPM served no local needs. Downtown transit distribution was already being carried out by an extensive and efficient bus loop service, and the DPM would provide less efficient service at astronomical costs. The DPM was also a clear negative in aesthetic terms, the elevated structure being the prime complaint. Cleveland is one of the greyest, most overcast cities in the United States; the last thing it needed was a massive structure to cast still more shadows over the downtown area.

The DPM was also a loser in functional terms because, operating as a one-way loop, its levels of speed and service were actually lower than those of the existing bus system. Finally, it represented an indirect threat to all the fare reductions and service improvements we had just won for the senior citizens and transit-dependent people of the city. All this was to be given up for a development proposal that would never have been considered at all except for the fact that the UMTA was offering "free" federal money, and the mayor's "favorite architect" stood to make a handsome fee. In our view, the merits of the proposal had nothing to do with its important status on the public agenda.

My staff and I (mostly Janice Cogger and Himanshu Patel, who had labored so long and so hard on the RTA negotiations) considered our options. We could, of course, do nothing and let the politicians do what they wanted to. This would have been safe, but it would have been contrary to many of our stated positions and to all the work we had done on transit over the last few years. We could try to lobby the mayor to withdraw his support for the DPM, and, failing in that, we could resign in protest. The problem with this was that we wanted to keep our jobs, and we doubted that our resignations would make much difference to the outcome of the issue. Or we could stay in City Hall, try to get the mayor to change his mind, and work behind the scenes to hamstring the DPM proposal as best we could.

It seemed to us that although city planners and other public administrators had normal obligations of loyalty to their boss, the mayor, they also had obligations to the public as well. Public service, we thought, involved values, ethics, benefits, and power. Even if an elected official tells his or her planners to steal, for example, or support racially discriminatory acts, they have no right to do so, since that would be a clear betrayal of a higher trust. Planners are agents of society, and they make choices that affect society's welfare. Their scope of activity is wide, and so is their discretion. To a great extent, planners must rely on the ethical traditions of their society, their own value systems, the considered procedures of professional planning practice, and their sense of justice and fair play.

As we considered our options, it was reassuring to us that planners operate within a network of professionals that is quite open and informal. Planners frequently swap experiences and resumes. One advantage of this system is that it provides many alternative opportunities for employment. In so doing, it weakens the absolute control any mayor has over his or her planners. The system provides many opportunities for planners to stand on their own values and professional principles and avoid simply being used to legitimate a mayor's pet project.

We decided to stay in City Hall and try to persuade the mayor to withdraw his support for the DPM. If that proved to be impossible, we would try to derail the DPM any way we could. I would be as open in my opposition as I possibly could, arguing against the project in meetings with the mayor and cabinet members, hoping to change their minds. But I would also try to inform and energize other possible opponents to the DPM, even if that meant going underground.

My plan was to work with as many people as I could to engage their interest and influence them to take a public position against the DPM. Naturally, I hoped these contacts would not expose my role. In some cases, particularly when dealing with newspaper people, who could normally be depended on not to reveal sources, I was confident that my anonymity would be protected; in other cases, I was not sure. In any event, I thought the issue was of the greatest importance, and I was prepared to take my chances, including the possible loss of my job. As it turned out, I must presume that no one revealed my role, because if someone had, I would have heard from the mayor in no uncertain terms.

I asked Cogger and Lazarz to talk to Margie Knipe, the director of the Senior Citizens Coalition. Knipe was their personal friend, and the planning staff had worked with her to capture an UMTA Dial-a-Bus demonstration in the Buckeye–

Woodland neighborhood and win fare reductions and community-responsive transit for the elderly in the CTS–RTA negotiations. Knipe, in turn, had helped orchestrate informal pressure from the seniors on the negotiators in the final days of the drafting of the memorandum of understanding. Knipe agreed with our evaluation. In a little while, the seniors were issuing press releases attacking the DPM as a "stupid idea." One of the releases questioned RTA's sense of priorities. "Why are they willing to give up $2 million for such a far-fetched project as the DPM when the Seniors' Coalition had to fight an eight-month battle for $250,000 to start up Community Responsive Transit? . . . Put money where it's *asked for and needed*—i.e., for transit-dependent people." The seniors were alert to the threat to their interests and were happy to fight the proposal.

We tried carefully to interject an anti-DPM point of view whenever the subject came up in private meetings with the mayor and at cabinet meetings. The argument stressed Perk's great victory in the recently concluded CTS–RTA negotiations and how the DPM represented a threat to his accomplishments. We implied that our neighborhood contacts were unhappy that more resources were being taken out of the neighborhoods and focused on downtown and that members of the business establishment were unhappy about the DPM's aesthetic impact.

Arguing in cabinet meetings against proposals favored by the mayor requires considerable tact. One must choose one's words with care, but one must argue, not merely defer. The terms and words of such arguments must be respectful and must not preclude future agreement. If other agencies and directors support the mayor, one's criticisms of their positions must be gentle but revealing. The objective is to give the mayor an opportunity to see different technical viewpoints, choose between competent old friends, and perhaps develop a new position.

The mayor frequently wants to know what the planners are thinking on an issue—even though their advice may ultimately be put aside. Searching for opportunities, the mayor may call the planners in and, even more importantly, agree to see them when they press for an appointment. These occasions provide the planners with great openings, but their presentations must be clear, condensed, and practical. Technical back-up may be discussed, but only briefly. The mayor will be much more interested in how the matter will affect relevant publics and how it can best be explained to them. The planners had better not lecture. The mayor's time is very limited, and the mayor's willingness to listen will also limit what information the planners can convey.

Nothing worked. Our arguments against the DPM in cabinet meetings and in private meetings with the mayor failed to dampen Perk's support for the project.

We spoke to Dick Feagler, Don Silver, and Herb Kamm at the Cleveland *Press*. We knew them pretty well, having spoken to them about different stories through the years. Feagler in particular was a brilliant writer, acerbic and humorous, a local version of Chicago's Mike Royko. We figured that if we could suggest some bizarre angles on the DPM, he might make a funny story out of them and we might laugh the DPM out of town. I brought him a couple of ideas, including a mock-serious "planning survey" in the form of a memo. The memo said that the planning staff had run a survey of comparative speeds to various downtown destinations. It had compared a trip on the DPM with a bus ride or a walk from Public Square to various destinations along the DPM route. Using figures from the DPM's own consultant, we had found that the DPM was 75 percent slower than the present bus loop and 50 percent slower than the time it would take a pedestrian to walk various distances. This was not a joke; it was actually the case, since the DPM was a one-way loop that started off in the opposite direction from the destinations we were measuring (see figure). We also pointed out some of the tortured professional jargon in the DPM report (the amount of time the vehicle would pause to take on passengers was called "dwell-time"). Feagler loved it and wrote two columns on the DPM.

Silver, who had covered the CTS–RTA negotiations for the Cleveland *Press*, and Kamm, an editor, were both interested in our views, thinking of us, I suppose, as nonpolitical professionals whose views were honest and oriented to the public interest. A few weeks after our meeting, the *Press* ran an editorial that reflected our skepticism.

I also gave information, background material, and our point of view to a local reporter named Diana Tittle, who was working on a devastatingly critical story for *Cleveland Magazine* entitled, "Is This Any Way to Move People? . . ." The article was brilliantly written and perhaps made lots of people rethink the merits of the DPM project.

Travel Time via DPM

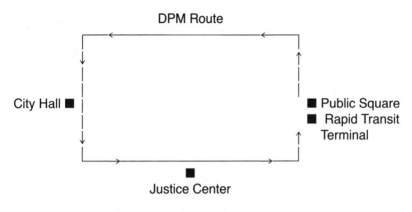

DPM Route

City Hall ■

■ Public Square
■ Rapid Transit
Terminal

■
Justice Center

Public Square to Justice Center

Bus Route Time	3 minutes
Walking Time	5 minutes
DPM Time	12 minutes

We also solicited and found three supporters in the wonderful world of Cleveland politics: County Commissioner Robert Sweeney, then–County Auditor George V. Voinovich, and Councilman Dennis J. Kucinich. For whatever reasons (I presumed that all three were working on their own political agendas), they were interested in the hard analysis and information we could supply. For close to a year, on an irregular, nonscheduled basis, we kept them supplied with our position papers, analyses, and views. When circumstances would change, or the DPM's progress would move to a different level for review (and publicity), we would come up with a bit of information or an insight we thought was useful, and we would relay it to one or all of the three politicians.

Voinovich, who was elected lieutenant governor of Ohio in 1978 and mayor of Cleveland in 1979, emerged as the political leader against the DPM, flatly denouncing it as a "federal boondoggle" and spending a good deal of time calculating how to dry up local funding for the project while dodging potshots from Mayor Perk, who denounced his fellow Republican as an "opponent of progress." We supplied Voinovich with the facts for statements he presented at a NOACA board meeting. "Whatever it costs," he said, "will be too much, because it is not needed. We have more than an adequate loop bus service. But even assuming there was a need, the $52 million figure is not realistic. Historically, planners' estimates are much lower than final costs. Just look at Morgantown."

Kucinich, who had begun the successful race that carried him to the mayor's office in 1977, called the DPM "a Disneyland contraption" and accused the federal government of having things backward. Instead of solving city transit problems, Kucinich said, the feds were trying to develop and sell state-of-the-art transit systems that were simply not needed. Other, more basic improvements were much more important, he argued. This was very much our point of view, although we would have used less flamboyant language.

Commissioner Robert Sweeney was running for re-election. He undoubtedly believed that opposition to the DPM would earn him votes as an opponent of waste and was very receptive to our anti-DPM material, which I would on occasion personally deliver on weekends to his law office. Ironically, although Sweeney and I worked closely and amicably on the DPM and other issues, I had years before publicly criticized him when his vote fired Irving Kriegsfeld from his position as director of the Cleveland Metropolitan Housing Authority. In politics, landscapes and coalitions shift, and strange partners turn up in bed together. It is always best to consider that reality in framing strategy: avoid bitter personal attacks that may be impossible to reconcile later.

We also attempted to stimulate some anti-DPM activity from downtown business interests, but were not, so far as we knew, successful. For example, I spoke to Brock Weir, chairman and chief executive officer of Cleveland Trust Bank, and Herbert Strawbridge, CEO of the Higbee department store. In both cases, I attempted to stress the disastrous aesthetic impact of the twenty-foot-high people-mover structure cutting across the façade of their buildings, partially covering the sidewalks, and turning them into gloomy, dark, and potentially scary tunnels. For Weir, I had a local designer prepare an "artist's conception" of the DPM creeping past the domed façade of the elegant, original, and historically significant Cleveland Trust Bank, built in 1905. Unlike most architectural renderings, which picture buildings on bright, sunny days, with blue skies, surrounded by fashionably dressed, slim people, my rendering was rather more ominous, showing the DPM on its massive concrete structure, twenty feet in the air, completely obscuring the exquisite domed, Renaissance-style rotunda and its eight fluted Corinthian columns, and casting Euclid Avenue into deep shadow.

I also pointed out to both businessmen that the proposed DPM route ran right through the middle of three districts listed on the National Register of Historic Places—the Terminal Group, the Public Square, and Daniel Burnham's Cleveland Mall Plan. These overtures were without apparent effect. The members of the establishment in Cleveland may disagree from time to time with public policy and with one another, but they never disagree in public. Still, I always had the feeling during the DPM controversy that powerful forces in the business community, moving just below the surface, were as bitterly opposed to the DPM as I was, although for different reasons. We suspected that some of our political allies may have been more energized in their opposition by establishment forces than by our arguments.

Curiously, the city's economic notables, who were seen as all-powerful on many issues, may have been too compromised to deal head-on with the DPM proposal. They had so many favors to request of the mayor—zoning changes, legal business, Urban Development Action Grants, tax abatements, deposits of city funds—that they could hardly afford to publicly oppose one of his pet projects. In that case, they might have felt that it was necessary to make a public show of support for DPM while using surrogates and pressures at other levels to defeat the proposal. Unbeknownst to me, they may have been on our side all along.

In spite of the controversy, either spontaneous or orchestrated, UMTA announced in 1977 that Cleveland would receive some $40 million to begin the detailed planning, engineering, and first-phase construction of the DPM. The news was greeted with enthusiasm by the mayor and other proponents. Dave Goss, RTA's assistant general manager, speaking a few years later, recalled that agency officials began thinking of how to reshape the DPM into the downtown distribution system they really wanted, and Dennis Kucinich, plotting his campaign for the mayor's office, seized upon it as another campaign issue. Kucinich described the DPM, along with the sale of Muny Light and the granting of tax abatements, as yet another reason to "throw the rascals out." It was a successful appeal.

Had it not been for the election of Dennis Kucinich later in 1977, I believe Cleveland, like Detroit and other cities, would have begun this project. (In Detroit the People Mover was supposed to cost $137 million and carry 55,000 riders a day. In 1988, after completion, the actual cost was $200 million to build, and it carried about 10,000 passengers a day. It is popularly known as the "mugger mover.") Once elected, Kucinich put his prior verbal opposition to the DPM into practice and ordered it killed. He asked me, then serving as community development director in his new administration, to write the letter to UMTA declining to proceed with the grant and, in effect, returning the money to Washington.

Kucinich personally presented the letter to President Jimmy Carter at a White House meeting. It allegedly caused a stir. It seemed no city had ever sent money back to Washington, and no one knew quite what to do with the returned grant.

For myself, and other members of the planning staff who were involved, there was a feeling of great satisfaction and relief. Ambivalent to this day about resisting the mayor's wishes, I believe the planning staff did the right thing and fulfilled its obligation to the public interest. I suspect that our role in defeating the DPM was not central, but it helped. Perhaps we had succeeded in changing some minds. We had fought off the downtown brick and mortar coalition and had lived to fight another day.

10

A State Lakefront Park System for Cleveland

From the moment in 1969 that we tried (and failed) to create a public beach at Euclid Beach Park (Chapter 4), we had been interested in Cleveland's lakefront, which seemed to offer so many recreational possibilities. Most of these were going unrealized because of the city's dismal fiscal condition and the fact that the city could not conceive a new administrative approach to the parks. But financial and political circumstances came together in the mid-1970s, aided by the persistence of the planners, to produce a marvelous park facility for Cleveland.

The city had four public parks on Lake Erie—Edgewater, Gordon, White City, and Wildwood—and all were in deplorable shape. The best beach was at Edgewater, and the water at that beach was so polluted that swimming had been prohibited by the Board of Health. In a pathetic attempt to provide some bathing here, the city in 1969 had stretched a waterproof curtain ten feet off Edgewater's shore and had heavily chlorinated the water inside the curtain so that it met minimum health standards. Safe bathing was provided inside the curtain. How sad! Here was Lake Erie, one of the largest fresh water lakes in the world, with no safe swimming beaches to offer except for a speck in one tiny corner. It had not always been this way.

Cleveland's park system had been spliced together over the years through cycles of inspiration and neglect. In 1871, the city established its first Board of Park Commissioners. That body purchased land for park development and accepted gifts of land for parks from such wealthy Cleveland citizens as Jeptha Wade, founder of Western Union, and John D. Rockefeller of Standard Oil. In the early 1900s, the park commission system was abandoned and the parks were turned over to a city department. During the golden age of Cleveland's parks, before World War I, Cleveland introduced many innovations in parks and recreation, and the parks were well used and admired. Midwesterners would come to Cleveland for summer vacations on the beaches and in the parks. But other parks, such as the Cleveland area's 18,000-acre Emerald Necklace in Cuyahoga County, and other pastimes like Sunday driving, weakened the position of the city parks.

By the 1960s, Cleveland's parks had fallen on hard times, and the city was spending only 3 percent of its local funds for park development and maintenance. In the early 1970s, the situation worsened, and maintenance was given over largely to part-time, often inexperienced, employees who worked with inadequate equipment. Many park employees were diverted to street repairs and snow removal. The parks fell into disuse and dreary disrepair. Given the city's dismal fiscal condition, it was clear that improvement would require an entirely new approach to funding or administration or both.

The planning and Parks Department staffs felt that Lake Erie's water quality would ultimately improve and that the lakefront parks should be put into better shape for bathing, picnicking, and other recreational uses. Their problem, however, was twofold: money and political will. First, the city lacked the money to hire more trained parks personnel. Large numbers of low-income kids would be hired through the federal Comprehensive Employment Training Act (CETA) program each summer to help clean up park properties, but the kids would be gone in the fall, and the Parks Department never had the political strength to argue successfully for hiring more permanent maintenance staff. Indeed, every city fiscal crisis resulted in further cuts to the parks budget. The second problem was a lack of administrative determination to keep the lakefront parks up. The limited resources of the department were heavily focused on an extensive softball program, so that very little was left for other activities. The traditional approaches to solving the parks problems were, first, to capture more resources, personnel, and equipment, and, second, to tighten managerial control; but Mayor Perk was a no-tax mayor, and the city had higher priorities for its limited resources.

The lakefront parks continued to deteriorate. Highly visible symbols of this deterioration were the eroded beaches, the vandalized and unusable beachhouses and pavilions, the sunken and rusted ore boats at Gordon Park, and open dumping everywhere. People were beginning to see the parks as dumps, and the small amount of police surveillance the city could provide was not an adequate deterrent.

Layton Washburn, Bill Whitney, and I had many meetings with long-time Commissioner of Parks John Nagy trying to figure a way out of the impasse. Nagy had been commissioner for over twenty years; for most of that time, his closest professional and personal friend in City Hall had been Layton Washburn of the City Planning Commission staff. Their friendship provided our entree into park and recreation issues. Most of our meetings were set up by Washburn, who was deeply distressed by the situation. He had been working with the Parks Department in one way or another since he came to Cleveland city government in the 1930s; he had never seen the parks in such bad shape.

The two staffs decided in the early 1970s that one thing we could do to improve park safety and reduce dumping and vandalism was to put as many uniformed rangers as we could into the parks. In our plan, these "rangers" would wear park-ranger-type uniforms but not be sworn police officers, who were in short supply and expensive to hire. We planned to hire these "smokies" on short-term contracts out of federal manpower assistance funds, help reduce unemployment in the city, and provide more surveillance and security in the lakefront parks, thus improving usage and discouraging vandalism. The few sworn police officers who included the lakefront parks in their beats could be released from that obligation until called in to handle an actual emergency and could concentrate more of their patrol time in the neighborhoods. Our strategy was to develop the idea as completely as we could, get tentative commitments from the CETA people, discuss it with Mayor Perk and enlist his support, and then sell it to the Police Department.

The idea had the full support of the planning and Parks Department staffs and of James Zingale, who was parks director and Commissioner Nagy's supervisor at that time. The CETA people were eager to provide the slots. When we briefed the mayor, he was also supportive, since the plan seemed to provide a way out of a growing parks problem with no need for increased taxes, a central tenet of the Perk administration. The

Police Department, however, was a different story. Police officials were adamantly opposed to the notion that other uniformed personnel would be providing security in the city, no matter how "quasi" their role. The Police Department was the agency responsible for security in Cleveland; if we wanted better security, their solution was to raise taxes, hire more sworn officers, and pay them better. Mayor Perk declined to challenge their view of the situation, and our idea never went any further.

This is only one small example of the power of the Police Department in Cleveland. Fear of crime against one's person or property was the most important issue in the city. The Hough and Glenville racial riots of the 1960s had intensified that fear. In response, Council and successive mayors had allocated to the police as much of the city's resources as they could. The police were deeply involved in politics. In the late 1960s, they had successfully changed the city charter so that they would automatically be paid 3 percent more than any other police force in cities over 50,000 in the state. By reporting or not reporting crimes, handling responses to emergency calls, declaring "blue flu" strikes when displeased, or alleging that such-and-such a politician was "soft on crime" or was weakening their morale, they could destroy a politician's career. Politicians and planners alike rarely moved against stated Police Department wishes, and then only with great reluctance and caution.

In 1973, Hurricane Agnes battered the lakefront parks, tearing up the breakwalls, marinas, and shoreline and destroying many groins and other erosion-controlling devices. In a sense, Hurricane Agnes provided the crisis for the lakefront parks, and crisis is a necessary ingredient for much of the change that takes place in local urban government.

Crisis is essential because local governments rarely lead, innovate, or anticipate their needs. Rather, government responds to pressure to "do something" about a problem that results from changing circumstances. If the problem is sufficiently large in scale or the people involved are sufficiently numerous or powerful, the problem registers as a "crisis." Then local governments move cautiously to resolve it. One may be critical of government's lack of interest in anticipating problems or initiating preventive programs, but without a crisis to spur a new policy, local governments are likely to prefer the status quo.

Given this reality, a planner with a good idea, policy, or program that has been tried and rejected would be wise to file it away where it can be recovered against the day when a crisis might convert his or her unsalable idea into one with broad support.

By leaving Cleveland's lakefront parks in a shambles, Hurricane Agnes provided the crisis through which change might occur. To help repair some of the storm damage, the city turned to the federal government for aid. During council's hearings on this request, the planners had the opportunity to talk to a number of councilmembers about an idea for moving the responsibilities for the maintenance and capital improvement of the lakefront parks to a broader taxing base. The notion began by considering the parks as a regional or state resource rather than merely a local one. Once they were seen in that light, it made perfect sense to lease them either to the Cleveland Metroparks system, which was supported by a property tax levy on all the real property in the county, or to the Ohio Department of Natural Resources (ODNR), which ran the extensive system of state parks. Both Metroparks and ODNR had adequate resources; both had a good reputation for professional park administration; both enjoyed a good deal of political support. Of the two agencies, I thought we might be able to bring off our plans more easily with the state, since at the time Cleveland City Council was 100 percent Democratic, as was the governor, John J. Gilligan.

When we mentioned this idea in a City Council committee hearing, a number of councilpersons, especially Councilwoman Carol McClendon, seemed interested and asked many questions. A few months later, Council introduced an emergency resolution that "declared the intention of the city to enter into a lease with the State of Ohio . . . to operate . . . and maintain [Cleveland's lakefront parks] . . . as state recreational facilities." Council passed the resolution and sent it along to the administration for its review.

Layton Washburn and I had a quiet meeting with Commissioner Nagy and Director James Zingale. Both were very supportive of the transfer, but wanted to see how Mayor Perk would react. As part of Perk's administration, directly responsible to the mayor, the director of the Parks Department was clearly going to follow the mayor's lead regardless of how he might personally feel about the issue. Rather than be seen as trying to pressure the mayor into supporting a proposal initiated by the Democratic City Council, Zingale suggested that Washburn and I, the "nonpolitical professionals" who were deeply interested in the proposal, feel out the mayor. We were more than willing.

We went to see Perk privately about Council's resolution, pointing out that the resolution offered a way out of the growing embarrassment of the condition of the parks. Here we would have another arm of government with state money maintaining, operating, supervising, and spending capital improvement dollars on parks that would continue to provide recreation for our citizens. The transfer would cost us nothing except direct control and some patronage, and we could fold the parks personnel now assigned to the lakefront parks into the neighborhood part of our parks system. We might be able to bargain (or appear to bargain, for public consumption) for specific capital improvements as a condition of the lease, and we could also ask for program review of other elements of the state plan as it emerged. We could represent the lease as a new approach to public administration in which the mayor could provide vastly improved facilities with no increase in taxes. I represented the lease as the good deal I was sure it was.

The mayor listened but clearly had some reservations. Like most mayors I have known, he thought of issues, not in long-range terms, or in terms of elegance of fit or appropriateness within a larger policy construct, but in short-run political terms, and the proposed lease had many dangers in the mayor's judgment. For one thing, he had come under some criticism for "selling" the city's sewer system to a new regional sewer authority for $36 million. His critics had charged that his (and Council's) reluctance to raise wastewater treatment fees had resulted in the unnecessary deterioration of the wastewater treatment system, a rate suit by the suburbs served by our treatment system, a moratorium on new building in the drainage area ordered by the court hearing the suit, and ultimately the "sale" of the system to the regional authority. The criticism was pure poppycock, since the decline of our sewer system went back at least thirty years, far before the Perk administration. As a low-tax, caretaker-type executive, Perk was in the tradition of most Cleveland mayors. Nonetheless, Perk was afraid that leasing the lakefront parks to the state would give his political opponents at the state and local levels an opportunity to charge him with another "give-away" and accuse his administration of being incapable of managing the city's resources. Our arguments against this point of view were in vain; ultimately Perk refused to approve the resolution, and Council's initiative died. In retrospect, although we were deeply disappointed at the time, his political judgment was probably right on the mark. A Democratic Council and a Democratic governor up for re-election would have been sure to inflate their role in any take-over of Cleveland's parks, and would have been likely to belabor the Republican mayor in the process.

Although Council's resolution died, the city's problem with its lakefront parks did not go away. They continued to be operated by the city, of course, but there was no stopping the long, cold slide of deterioration. More and more "publics" became aware of the decline. No one—citizens at large, the business community anxious to "sell" Cleveland's image, politicians—could ignore the deterioration.

In 1976, the Cleveland Foundation, anxious to nudge the park issue off dead center, published its "Cleveland Parks and Recreation Study." Layton Washburn and I were extensively interviewed in the course of the study. Our arguments, probably shared by many other observers, were essentially adopted by the report's authors. They were a combination of facts and political advice on how to accomplish change, how the issue should be seen, and what opportunities and constraints existed. The facts we presented were designed to shift the problem away from Perk and Cleveland's budget to the state. Our message was: "Don't criticize the administration's supposed incompetence or lack of managerial talent. That will harden resistance to any change. Focus on the Parks Department's continually shrinking budget and lack of full-time professional maintenance staff. Make a point of emphasizing how the city's chronic fiscal bind and the Parks Department's lack of political clout always translate into greater budget cuts in parks than elsewhere. And play up the notion that Cleveland's lakefront parks are not only a city resource, but a prime resource for the Cleveland region and the entire state of Ohio." The report, when published, received a good deal of publicity and newspaper comment, and may have helped sway Mayor Perk's mind in the right direction, since politicians read more newspapers than technical reports.

By mid-1976 the lakefront park problem had worsened. The city had gotten some money in 1974 from the federal government's flood relief program, but not enough to repair the damage caused by the storm, let alone keep up with continual maintenance needs. Garbage dumping continued at Gordon Park; the outbuildings and public bathrooms at all parks were badly dilapidated; the beaches and the fishing jetties were filthy and unusable. The newspapers had focused on the issue and had turned the parks into a highly visible reproach to the Perk administration's managerial capacity. With another election coming up, Mayor Perk was looking for a way out. To me, a good way out was obvious, and I mentioned it at a cabinet meeting when the subject came up—a replay of the earlier lease proposal. Only this time, instead of the visionary leadership coming from City Council, it would come from the mayor and the Republican governor, James A. Rhodes. This time, the mayor could be in control of the whole scenario. With some behind-the-scenes prearranged negotiation with the state, the mayor could enjoy a public negotiation process that was bound to succeed. The mayor seemed impressed with the idea, and none of the other directors objected.

We explained the idea in greater detail to Mayor Perk after the cabinet meeting, noting that City Council was already on record in favor of the transfer lease and that the establishment, as represented by the Cleveland Foundation and the newspapers, was sure to be supportive. If the mayor could clear the deal with his old friend the governor, we had a no-lose situation. I asked the mayor to appoint me as the chairperson of a new Lakefront Development Task Force, whose only purpose would be to work out the details of the lease with ODNR, develop a list of high-priority capital improvements, draft the legislation, sell it to City Council, and go out of existence. I told Mayor Perk that if he would do this, we could have the deal completed in time for the 1977 elections. And if, for some reason, the lease negotiation was unsuccessful, Perk's planners, not the mayor, would bear the onus of failure.

Here, as in other issues we were trying to sell, the planning staff was to function as a lightning rod for possible political criticism. It is a useful arrangement for planners in City Hall and for their superiors. We would be the up-front proponents who would test ideas and take all the flak from the opposition as it emerged. If the opposition proved overwhelming, the proposal would be withdrawn and the planners would wear the jacket. If no opposition emerged and the proposal was successful, the mayor would get all the glory. This time Mayor Perk thought it was a wonderful idea and appointed me head of the new committee as suggested.

Since I thought all the principals to the deal (the mayor, City Council, the establishment, and the governor) already were lined up or could be quickly lined up, I decided to appoint a small committee that would move fast. I did not seek broad citizen participation but included only representatives of those organizations that would be needed to put the deal together. Speed was, it seemed to me, urgent: with councilmembers, the mayor, and the governor all favoring the lease transfer, we had to move before one or more was replaced or changed his mind. As we figured it, the Lakefront Development Task Force would need some foundation support for a consultant study to put a technical framework around the proposal and identify capital improvement needs; a representative of City Council to help other members understand and support the legislation; a representative of ODNR to assist the state with the lease; and some visible support from the business community in the form of verbal endorsements. The composition of the task force reflected those needs. It consisted of Thomas Patton (head of the Cleveland Foundation's distribution committee and retired chairman of the board of the Republic Steel Corporation, who proved to be particularly helpful); Campbell W. Elliott (executive director of the Growth Association); Richard Adler (former Growth Association leader); Robert Teater (director of ODNR); George Forbes (City Council president); and Harold Schick (director of the Cleveland Metroparks system). Schick was on the committee in case it became more expedient to deal with Metroparks instead of ODNR. Patton, Elliott, and Adler were all well-known business leaders and long-time supporters of Governor Rhodes. None of them was likely to oppose something the mayor and governor might want to do. Patton, Elliott, and Adler came to all three of the meetings held by the task force over the next year; Teater sent a key assistant; and Forbes designated an alternate from Council who did not come to any meetings at all.

At our first meeting at the Planning Commission offices, I laid out the mayor's objective—a fast turn-over of the lakefront parks to ODNR. Everyone was in agreement except Bob Teater's alternate from ODNR. He explained that ODNR had no interest in running urban parks. All its parks were in rural areas, and the agency enjoyed an excellent reputation for its development and running of them. Its officials were afraid that if they began taking over distressed lakefront parkland in Cleveland, they would be deluged by similar requests from all of Ohio's lakefront communities from Ashtabula to Toledo. Taking on all those facilities would overwhelm ODNR's budget and administrative capabilities.

Obviously, reluctance on ODNR's part could have killed the whole plan. We were flabbergasted by this position because we had thought ODNR was already in on the deal. We quickly related the problem to Mayor Perk and urged him to call Governor Rhodes and straighten it out. Tom Patton, an old friend and influential supporter of Rhodes, also agreed to visit the governor and urge him to cooperate. Later that week, I received a call from Bob Teater indicating that ODNR had rethought its position and would now be pleased to consider a long-term lease on the city's parks. It seems probable that this prompt change of heart was due to Patton's visit and two phone calls, one from Perk to Rhodes and a second from Rhodes to Teater encouraging him to rethink his stand. Directors in Governor Rhodes's administration did not argue with the governor's decisions.

In its first meeting, the task force agreed to ask the Cleveland Foundation for an emergency grant of $5,000 ("emergency" because we did not want to wait for the foundation's normal award cycle) to employ a planning firm to determine the capital expenditures needed to bring Edgewater and Gordon Parks back to first-class condition. As usual, Homer Wadsworth, the Foundation's executive director, understood the issue, empathized with the objective, and was immediately supportive. Wadsworth was one of the most creative foundation officials I have ever met. His hands were all over many of the most innovative and successful projects in the city. He was a great friend of the lakefront parks concept and a great friend of planning. Wadsworth made the grant we requested within a week, and we hired the consultants just as fast.

Wadsworth also sponsored a subtle educational sideshow:

a three-week trip to several port cities in northern Europe to examine how land adjacent to their waterways was used for commercial and recreational purposes. Bob Teater attended along with others, including the majority whip of the Ohio House of Representatives. Teater, who began the trip as a partisan of rural park development, returned full of enthusiasm and ideas about the potential of urban waterfront parks.

The consultant's study, "Gordon Park, Edgewater Park Transfer Feasibility and Rehabilitation Study," was completed in less than two months by Dalton, Dalton, & Little, as we had ordered. It pinpointed more than $13 million in capital outlay needed to halt disastrous erosion along the shoreline as well as create or improve beaches, buildings, marinas, fishing piers, paths, picnic areas, and playing fields. This $13 million became part of our request for improvements to the state; ultimately, the parks received $7 million in the state's first two-year park budget. This capital improvement concession helped the mayor maintain the image of driving a hard bargain, and succeeding—an image important to his continuing support.

The second meeting of the task force (we were to hold only one more—to congratulate ourselves and then go out of business) was held for two reasons: to accept the consultant's capital improvement report and to authorize the Law Department to begin drafting the lease legislation for introduction to City Council. The legislation (drafted by attorney Steve Garfunkel of the Law Department) called for a turn-over of Edgewater, Gordon, White City, and Wildwood parks to the ODNR and set the terms and conditions of the lease to be "substantially in conformity with the 'Gordon Park, Edgewater Park Transfer Feasibility and Rehabilitation Study' " (Map 3). The Planning Commission passed the legislation at its meeting of October 21, 1977. The commission had been briefed periodically by Washburn and myself on the progress of the lease, but this was the first and only time it took an official action.

The final lease agreement, for fifty years with an option to renew, ironed out a number of details that came up in Council's public hearings. Marinas and yacht clubs, left out of the earlier draft, were specifically included in the final lease, and the city's use of the parks for its extensive organized sports programs, especially softball, was to be phased out over five years. Later on, we discovered that we had already leased the smallest

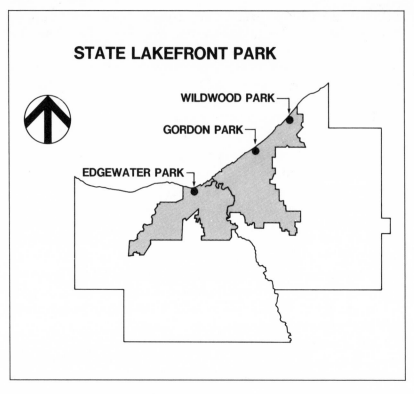

STATE LAKEFRONT PARK

WILDWOOD PARK

GORDON PARK

EDGEWATER PARK

**MAP 3. Cleveland Lakefront parks leased to the Ohio Department
of Natural Resources for a New State Lakefront Park**

park, White City, to the Regional Sewer Authority, and, because
you can only lease a thing once, we had to delete it from the
state lease. The lease now became a reality.

The importance of speed and timing was underscored by
the fact that Mayor Perk and Governor Rhodes ceremonially
signed the final lease agreement during the first week of November 1977. In the second week of November, Dennis J. Kucinich took over as mayor of Cleveland. If the deal had not been
signed, sealed, and delivered before the new mayor entered
City Hall, we might have had to begin again.

In retrospect, the lakefront park system in Cleveland was
one of the most satisfying and rewarding planning efforts in
which the city planners had ever been involved. In a sense,
those efforts did not involve planning, or organization, or management—they were closer to implementation. It was, in its

way, a perfect example of the way real progress is achieved in an urban area—bit by bit, with patience and determination and an openness to opportunity wherever it is found.

The case goes back at least to the early seventies; it is still developing. From a group of formerly elegant parks temporarily in a shambles that defied planning, management, or even basic maintenance, the lakefront parks have been transformed into pleasant and popular recreation spaces. The $7 million committed by the state of Ohio to Cleveland's lakefront park system in 1976 was the beginning of a flood of supporting dollars that by 1987 totaled over $32 million in capital improvements and another $11 million in personnel and operating funds. This money was being spent on operations, the acquisition of over two hundred acres of additional parkland (including the beach at Euclid Beach Park that we had sought to acquire in 1970 for free), off-shore erosion-control devices, major new facilities and complete rehabilitation of existing facilities, and the first stages of Cleveland's downtown Inner Harbor project. Swimming beaches, fishing piers, picnic areas, and marinas have been restored. In 1985, 6 million people visited these parks, and they stand as an essential and attractive building block upon which the future of Cleveland will be built.

11

Helping Cleveland's Neighborhood Organizations

The basement of St. Benedictine High School in the Buckeye–Woodland neighborhood was filled with about a thousand excited people. It was the first Buckeye–Woodland Community Congress Convention in 1976. Older white ladies exchanged pleasantries with younger black men. Clerks from two local Hungarian bakeries were offering kolatchy and coffee to anyone who seemed interested. Politicians and downtown bureaucrats, some of whom had never been in the neighborhood before, were circulating, smiling and pressing the flesh. On the walls and stapled to poles marking different areas of the auditorium were the names of the different block clubs and organizations that testified to the area's diversity. The atmosphere and the attire of the participants represented a cross between a 1960s anti-war rally and a Polish wedding.

The meeting began more like a celebration than an occasion for business. The nomination and election of officers was punctuated by good-humored partisan demonstrations, and the balloting for the president was followed by a snake-dance that went around the hall. The elected president, Diane Yambor, began her acceptance speech by saying, "I never thought I'd be doing such a thing." She went on, "Six years ago, I thought Buckeye–Woodland was going to the dogs because blacks were moving in. Now I know that neighborhoods are destroyed, not by blacks, but by people who make lots of money off racial change."

When the meeting adjourned a few hours later, a dozen people remained behind to socialize and talk about their hopes for their new organization. Included in the group were four members of the Cleveland City Planning Commission staff.

They were regarded not with indifference or hostility, as planners sometimes are—as part of the "downtown crowd"—but as a trusted and respected part of the organization. They had worked long hours on several of the "victories" proclaimed during the meeting and, indeed, on coordinating the meeting itself. They had earned the trust of the group. How did they get to that point?

The involvement of the city planning staff with Cleveland's neighborhood movement began in 1972 when a young Roman Catholic priest named Dan Reidy was named executive director of the Commission on Catholic Community Action (CCCA). CCCA reflected the concern that infused many Catholics for civil rights, anti–Vietnam War issues, and urban poverty. The organization, which began by conducting adult education seminars in some of the parishes of the diocese, moved quickly from general issues to the consideration of advocacy as a strategy and decided to focus on organizing the neighborhoods of Cleveland. The concept harked back to the old American ideal of cooperative group action by ordinary citizens motivated by specific grievances and civic idealism. In 1976 CCCA hired Harry Fagan, a Catholic layman and former advertising executive, as director. Together, in their first organizing effort, Reidy and Fagan brought six parishes together to form the Buckeye–Woodland Community Congress, whose purpose was to ease racial tensions in a neighborhood experiencing rapid racial change. There was ample evidence that the Buckeye neighborhood, once one of the largest ethnic Hungarian neighborhoods in the United States, had been targeted for racial steering and block-busting by unscrupulous real estate interests anxious to make high profits from high turn-over rates. The congress was intended to help calm and stabilize the neighborhood.

At the time he was director of CCCA, Reidy was also a member of the Cleveland City Planning Commission and had become a supportive personal friend. He was interested in seeing if the planning staff and the young neighborhood organizers of CCCA shared mutual interests and could work together. The same course of action had been pressed on me by some of my new staff members. Janice Cogger, Joanne Lazarz, Ernie Bonner, and John Linner all lived in Buckeye, and the two women were already friends of the Buckeye–Woodland Congress staff.

Quite apart from these recommendations, it seemed a logical and appropriate idea. Planners going back to Ebenezer Howard had emphasized the importance of the neighborhood unit. More recently, planners had been directed to work with low-income neighborhoods in the Great Society programs of the 1960s, which required maximum feasible participation. Beyond that, I had met Harry Fagan, and I liked and trusted him. At the time, Fagan was promoting and supporting thirteen separate, autonomous community organizations. The advocacy work of his group was certainly reflective of our own interests. We also realized that it would be very useful for our own Planning Commission programs if we could turn out real, live neighborhood constituents at City Council meetings in support of our joint programs. It was obviously important for members of the planning staff to support their recommendations to Council with arguments based on good data analysis and graphics. However, many of the planners may have seemed strange to City Council, college-trained newcomers with new and perhaps threatening ideas. Although I tried to dress and talk to councilmembers in ways they would find familiar, I was still new in town and, so far as they knew, might be a bird of rapid passage. By contrast, members of the neighborhood organizations were real, live, recognizable constituents who had needs and demands councilmembers could understand. It would help to have them on our side.

There were also less personal reasons for our involvement with neighborhoods. Both the neighborhood organizations and planning staff members shared the belief that crucial decisions bearing on the lives of Cleveland's citizens were becoming more and more removed from their control. We also believed that the growing symbiosis between government and business did not necessarily bode well for low-income and working-class neighborhoods. And we both rejected the view that neighborhood interests, however urgent, should always be overridden by regional interests, however trivial.

AN EARLY COLLABORATIVE STRATEGY

There was another powerful reason for beginning our neighborhood involvement with the Buckeye group. A year before, Cogger and Lazarz had helped the Cleveland Senior Citizens

Coalition develop a Dial-a-Bus proposal to the Urban Mass Transportation Administration (UMTA). We had succeeded in getting the Buckeye neighborhood designated as the location for the demonstration project, and some of the seniors who knew of our involvement in Dial-a-Bus were also part of the Buckeye–Woodland Community Congress leadership.

Our involvement in the Dial-a-Bus demonstration program in Buckeye exemplifies the format we followed in much of our neighborhood-based work in the years to come. In this case, the seniors were looking for a way to improve transit for their members, many of whom had no regular access to an automobile and depended entirely on the Cleveland Transit System (CTS) for mobility around the metropolitan area. CTS offered mostly long-distance, downtown-oriented service, with little off-peak or cross-town service, the type needed by the seniors. The older people were also afraid to stand on corners waiting for a bus. A few of their members had been mugged while doing so, and a number of the seniors were so fearful, that they had become prisoners in their own homes. Margie Knipe, director of the Seniors Coalition (which was funded by CCCA), had heard that the Planning Commission staff was interested in providing technical assistance to citizen groups. Knipe came to our offices in City Hall and asked if we would be willing to help. After a staff discussion, Cogger agreed to work on the project, and she, Lazarz, and Knipe became fast friends.

Together, they discovered the UMTA Dial-a-Bus Demonstration Grant, discussed it with members of the seniors' organization, and wrote the grant application in conjunction with a staff member at CTS, which was to be the operating agency. The necessary lobbying, endorsements, and political support were provided by the leadership of the Seniors Coalition.

When Cleveland was awarded the grant, Cogger, Lazarz, and Knipe continued to work closely together. They were key, along with Seniors Coalition leadership, in selecting Goldie Lake, a local administrator, as director of the demonstration. They also worked with the entire seniors' group membership in selecting the mini-bus Argosy vehicle for the service. But that was not the end of their efforts.

When the eighteen-month Dial-a-Bus demonstration was about to expire, all of us—seniors, CTS, and planners—were waiting for program evaluations that had been contracted out to consultants. If their evaluation was reasonably positive, those of us who believed in the need for some kind of demand-responsive system to supplement CTS's line-haul service would have an important document to support our beliefs. But it soon became clear that the demonstration would run out of money before the evaluation report was completed. The consultants refused to be hurried. They refused to issue a report until they had carefully tested their data and had at least a 95 percent confidence level in it. They expected to have a final evaluation report in hand about two months after the actual project had shut down for lack of funds. We could not accept that; if we were to persuade CTS to make Dial-a-Bus part of its regular service, we would have to have an evaluation of the program while it was still running and still fresh in people's minds.

We decided not to wait for the consultants' report. Instead, Cogger spent a week riding the Dial-a-Bus, interviewing riders, and filling out questionnaires. She then hand-tabulated the results. Her analysis made clear that the people who were using Dial-a-Bus were poor and transit-dependent, could not use the regular line-based service for their needs, and considered the door-to-door aspect of the Dial-a-Bus its most valuable characteristic. It was exactly the profile of the rider we (and UMTA) had hoped to reach. Mindful of a key CTS board meeting coming up in a few days, Cogger and I then wrote a press release, which we gave to the media and the Seniors Coalition. The coalition, in turn, developed a media event in which they distributed copies of the release, along with heart-shaped cookies, to the CTS board meeting a few days later and successfully lobbied for the continuation of the Dial-a-Bus service. After this, the seniors and the Buckeye group knew we were friends.

WORKING WITH NEIGHBORHOOD ORGANIZATIONS

The first meetings between the planning staff and the staff of the CCCA took place in their offices in the evening. It was a crowded scene, with people sitting on the floor and out in the hallways. At that time, CCCA had about thirty dedicated young people working as organizers for sixty or seventy hours a week for about $9,000 a year. Most of the organizers considered themselves to be rebels, outside the system; they expressed amazement that members of the City Hall establishment would show up and talk to them. We told Fagan and his people that we were indeed interested in helping them, that both organizations were working the same side of many issues and hoping for the same outcomes, and that we hoped we would earn their trust. We also told them that situations would probably arise where it could be dangerous for us to be too closely and too publicly identified with them. For example, their strategies might demand that they mobilize an "action" or demonstration against City Hall or, indeed, against the City Planning Commission. That was OK, in our view, since we appreciated the dynamics of their work. When those cases arose, we would tell them to respect our confidence, and we hoped that they would. They responded with considerable enthusiasm, and from then forward, on one issue or another, or in one guise or another, they knew the door of the city planning offices was open to them.

In a series of Planning Commission staff meetings over the next few months, we evolved a strategy for helping neighborhood organizations. The rough guidelines we agreed on were these:

- If we had to choose among many different requests for assistance, we would try to serve black or racially integrated groups representing poor neighborhoods first. In doing so, we hoped to be most helpful to those groups lacking access to the normal channels of money and power.
- Planners would volunteer for assignments whenever possible, rather than being ordered to serve certain neighborhoods.
- Planners who were residents of a given area would get priority assignments there, but they would be urged to be actively involved with the neighborhood organization as well.
- Work assignments would evolve from the needs of the neighborhood organization as expressed by its leadership. If planners perceived other needs, it was fair to suggest them and work on them, but only if the group's resident leadership approved.
- Planners could provide direct technical assistance such as preparing surveys, Community Reinvestment Act (CRA) complaints, or grant requests. They could also function as brokers for services that lay outside the Planning Commission. This would include facilitating relations with public agencies, lenders, insurers, developers, and teaching/training institutions. The aim would be the development of an informal network, a sort of Growth Association for the

neighborhoods, which could help support and educate neighborhood people.

- Neighborhood-based planners could act as advocates for the capital spending needs of their turf as opposed to focusing exclusively on comprehensive city-wide proposals.

Using these guidelines, members of the planning staff initiated support efforts with two other neighborhood groups in the next few months: the St. Clair–Superior Coalition, a working-class, racially integrated neighborhood on Cleveland's east side, and the Detroit–Shoreway Community Organization on the west side. We had had past contacts with both groups and knew and respected their leadership.

In Detroit–Shoreway, we helped the group buy, rehabilitate, and preserve the Gordon Arcade through the city's first neighborhood-oriented Urban Development Action Grant (UDAG). The Arcade, which was the centerpiece of the neighborhood's commercial strip, was deteriorating and in danger of demolition. We prepared the UDAG (although the city's Community Development Department was formally responsible for the program) because our planner John Finke understood the UDAG program better than the person assigned by the Community Development Department. Finke offered to teach his opposite number about the program by working through an actual application—for a UDAG we favored. We also helped prepare applications for two Small Business Administration 503 low-interest loans and generally initiated a broad technical-assistance program that has continued up to the present. In St. Clair, we helped the coalition produce a long-range development plan, while a neighborhood improvement program detailed short-range public service improvements that were in high demand.

The neighborhood improvement program (NIP)—a commitment to gain specific improvements within three months—was a unique document. It grew out of a series of neighborhood meetings attended by Janice Cogger and myself. These meetings were filled with complaints from neighborhood residents. It seemed that they could not get any response from City Hall for a great number of basic housekeeping chores. The complaints were mostly minor and specific. Nobody asked for an improved public school system or for an end to racial discrimination. It was almost as if the group had decided they couldn't do anything about such cosmic issues and should restrict themselves to dealing with things that the city could and should do. They asked for the stray dogs that were running wild in the neighborhood to be picked up; a stop sign to be installed at a busy intersection; an abandoned, burned-out house to be demolished. It seemed to Cogger and me that what the folks were asking for was clearly part of our agenda of responsiveness to the grass roots, and that we ought to be able to broker a deal that would put together a package of complaints and the means to resolve them by city agencies. This presumably would make the St. Clair–Superior coalition members happy and reflect positively on Mayor Perk and his entire administration.

We discussed the idea of a NIP with the coalition leadership, and they were enthusiastic. Then I discussed it with Mayor Perk, emphasizing that once we adopted such an approach, we were under an obligation to follow through. The mayor took to the idea immediately, perhaps because he was particularly strong in this ward. Cogger and I then returned to the coalition and enlisted volunteer residents to survey the neighborhood and document specific needs in such housekeeping areas as building demolition, lot clean-up, street and sidewalk repairs, tree trimming and planting, needed stop signs, and the like. The items, we told our field volunteers, were to be documented as precisely as possible by street and address. When the neighborhood volunteers had completed their work, Cogger and I collected the rough worksheets and arranged the items by categories. We then typed and reproduced a number of copies for review by the group. The format looked like this:

Item	Location	Status	Responsible Dept. & Official
STREET REPAIR	Pothole at 344 E. 56 St.		Services Dept., Commissioner Joe Smith 664–2210
DEMOLITIONS	1176 St. Clair 37 Glass Avenue		Community Development Dept., Comm. Lisa Thomas 664–7865

The coalition members reviewed the document, made some slight changes, approved it, and sat back to await results. We then presented the entire NIP at a cabinet meeting at which the mayor was present, and the other directors were advised that the NIP idea had the full support of Mayor Perk. We also told them that they could strike certain items from the list if they thought their departments could not deliver within ninety days, but if they approved an item, the mayor and the St. Clair Coalition would expect results. Although a few of the directors modified the list a bit, none rejected it out of hand. Most of them signed off on the entire list (the items were, after all, merely housekeeping tasks for which their departments had responsibility in any event). Surely they were all busy people, but the mayor wanted this done, the work items would not take a great deal of extra effort or money, and the administration would have a chance to look good.

We then printed about five hundred copies of the approved list for distribution in the St. Clair neighborhood. Included in the final document were the names and telephone numbers of the city officials who were responsible for execution. Given such clear direction (and such relatively simple assignments), the city departments executed 90 percent of the items within three months, and everybody was happy.

The NIP idea was a triumph of simplicity. It enlisted the citizens in resolving some of their own perceived problems. It involved modest housekeeping complaints that could be handled cheaply and quickly by the operating departments. It improved the neighborhood and the neighborhood's view of City Hall responsiveness and made the mayor look good. And it could be replicated in any city in America and repeated at intervals.

Some of our other activities in support of neighborhood organizations over the next few years are shown in the accompanying table. By and large, our work with neighborhood and other advocacy groups was emotionally satisfying and professionally rewarding. Thinking carefully about how we could relate to neighborhood-based organizations had helped shape our original work program as well as the *Policy Planning Report* (Chapter 3). We worked with neighborhood organizations in various phases of the transit negotiations (Chapter 8), the CASH program (Chapter 6), and the land banking program (Chapter 7). The work on land banking was helpful in the development of a number of projects, including Lexington Village.

The Lexington Village project consisted of a large new townhouse development (183 units in Phase 1) built at East 79th & Hough Avenue, the flash-point for the 1966 Hough racial riots, which had degenerated into one of the most thoroughly abandoned and demolished sites in Cleveland. The planning

Selected List of Cleveland Planning Commission (CPC) Neighborhood Projects, 1973–1979

Issue	How CPC Came to Be Involved	CPC Expertise/Resources Employed
Housing		
1. Tremont housing abandonment; high property speculation; potential need to increase home-ownership	• Request initiated by Chris Warren, director of Tremont-West Development Corporation.	• General familarity with inner-city housing problems • Knowledge of corrective approaches employed elsewhere • Knowledge of specific forces at play in the neighborhood in question
2. Multi-family housing abandonment in Glenville	• Work with Glenville Housing Corporation initiated by CPC staff. Staff member lobbied HUD to consider Cleveland for pilot program; Glenville neighborhood was selected for demonstration.	• Staff familiarity with problems of multi-family abandonment in the city and elsewhere • Contacts with other local and national organizations concerned about multi-family abandonment
3. St. Clair–Superior Aetna investment negotiations	• Initiated by St. Clair–Superior Coalition director, Tom Gannon.	• Staff knowledge of area • Housing market analysis skills • Familiarity with specific problems in that neighborhood market • General research, analytical, and writing skills
4. Unavailability of conventional mortgage money and reasonable rates and terms	• Staff initiated, following complaints by many neighborhoods about restricted mortgage availability.	• A staff expert on Urban Development Action Grants (UDAGs) • Staff housing expertise • Staff liaison with local lending institutions

Tasks Performed by Staff	Outside Institutions, Brought in and Coordinated by CPC	Apparent Outcomes
• Gathered information • Attended many meetings with neighborhood groups and community house staff • Arranged meetings between community representatives and other resources within and outside the neighborhood	• Famicos Foundation, to provide advice and start-up assistance • City Demolition Division contact, to delay demolition on houses selected for rehabilitation and resale to residents • Center for Community Change, a national organization, to decide with neighborhood what additional technical assistance was needed and arrange to get it	• A new community-run housing rehabilitation program offers home-ownership opportunities to the neighborhood's low- and moderate-income residents. This approach to homeownership for poor families became the most important program for the Cleveland Housing Network, which had produced over 600 homes for the poor by 1989.
• Made preliminary inquiries with HUD about program specifics • Held discussions with local groups concerned about the issue • Prepared problem statement and proposal for HUD • Held on-going negotiations • Contributed to building-selection process • Generally coordinated local and national actors	• Famicos Foundation, to share general rehab expertise as well as assist in recruiting potential co-op members • Lutheran Housing Corp., to provide rehab expertise • Cleveland Tenants Organization, to provide assistance with co-op formation and other matters • U-HAB, a national technical assistance organization, to advise about the creation and operation of such a project • Local Community Development officials, to assist with rehab cost estimates • Local HUD officials, to secure the donation of a HUD-owned property to Famicos	• A low-income, apartment was rehabbed, but the low-income co-op demonstration program in Glenville failed to be established.
• Analyzed numerous housing investment strategies, listing positive and negative aspects for this neighborhood • Provided written analysis of housing market • Met with coalition staff to discuss housing investment needs in the area	• None (coalition had already begun negotiations with Aetna)	• Aetna made grants in support of Co-Hab, a new, nonprofit neighborhood housing corporation.
• Developed preliminary proposal for CASH program • Met with local lenders to explain concept, discuss their role, and determine their interest • Garnered support of mayor	• Community Development and Economic Development departments • Local S&L League • 22 commercial banks and S&Ls • Mayor's office • City Council	• CRA complaints were filed. • CASH program was established to ensure lending. • Bank participation in several new community development corporations was initiated.

(Table continued on following page)

Issue	How CPC Came to Be Involved	CPC Expertise/Resources Employed
Housing (*cont.*)		
5. Lexington Square abandonment/need for redevelopment	• Bob Wolf, director of Famicos Foundation in Hough, asked for assistance of staff member who had worked with them on other projects.	• Staff familiarity with possible funding source and CRA pressure on lenders to behave responsibly • Informal connections with banks • Understanding of and access to information about the city's land banking program • Understanding of related land acquisition procedures
6. Arson	• Initiated by Near West Neighbors in Action.	• General research capability • Knowledge of areas in the city where arson was a particular problem
Commercial and Economic Development		
1. Commercial and industrial decline in Detroit–Shoreway; industrial traffic congestion on residential streets; decay of Gordon Square Arcade, a key commercial building	• Ray Pianka, director of community group, requested assistance.	• Working knowledge of key actors and issues in neighborhood • UDAG expertise • Loan-packaging knowledge • Contacts with related city departments • Skills in working with neighborhood block clubs to explain city's intent
2. Industrial expansion and employment needs in the Woodland East Community Organization area	• Staff assumed responsibility for UDAG applications from another city division.	• UDAG expertise • Familiarity with other city officials overseeing land acquisition, relocations, etc. • Informal contacts with community group in industrial expansion area

Tasks Performed by Staff	Outside Institutions, Brought in and Coordinated by CPC	Apparent Outcomes
• Researched property records for Famicos Foundation • Arranged meetings between Famicos Foundation and lenders • Instructed community developer about land acquisition procedures	• Community Development Department, to cooperate in land acquisition • Famicos Foundation, to assume primary development responsibilities • Lenders, to consider project financing • Private developers • Financial assistance from local and national foundations	• Famicos acquired one-third of the land needed by 1979 and the complete site a few years later. • S&L commitment for mortgage money was secured. • Construction on Lexington Village project began in 1984. Phase 1 (183 units) was completed in 1986. Phase 2 (94 units) was completed in 1989. Twenty percent of all units are set aside for the poor using Section 8 certificates.
• Gained membership on local arson task force • Arranged to receive daily fire reports, from which arson data were extracted and classified by ward, target areas, and census tracts • Supplied monthly statistics to neighborhood anti-arson group • Supplied data to councilmembers upon request	• Arson Task Force of Greater Cleveland Crime Prevention Committee • Tremont, Ohio City, Neighborhood Housing Service (NHS), Detroit–Shoreway, and St. Clair–Superior groups • City's Fire Statistical Unit • Two councilmembers	• Neighborhood anti-arson group was formed after CPC supplied data on similar efforts elsewhere. • An innovative grant application to the Law Enforcement Assistance Agency was successful. • Two additional arson investigators were assigned to the organized neighborhood.
• Attended and arranged numerous meetings • Developed contact with HUD–UDAG officials • Developed and pushed through UDAG application; won funding • Oversaw contractual agreements between city, HUD, neighborhood limited partnerships, etc. • Served generally as project trouble-shooters and coordinators	• Two expanding industries • Partnership of neighborhood investors • City Planning, Law, Community Development, and Economic Development departments • HUD	• UDAG funding supported: relocation of two industries within neighborhood construction of industrial access road complete rehabilitation of Gordon Square Arcade, including 66 low-income units completed in 1989.
• Met and negotiated with industries in question • Discussed the desire for a community-run job-screening and referral service • Prepared and submitted UDAG application	• Two expanding industries • Garden Valley Community House • Appropriate city departments • HUD	• UDAG funding supported: jobs for area job-screening program for public housing tenants and preferential hiring for Garden Valley public housing tenants

(Table continued on following page)

Issue	How CPC Came to Be Involved	CPC Expertise/Resources Employed
Commercial and Economic Development (*cont.*)		
3. Lack of commercial amenities near public housing estates	• CMHA Central Advisory Council (CAC) requested staff assistance. This tenants' group was aware of funding possibility but needed help in formulating a proposal.	• Attendance of two staff members at CAC meetings • Proposal-writing expertise, including access to program regulations
4. Desire for a community-based cannery to process foods raised in community garden of public housing estate	• Spencer Wells, director of Garden Valley, requested assistance.	• General research skills
5. Vacant, tax-delinquent parcels	• Staff initiated research with support of several CDCs.	• Knowledge of extent of tax-delinquency problem in Cleveland, as well as the snags in old foreclosure process • General research abilities • Legal expertise on staff
General Planning		
1. Need for a neighborhood plan in St. Clair–Superior	• Tom Gannon, director of St. Clair–Superior Coalition, approached staff for assistance.	• Staff knowledge of the necessary elements of a neighborhood plan • Questionnaire/survey research expertise • Computer processing skills and hardware • Survey analysis and writing skills

Tasks Performed by Staff	Outside Institutions, Brought in and Coordinated by CPC	Apparent Outcomes
• Met with CAC to discuss funding possibilities, desired projects • Held staff meetings to discuss ideas for commercial co-ops approved by CAC • Wrote and submitted proposal to HUD	• HUD • Cleveland Tenants Organization for initial ideas and advice	• Application was successful. • CMHA neglected to fulfill commitments, and project was ultimately abandoned. • Experience formed basis for a successful laundromat developed in the 1980s.
• Researched community canneries elsewhere • Explored potential funding sources	• Area Agency on Aging • Community Services Administration • U.S. Department of Agriculture • State Department of Agriculture	• Work was abandoned because of community uncertainty about scale of operation.
• Researched alternative foreclosure processes • Sought and received foundation grant of $50,000 • Wrote legislation to change Ohio foreclosure laws • Found legislative sponsor and lobbied on behalf of legislation • Upon passage, worked with county to develop administrative machinery to implement land banking	• State legislators • Real Estate Research Corp. • Ohio Municipal League • County officials • Inner-City Land Re-Use Task Force • Auditors and planning officials throughout Ohio	• Land banking machinery is now in place. • City owns about 2,500 parcels in 1989, with about 10,000 working their way through the system. • CPC is equipped to advise groups about land bank program. • CPC staff members sit on a city-wide Land Re-Use Task Force. • Many land-banked parcels already used for new developments such as Lexington Village.
• Met repeatedly with coalition staff to discuss their perceived needs • Designed survey tool • Analyzed survey data • Wrote two reports and produced series of charts for visual display purposes on survey results • Produced computer runs, including part of coding and key punching required	• None	• Current, reliable data on neighborhood were analyzed and presented in usable form in neighborhood plan (1976).

staff, led by Mindy Turbov, became involved at the request of Bob Wolf, director of the Hough-based Famicos Foundation, a neighborhood-based Community Development Corporation (CDC). Our city planners researched property records, set up key meetings, instructed the CDC on proper land acquisition procedures under the land bank law we had helped to pass, and interested prospective lenders and developers in the project. We also helped facilitate the process whereby Famicos ultimately obtained from the land bank several key parcels without which the project could not have gone forward at its planned financial level. The first phase of Lexington Village was completed in 1986, and the 183 units (including the 20 percent set aside as Section 8 subsidized units) were fully rented a year later. Turbov later left the City Planning Commission and joined the staff of the project developer. A second phase of 94 units was completed in 1989.

Although these projects were successful and satisfying, there are at least two other neighborhood projects I would prefer to forget. One involved a proposed cannery, which was to be built at the Garden Valley Estates (in Cleveland, public housing projects are called "estates"). The canning factory was supposed to preserve the vegetables grown at the Garden Valley neighborhood garden and the other community gardens throughout the city. My staff and I thought the neighborhood's interest in this was very positive; we envisioned self-sufficiency in good, home-grown food, money saved, and possible commercial potential as well as a few jobs in the cannery. We also thought that visits to the Garden Valley cannery by neighborhood organizations from around the city would help break down the tragic isolation of the people in public housing. The planners, working with the Garden Valley community organization, made contact with local, state, and federal agricultural extension agencies and with a variety of funding sources. We helped draw up a prospectus for the cannery, but had to stop there. We were unable to get the members of the organization to decide on the scale of their participation in the project or the amount of work they were willing to invest, and the proposal went no further.

The second neighborhood-related project that proved unsuccessful, in my judgment, was an effort to complete Cleveland's first multi-family, low-income co-op apartment. Mary Niebling, the lead planner in this effort, did not consider this project "unsuccessful." "The program was successful in providing low-income housing," she recalled in a 1989 interview. "Its failure was in not being able to convince the low-income tenants that it was in their best interest to participate in a housing cooperative." Niebling initiated the effort in conjunction with Glenco, a subsidiary of the Famicos Foundation based in the Glenville neighborhood. Niebling and Glenco lobbied HUD to select Cleveland as a demonstration site for the co-op and were successful. The demonstration was to use Section 312 multi-family loans for the rehab. In the months that followed, Niebling and the CDC staff brought in technical assistance from the U-HAB Consultants in New York City to provide overall help; Cleveland's Lutheran Housing Corporation to advise on the rehabilitation and train the homesteaders; the Famicos Foundation to help recruit members for the co-op; the Cleveland Tenants Organization to form the co-op and provide legal help; the local Council of Economic Opportunities to provide weatherization and solar water heaters; and local HUD officials to secure the donation of a foreclosed HUD property as the actual demonstration site. But in spite of all the time, money, and effort invested, the participants preferred to rent rather than join in a low-income co-op.

I think the reason we failed to put the co-op together had less to do with a lack of expertise and effort on the part of the planners and other groups than it did with a lack of interest in co-ops at any price level in Cleveland. As late as 1987, there were still very few co-ops or condominiums anywhere in the city. They exist in profusion elsewhere, but not in Cleveland. Apparently, other, more preferred housing opportunities exist in Cleveland's soft real estate market. Nonetheless, in spite of the large investment of time and the unsuccessful outcome of the Glenville project, I would probably choose to get involved in the same kind of project today if the chance came along because of its potential for housing low-income families.

After ten years of working with neighborhood-based organizations in Cleveland (four years at the Cleveland City Planning Commission and six years at the Cleveland State University Center for Neighborhood Development), I feel that some comments are in order.

First, neighborhood planning—planning from the point of view of existing neighborhoods and their residents—works: that is, it focuses attention on neighborhood needs and helps build and repair parts of the neighborhood infrastructure. Since our first halting efforts in the early 1970s, Cleveland has evolved a sophisticated network of neighborhood organizations, nonprofit housing corporations, and CDCs. Almost all of them have had some technical assistance rendered by Cleveland's city planners. Some of them have been our clients for ten years or more. These groups now rehabilitate and build low-income housing (faster and more cost-effectively than the local housing authority), provide effective energy-conservation services, and do commercial and economic development. They also offer anti-arson and neighborhood safety services. They may offer an entirely new way of delivering public goods and services—perhaps an entirely new approach to public administration. They also involve some number of neighborhood residents in resolving some neighborhood problems, although it is never clear how many of the residents either belong to or support the organizations that speak in their name. Planners who work with these groups are investing their time well. Indeed, they may be investing their time in the only way that can revive dispirited people and disinvested urban neighborhoods.

Second, while the neighborhood organizations have become effective vehicles for dealing with certain types of problems—mostly of a physical or administrative nature—they have not been effective in confronting more fundamental issues. Many of Cleveland's neighborhood organizations were formed by organizers schooled in the techniques of Saul Alinsky, whose approach emphasized three essential elements. First, Alinsky recommended organizing people to act in their own behalf, in their own interests, on short-range issues. Second, Alinsky stressed the need to build indigenous, grassroots leadership; the organizer was to try in every way to organize himself out of a job by strengthening existing neighborhood institutions and residents. Third, Alinsky stressed the need to win; the organization had to build its confidence and capacity with "victories"—no matter how small.

But the problems that vex our distressed neighborhoods and cities are far more structural than isolated, short-term issues. The devastating effects of concentrated poverty and of racial discrimination will not be cured by demolishing some vandalized homes and rebuilding some sidewalks. Victories dealing with the basic inequities of our economic system are few and far between because neighborhoods cannot deal with the underlying basis for inequality. While the staff and some of the leaders of neighborhood organizations in Cleveland agreed on the need to address more structural issues, they were unable to do so.

For example, industrial plant closings were a major problem in Cleveland during the 1970s. Neighborhoods did not organize around this issue at all. Another major issue was school desegregation. A federal court ordered busing for integration and educational improvement. A peaceful resolution of this issue was essential to the city, yet in spite of suggestions by various members of the neighborhood leadership and the city planning staff, no neighborhood group in the city took a public position in support of busing or the peaceful integration of the schools. (At the same time, it is important to note that the neighborhood groups did not forcefully *oppose* busing, as they did in some cities, thus precipitating urban disorder and violence.) Tax abatement and the proposed sale of the municipal light plant were other major issues affecting the city and the neighborhoods. Yet, again in spite of urging from planners and neighborhood leaders, no neighborhood position was taken. It was almost as if the focus on short-term "victories" precluded involvement with issues that were more difficult or longer-term. While the planning staff members were trusted by the neighborhood groups, their influence was not deep enough to have the groups adopt broader goals and objectives.

Third, the members of the planning staff who worked with the neighborhood groups were pleased and enthusiastic about their assignments. Janice Cogger, the staff member who became most deeply involved with neighborhood work, later left the city planning staff, took a cut in pay, and became a director for the St. Clair–Superior Coalition. She was still working in Cleveland for a neighborhood-based CDC in 1989. Barbara Clint, Mindy Turbov, Bill Whitney, Mary Niebling, Joanne Lazarz, and Ruth O'Leary were also interested in and pleased with their neighborhood assignments. The idea of neighborhood planners in City Hall has spread. Today, neighborhood planners can be found not only in the City Planning Commission but in the Economic and Community Development Departments as well.

The planners working with neighborhood organizations had to adjust to different styles of discussion and negotiation than they might have grown accustomed to in City Hall. When a planner is reviewing a developer's proposal, for example, he or she generally talks directly to the developer or his lawyer. Both parties are well-educated, observe similar rules, and use similar patterns of speech. Rules are understood and accepted, and distractions are held to a minimum. Meetings take place from nine to five in well-maintained and occasionally elegant surroundings. By contrast, when planners work with neighborhood organizations, the meetings are held at night, and in the storefronts of old buildings or in church basements. The members of neighborhood organizations in cities like Cleveland rarely hold master's degrees, and their style of discussion is apt to be blunt and conditioned by deep, well-justified suspicion. Informality is often the rule, and the expressive style sometimes includes shouting and confrontation. Trust is the absolutely essential commodity, and it must be earned. Planners who understand the peculiar rules of neighborhood participation can be very effective, but respectful and patient listening is important to that success.

Most of the older, inherited planning staff members were uninterested in neighborhood assignments. This tended to widen the gap between the "older" and the "newer" planners. Ironically, the "older" group may have resented the "newer" one for getting the interesting assignments even though they themselves did not want to accept them. They may have felt that the boss preferred the new planners, a charge that was generally true (with some exceptions). Although none of this resentment ever flared into open hostility, the Council president once refused to approve the Planning Commission's budget for a time, accusing me of "running two different operations upstairs." Ultimately, we got the budget approved, but not before assuring him that everything possible would be done to close the gap.

Fourth, although we worried about being linked publicly to some of the more confrontational neighborhood organizations, such exposure was never a problem. Much of our work with the neighborhoods, such as the St. Clair NIP, was of course open and above-board and required support from the administration in order to be successful. From time to time, however, we had to operate underground. We took such action only after the most careful consideration of our conflicting obligations. For example, when the Perk administration planned to buy the dilapidated Civic Arena for $2 million in CDBG money (an idea that our analysis made clear was absurd), we passed along the proposal and our analysis to neighborhood groups, suggested that it was *their* CDBG money which would be spent for the purchase, and discussed with them the tactics that successfully stopped the proposal before City Council. We also helped organize neighborhood pressure in favor of various housing rehabilitation proposals such as the Lutheran Housing Corporation's proposal in the Buckeye neighborhood. In this case, the neighborhood organization wanted the corporation to be funded and the Community Development Department was inclined not to fund. We helped orchestrate the neighborhood's support for the Lutheran Housing Corporation and were successful in attracting the necessary funding from the city. Our covert role was never revealed.

Finally, one of the strongest arguments in favor of neighborhood planning is the fact that it has a public and a private side. On the one hand it sensitizes government to the diversity of communities within the city; on the other, it enhances cooperation and investment between neighborhood groups and private investors, developing, in the process, parts of the city that might otherwise have been completely overlooked.

12

Improving Planning, Management, and Administration in Other City Agencies

City planners have rarely attempted to provide analytic staff support to other city agencies in order to improve their performance; few city tables of organization provide for such linked support. Yet the quality of life in the present and future city depends heavily on the quality of services provided by a city's line departments. These departments may lack any internal planning capacity at all or may be unable, because of structural constraints, to analyze their present operations in order to modify and improve them. In that case, it is appropriate for the planning staff, if it has slack time and analytic talent, to help.

This chapter is about efforts the Cleveland planners made to assist four line agencies in local government—the Police Department, the Solid Waste Division, the Municipal Electric Light Plant, and the Community Development Department—to improve their management and services. Planners can, of course, ignore such opportunities, but if they do, they will miss chances to improve conditions in their cities as well as to broaden their own influence with other important actors in local government.

Providing staff support to line agencies is not easy. Urban problems are very complex; objectives are frequently unclear; political leadership, in order to ensure the broadest possible support for a policy, invariably will prefer ambiguity of purpose to clarity. And even when objectives are clear and political will exists, actual goals may be difficult to attain because of the rigidity of rules, procedures, and union arrangements. Still, with all its problems, helping other city agencies to do their jobs better is worth doing. We began our work with them in the early 1970s at what we called the Thursday afternoon policy seminars.

The Thursday afternoon policy seminars, which we invented and which were convened in the Planning Commission conference room, were intended to help professionals in all city departments talk about their work and their work-related problems. The meetings were attended mostly by new members of the planning staff and by members of the Community Development Improvement Program (CDIP) of the Community Development Department. A sprinkling of others came from the Health, Parks, Budget and Management, and Human Resources Departments. It was an informal group whose size and membership shifted from meeting to meeting.

The meetings were a useful strategy in a number of respects. First, they introduced the new city planning staff to the opposite numbers in the other agencies with whom the planners would have to work. This signaled a decided departure from the past. The meetings told others that the new people at city planning were competent, were looking for things to do cooperatively, and were going to work hard and professionally. The meeting also helped us identify potential clients and allies for our work. In the discussions that went on around the huge, boomerang-shaped table on the fifth floor of City Hall, it was easy to tell where policy interests and points of view coincided and where people talked the same language. Circumstances that eased communication among professionals from different departments included great similarity in social class, training, professional style, and ideology. With a few exceptions, most attendees were white, liberal, master's-degree-holders. Few were originally from Cleveland, and many had come to Cleveland specifically to work for Mayor Carl B. Stokes. Though members of this group communicated very well with one another, they realized that the test of their work would be its adoption or rejection by politicians and important bureaucrats who might be less well educated than they, and that implementation might depend on other city employees who might be considerably less articulate. For our part, as the planners and conveners, we felt that if other participants shared our views, they might help us generate our work program, suggest studies that needed to be undertaken, or even lobby for our positions with their own directors, who might otherwise be reluctant to cooperate. Parenthetically, it was also an opportunity for single people who were new in town to meet other single people who were new in town.

The seminars were also comforting to the new planning staff and to the CDIP groups, since members of both groups were struggling with questions of what goals to serve, what to do, and how to be most helpful and effective. Characteristics of this process are self-questioning, agonizing over issues, and feeling that no one else cares about what you are doing. The seminars showed the participants that their concerns were real and shared by others. The seminars also helped define parts of our work program and helped us to identify important old ideas to restate and important new ideas to introduce into the Cleveland political system.

This last element—stating and restating important ideas— is usually overlooked as a function of a city planning agency. Yet good ideas may be stated before their time; if they are restated and reintroduced to the system with some persistence, they may be adopted when the time is right.

The Muny Light and Tower City cases in this chapter and the state lakefront park case discussed earlier (Chapter 10) underscore the value of restating old but good ideas. The reasons to keep the city's municipal light plant have had to be repeated one way or another for almost a century. The idea of a state lakefront park, completely rejected in 1974, was embraced by the same administration just a few years later. Politicians have short time horizons, and they place much more value on feasibility in operational terms than they do on consistency. A planner who persistently repeats good ideas may sell some as circumstances change. And it is rare that other agencies in city government, burdened as they are with daily responsibilities, will perform this function.

FAILING: LEARNING THE HARD WAY WITH THE POLICE

One of the ideas that came out of the policy seminars was an attempt to reshape the deployment of manpower in the Cleveland Police Department. Seminar attendees had listened to citizen complaints about inadequate police protection, were aware of the horrendous response-time figures provided by the Police Department itself, and decided that this was a top-priority issue to address. The group asked John Little, Mayor Stokes's executive assistant, to join us in a meeting in order to discuss the matter and lend us his support. Little, a lawyer with one of Cleveland's most prestigious law firms before he signed on with Stokes, heard our arguments, agreed with most of our observations, graciously explained to us that the mayor already had considered this effort as a high priority and then rejected it, and left us to decide for ourselves how we might best move on the issue. In spite of the mayor's reluctance to approach it, we decided to study the problem because of its overwhelming significance for the quality of life in Cleveland. Analysts for CDIP were to take the lead role, and Ernie Bonner, of the planning staff, was to provide support. The project seemed like an excellent choice: it was clearly an important matter; a success would have great impact; and the project offered an exceptional opportunity to begin developing linkages among staffers from different departments.

We decided to concentrate on violent crime (murder, rape, robbery, and assault), since these were the crimes the public feared the most. We adjusted for unreported crime and factored out those crimes that we thought it would be impossible to prevent in any event. We then looked at the current deployment of patrol cars. Not surprisingly, we found that deployment bore little relation to location of crime.

Because the city's politics had long been organized on a ward basis, police services were more likely to be allocated by ward than by need. Allocations of manpower by police district were not made in proportion to the need for services but were spread evenly throughout the city; every councilmember got about one-thirty-third of the service. But violent crime did not occur evenly across the city; it was heavily concentrated in low-income east side wards.

Working with an interested sergeant in the Police Department (our attempts to involve the chief or assistant chief in our research had been bucked down to the sergeant level), our researchers produced an analysis of present patrol car deployment patterns, made clear their irrelevance to the actual location of reported violent crime, and developed a sophisticated allocation model that reflected our concerns. Then we made a number of recommendations for a more effective deployment pattern that would increase the number of patrol cars at high-crime times and in high-crime areas (while also, of course, reducing the number in low-crime zones). We were delighted; we had technically succeeded in getting many more patrol cars on the street in high-crime areas without hiring a single new police officer. Proudly, we handed the completed study to the mayor with a copy to John Little and sat back to see the changes unfold.

Nothing happened. We then delivered copies of the report to the public safety director and the chief of police, neither of whom even bothered to acknowledge receipt. When both were asked about their reaction to our labors a few weeks later, it became apparent that the report had gone unread. We considered various means of "pushing" our findings: leaking them to the media, finding a dissident "good administration" faction in the Police Department, or getting an ambitious councilmember to act as client. We ultimately rejected all of these courses of actions as potentially more dangerous than helpful to the mayor, and very dangerous to the analysts.

As in most cities, the Cleveland Police Department dominated the city budget and the concerns of most politicians and citizens at large. Their crime-fighting procedures had evolved over a long period of time. They powerfully insisted that they were the "experts" in dealing with that crucial urban problem: crime in the streets. An unknown group of technicians like us could hardly hope to implement important proposals on the redeployment of police manpower without the complete support of the mayor, the public safety director, or the chief of police.

We never did gain greater prominence for our proposals. So far as we were able to determine, our recommendations were never seriously considered by the Police Department, let alone adopted, and police manpower continued to be assigned as before.

In retrospect, the naivete of the seminar members with regard to the police policy study is embarrassing. We failed to consider even the most fundamental and essential elements of program modification and reform. As we came to understand more fully later, reform or change in city government is extraordinarily difficult to accomplish and requires much, much more than we gave it in this instance. For example, in no sense was the Police Department a serious client for our work—that is, anxious to have it and anxious to implement it. Sure, one sergeant was interested, and the chief of police and director of public safety indicated a general interest in the issue from time to time, but they did not view the problem as an urgent one. Indeed, most of the police brass saw little reason to make any changes at all. No important outside pressures to improve matters were focused on the department. We analysts, all planners and economists new to the city and completely unknown to the police, were not necessarily regarded as a friendly source of neutral and competent advice. The idea for the study did not originate in the Police Department or the mayor's office, but in an unknown and informal self-styled policy group. In a sense, we deserved to be ignored.

We discussed our frustration with the police study at a subsequent cabinet meeting with Mayor Stokes and other directors. We said something to the effect that we all had to be concerned with improving basic public services; service demands were high, and our likelihood of getting new revenues to hire more personnel were probably not good—at least until we could demonstrate convincingly that we were doing the best we could with the resources we had. We also said that the planning staff and the policy group would be willing to work with other agencies to the extent we could in trying to make service programs as cost-effective and efficient as possible.

Several of the directors voiced surprise that the planning staff could help perform a study like the police analysis and that we were interested in trying to be helpful to other departments as well. Mayor Stokes suggested that we talk to the people at the Solid Waste Division of the Service Department. The division, he said, had obvious problems and little internal planning capability and might make an interested client, since it was suffering from much public criticism. The criticism, in letters to the editor and on the floor of City Council, alleged a low quality of waste collection service ("they didn't pick it up or get it all" or "they dumped half of it on the street") relative to a large and ever-rising share of the city budget. We decided to begin in 1970 what became a long and successful association with the Solid Waste Division.

We also began working closely with the Municipal Electric Light Plant on matters originally having to do with our capital improvement program and ultimately having to do with the survival of the facility in public ownership.

SUCCEEDING: LEARNING TO PICK UP GARBAGE "HEURISTICALLY"

Cleveland's Solid Waste Division seemed an unlikely client. It consisted of some 450 employees who were members of the powerful Teamsters Union and were guided by a tough and resourceful union leader. Their political astuteness and power at the bargaining table were second only to those of the safety forces, who were prepared to litigate virtually any change proposed in their procedures. The 450 members of the division manned 110 trucks, collected and disposed of 1,300 tons of solid waste and bulk items each working day, and absorbed an annual budget of about $23 million. But while the division was large and politically potent, it was also burdened with an increasing amount of solid waste, rising collection and disposal costs, and a city budget that was increasingly straining for resources. Mayor Stokes was anxious to achieve efficiencies in city government and thought that perhaps this was one area in which research and analysis could help. Even if our efforts did not actually effect savings, the mayor may have reasoned that any publicity about the study as it progressed would suggest to the public that the administration was aware of the problem and was applying modern methods to its solution. This might result in positive publicity. Further, there would be no consultant's fees to explain to City Council and the media. In the past, the administration had been criticized for "steering" an excessive amount of consulting work to political supporters.

We introduced ourselves to the commissioner of the division, Bob Beasley. He was skeptical; what did some city planners, new to Cleveland, know about garbage and his specific problems? We persisted, mentioning the mayor's interest in the study and the support of the director. We also offered to examine only those issues of interest to the division, to meet time schedules set by the division and to remain completely anonymous. We offered as analysts Ernie Bonner and Doug Wright, two of our best newcomers, and Charlie Volz, an older member of the planning staff who was known, liked, and trusted by the Solid Waste Division staff. Volz was a capable member of the planning staff who had been with the commission for many years. Although he was a respected technician, Charlie could also have a drink with the boys and make them feel comfortable. He was viewed by the members of the Solid Waste Division as potentially helpful and nonthreatening.

As it happened, the mayor and the local newspapers were pressing at the time for productivity gains or cuts in the Service Department's budget, while some of the sanitation crews were unhappy with their work schedules. Outside forces had come together to make our effort appropriate. The commissioner finally asked if we could provide an analysis of existing collection routes, disposal procedures, and manpower shifts. When we had them, he wanted us to make our recommendations confidentially to the mayor, his director, and him. We accepted the assignment with delight.

As it turned out, the choice of people for the assignment was fortuitous. The younger planners, Bonner and Wright, could apply the most current techniques to the research, and Volz, the more senior planner, could help translate the findings to the division's staff in a pleasant manner. Volz became so committed to the implementation of the recommendations that he remained on part-time assignment to the division for six years.

The results of the work completed by the planning staff in the first year after we accepted the assignment were impressive. At our urging, supported, of course, by the director of the department, a cabinet-level task force on solid waste was established to give the issue the high-priority focus it deserved. The task force helped secure a federal grant for more detailed analysis. The grant funds also provided for a consultant who specialized in routing procedures, and he was hired to further study and systematize collection routes and procedures. Recommendations arising from the work done by the consultant, Bonner, and Wright were carefully developed with the division's employees. They included reassignment of personnel, rescheduling of routes, and a phased reduction in manpower.[1] The last recommendation, operating the collection vehicles with one fewer man, was the most difficult to sell. Ultimately, though, it was accepted as part of a revision of the union's contract. The set of proposals and reassignments was then generally approved. Within a year, our recommendations were

---

[1]Cleveland City Planning Commission, "Solid Waste Collection and Disposal," March 1971.

saving the division over a million dollars a year compared with previous budgets.

The research also led to the city's first two trash transfer stations, which greatly reduced costs due to over-the-road trips to distant disposal sites. Although there was a long dispute over the locations recommended, the research recommendations ultimately prevailed. The association between planning and the Solid Waste Division had two other benefits, one more directly useful than the other.

A striking contribution by Charlie Volz was the "discovery" of $6 million in voted bond authority. In order to avoid the risk of an increase in the property tax rate, it seemed that the Locher administration, which preceded that of Mayor Stokes, had decided not to issue waste collection and disposal bonds that had been approved by the voters in 1967. Following changes in the mayor's office and in top administrative personnel in the Service Department, the existence of the bond authority had been forgotten. While studying old capital fund records, Volz "rediscovered" it. Only weeks before the voted authority was to lapse, he organized the needed support from the commissioner, director, and mayor to have the bonds sold. The support was there, but it needed to be informed and energized. Volz hand-carried the legislation around, seeking the relevant approvals, and organized the action and support of others. This ensured the availability of the capital funds needed to carry out the division's program and further strengthened Volz's position as a key actor in the division's planning process.

In another, less dramatic side effect, the division's leadership began to receive well-deserved national publicity. As he became more and more at home with the planning staff and with the other technical consultants that we helped screen and bring in ("screen" because we were deeply concerned about the quality of the division's other advisors), the commissioner, who was a former garbageman, became a frequent speaker at national conventions, where he would tell how he turned his troubled division around and how his division learned to "pick up garbage heuristically." Much of his material was drafted by ghostwriters from the city planning staff. This, of course, was a service we were glad to provide, whether or not we received public recognition for our efforts.

KEEPING THE LIGHTS ON AT MUNY LIGHT

Another interagency issue in which we were deeply involved
was that of public versus private electric power. Cleveland is
served by two electrical systems—the Cleveland Electric Illuminating Company (CEI), an investor-owned regional utility
company that serves about 80 percent of the accounts in Cleveland, and the city's own Municipal Electric Light Plant (Muny
Light). Muny was established in 1905, during the administration of Tom L. Johnson, Cleveland's great reform mayor. One of
its original purposes was to act as a yardstick against which to
measure the performance of the privately owned utility. In this
regard, it functioned very well. When Muny began operating in
1914, it charged its customers three cents per kilowatt hour,
while CEI was charging ten cents. By 1931, Muny was still
charging three cents and CEI had been forced to cut its rates to
five cents. Even today, Muny's rates were lower than CEI's. In
1989, CEI's rate for a typical 500-kilowatt-hour-per-month residential customer was $50.67; for Muny it was $36.61.

In 1971, a series of power blackouts caused the city planning staff to examine Muny Light's physical needs as a routine
part of our preparation of the city's annual capital improvement program. Ernie Bonner and Doug Wright were our principal investigators, and they worked closely with Muny Commissioner Warren Hinchee. Hinchee had been introduced to us
by one of his staffers who attended the Thursday policy seminars.

As our capital needs analysis unfolded, it became apparent that the issue was more complex than Muny's need for a
few pipes and boilers.

Bonner and Wright found that CEI had for decades been
interested in purchasing Muny, presumably to eliminate competition. We also found that, apparently to injure Muny's competitive position, CEI, which completely surrounded the Muny
service area, had steadfastly refused to allow Muny to tie in to
other power sources. Therein lay Muny's problem. Nearly all
electric power companies have tie-ins to other power systems
so that they can continue service should their own facilities
need repair or fail. Because it had no such tie-in, Muny was
plagued with power failures. Every time something had to be
repaired, service was interrupted. This led to numerous com-

plaints about Muny's service, and several councilmembers were proposing to sell the facility to CEI.

Bonner and Wright concluded that this might solve the blackout problem, but it would also mean that Muny's customers would experience an immediate rate hike and that the city would no longer have an effective brake on future rate increases. Thus, the issue appeared to have serious economic implications for the city's poor. Because electricity is a relatively fixed item of household consumption, any change in rates would have a definite effect upon the real incomes of city residents. Moreover, a significant change upward in rates might influence the location of firms within the Cleveland region and, thus, the access of city residents to jobs.

Bonner and Wright worked closely with Commissioner Hinchee and his staff. They analyzed the fiscal and legal aspects of this question and the history of CEI's apparent long-term attempt to subvert and destroy Muny. Then they proposed something quite different from the sale of Muny to CEI. At a Planning Commission meeting attended by representatives from every newspaper and television station in town, whom we had thoughtfully invited, we proposed that Muny Light use state law to condemn the CEI plant and purchase CEI's transmission and generating facilities in the city for $280 million.[2] This would expand the small municipal power system into a citywide network, eliminate blackouts, and also provide electricity at much lower cost to city residents.

Our proposal was greeted with surprise and controversy by the members of the Planning Commission. Bob Storey, one of our strongest supporters on the commission, suggested that we had "made a mistake with this one." But his objection was good-humored. The proposal was greeted with derision by the news media. It did not result in the condemnation of CEI. However, it may have helped to forestall the sale of Muny Light to CEI and prevent rate increases. It also served to remind local decision-makers of the rationale for Muny Light's establishment. Beyond this, our study may have played a role in the events that followed.

In 1975, under Mayor Ralph Perk, James B. Davis, the city

---

[2]Cleveland City Planning Commission, "An Expanded Electric Power System for the City of Cleveland," April 1972.

law director, filed a $327 million anti-trust suit against CEI and four allied power companies for anti-competitive practices. A year later, the U.S. Justice Department filed a brief in support of the city, and the Atomic Safety and Licensing Board of the U.S. Nuclear Regulatory Commission (NRC) handed down a decision that elaborated on Bonner and Wright's findings of four years earlier and confirmed that CEI had a history of acting "individually and collectively to eliminate one or more electric entities and to preclude competition."[3]

In the years that followed, Mayor Perk reversed his longstanding support for Muny and proposed to sell the system to CEI. One of the terms of the sale provided that the city would drop its anti-trust suit. However, the sale was never consummated; Dennis Kucinich used the issue as a rallying point in his 1977 drive to the mayor's office and killed the deal. The administration of Mayor George V. Voinovich pursued the suit vigorously until the case was finally decided against the city in 1984.

Did the work of Cleveland's city planners in publishing our 1972 report, in making depositions in the city's suit, and in publicizing the CEI–Muny Light issue have anything to do with Muny's present cherished place in the hearts of the city's leadership? Perhaps, but for most of us it is enough to know that we used our skills in data gathering and analysis for the useful purpose of exposing CEI's effort to destroy a municipal institution. Muny (now renamed Cleveland Public Power) is a major asset still in the hands of the city.

WHO GETS, WHO PAYS, AT TOWER CITY

A final example of working with line agencies to improve their performance has to do with the Tower City development proposal. It provides an example of early "linked development" and an attempt to deny an application for regressive property tax abatement.

In the winter of 1974, a local real estate developer approached the city through the Community Development De-

---

[3]5 NRC 133 (1977): *Nuclear Regulatory Commission Issuances*, January 1, 1977–March 31, 1977, vol. 5 (Washington, D.C.: Government Printing Office, 1977), pp. 133–260.

partment with plans to construct a major downtown commercial complex called Tower City. The developer claimed that the total value of planned construction would reach $350 million. The media, the business community, and the city's political leadership hailed the proposal as a bold step toward revitalizing downtown Cleveland.

Craig Miller and Bill Resseger of the Planning Commission staff analyzed the legislation and the proposal and found several disturbing aspects. The city was asked both to waive rights it held to the development site and to agree to repair some roads and bridges at a cost that could exceed $15 million. Further, it appeared that the developer would request property tax abatement for twenty years.

We concluded that the city had little to gain from the Tower City proposal as it stood. The bridge repairs would be expensive, and our responsibility for them was unclear; the city might be forced to give away any new property tax revenue; the promise of new income tax revenue was not bright, since our studies showed that the market for downtown office space was not growing but simply shifting from one location to another; and the developer was not offering any new jobs to the city's unemployed.[4]

We were not opposed to new development per se. We realized that new development might keep in the downtown district firms that might otherwise have left the city completely; that development provides short-term construction jobs; and that it adds to the tax base (unless new tax revenues are abated). We wanted new development that was of clear net benefit to the city and its people.

We met with the Community Development Department staff and pointed out our concerns. First, we suggested that the city should delay action on the issue so that we could litigate and have a court declare the city's responsibility, or lack thereof, for the costly road and bridge repairs. Otherwise, these repairs would come out of our limited capital improvement budget. Second, we urged that the developer provide firm commitments on the number of city residents, preferably the unemployed, that he would be willing to hire. If we were "giving"

---

[4]Cleveland City Planning Commission, "Impact of New Construction on the Market for Existing Downtown Office Space: Implications for the City's Revenue Base," June 1974.

subsidies and authorizations, we were entitled to get something back. Finally, we argued that the developer should agree to forego property tax abatements. We pointed out that the property tax load in Cuyahoga County was already shifting in a regressive direction, from industry and large corporations to homeowners and small businesses; that new development would demand new services and that tax revenue must offset that demand if general service levels were not to fall; and that the strapped Cleveland school system would lose 60 percent of any abated property taxes. We stressed the inequity of subsidizing millionaire developers at the expense of low-income and working-class city residents. The Community Development staff took our arguments under advisement, but it was plain that they wanted the development and were not prepared to drive hard bargains.

We went to see Mayor Perk, explaining our concerns to him. The mayor's response was ambiguous: "Help the project move ahead," he said, "but protect the interests of the people." This, I thought, was clearly an invitation to do what we considered best. In effect the mayor was asking the Planning Commission to get out ahead of him. "You can do this," he was saying, "but I can't yet." We needed no further instruction.

Following the staff's recommendation, the City Planning Commission refused to approve the legislation unless several amendments were made under which the developer would undertake the bridge repairs on his own account, guarantee a number of new jobs to city residents, and agree to forego tax abatement and to pay full property taxes on the project. These conditions were not acceptable to the developer, and the commission disapproved the proposal.

Very quickly, our position came under fire from City Council and the newspapers. We were accused of obstructing progress and being anti-development. Our rebuttal was that the health and vitality of a city did not depend on the construction of new office buildings and hotels downtown but rather on how well the city helped provide jobs, opportunities, and services to its present and future residents. Our argument did not convince many people.

Attacks on the planners grew stronger and more personal throughout the City Council committee hearings. Council President George Forbes, until 1990 the ringmaster of City Hall, called the City Planning Commission "a bunch of baboons" and on television demanded my resignation. Eventually, Council overrode the commission's disapproval 32 to 1 and passed the legislation. As it turned out, Forbes's attack was largely theatrical; a week later, he was asking for the staff's help on a speech he needed written.

On this particular issue we lost badly, but we succeeded in placing some important issues on the public agendá. We pointed out that the city should go slowly in assuming costs that might belong to others; that money to subsidize projects such as Tower City would be obtained at the expense of high-priority capital improvements in the city's working-class and poor neighborhoods. We asked how far the city should go to underwrite the risk of private development. We also tried to make clear that the city's scarce resources should be applied to facilitating private development only if that development provided permanent, productive jobs for the city's people and net increases in tax revenues for the city's coffers. In short, we proposed the doctrine that the city spend its money and power in more "businesslike" ways. These arguments may have led the Community Development Department and City Council to begin considering resident hiring and minority set-asides. Perhaps more importantly, they may have led to the complete ending of tax abatements during the mayoralty of Dennis Kucinich and the first six years of George V. Voinovich's tenure as mayor.

LESSONS LEARNED

What do these stories tell us that may be useful to planners and other public administrators in local government? A number of lessons might be derived from our experience.

First, planners generally have been too timid. Beyond the relatively narrow powers delegated to planners by their charters, there are wide possibilities for useful interaction with other agencies in city government. The scope of planning activity is not specified by law or custom, nor is it uniform in practice. Planners, therefore, have great freedom to define their roles and responsibilities. Other decision-makers will not help in that definition; planners themselves must seize the initiative. If they do, they will find many ways to make things better for the people of their cities. It is important to note that planners, behind the buffer of the Planning Commission, are independent enough to be somewhat critical of city policies; isolated enough to work on underlying problems; and close enough to provide city agencies with recommendations that are both useful and timely. There will always be political space for planners to expand; it will not be found in the mandated responsibilities of the city charter but through an opportunity-scanning process.

Second, planners' technical training is very useful in working with other city agencies. That training consists of an ability to collect and analyze voluminous statistical information, familiarity with public financial practices, an understanding of basic economic precepts, a working knowledge of law, and an appreciation of the rules of bureaucracies. Information, analysis, and insight are powerful tools for shaping public outcomes.

Third, it is wise to use care in stating certain taboo words and concepts. Proposals, for example, to expand the public sector at the expense of the private sector (as in our Muny–CEI proposal) may be contrary to the general notion of how things ought to relate to each other. These notions are heavily influenced by words and language. If stated in the wrong way, the words can drag down the concept. But the discussion can reach the table if the concept is stated more skillfully in different words. Cleveland's municipal power plant is to be saved, then, not because it represents a triumph of public power over a private sector greedy for profits, but because it is a city asset that makes good business sense and, by lowering electricity costs, will make the city a more competitive location for investment. In the same way, opposition to public subsidies of the downtown area is to be couched in the language of a "bad deal" for the city (that is, one in which the city should negotiate more powerfully in the public interest, and not "give away the store"). Sensitive planners can often circumvent the constraints of language, but first they must recognize that these constraints exist.

The overriding point of the events described in this chapter has to do with broadening and seizing opportunities. Frequently the planning profession's stance seems a passive one, waiting for others to bring work through normal channels, then judging appropriateness through standards or regulations and presenting findings to the planning commission. Too often planners then stop, as if their work were done. But their work is not done, of course, and if they wish to see their ideas and recommendations implemented, they have to do more. If planners are truly interested in improving the future of cities and their residents, they must understand that the future only emerges through the present. Ends and means interact, and desirable outcomes require the planner's prolonged participation in the wide space beyond the commission.

PART TWO

LESSONS

13

Possibilities

> Involvement in policy and program formulation inevitably means involvement in politics. This did not *put* politics into planning: it has always been there. As our experience demonstrated, there were risks, but they were manageable. In light of the limited information available to local decision-makers and the shifting political coalitions characteristic of local government, planners with an informed, equity point of view could survive and prosper and even improve the quality of political decision making. (Chapter 3)

We now turn from the cases to explore their implications for planners in other locales. In this chapter, we argue that opportunities for equity planning like those found in Cleveland exist more generally. In many cities, planners can use their access to elected officials, for example, to shape decision-making agendas. They can use their research and analysis to support particular projects or oppose them, to encourage or inform citizen action.

In Chapter 14, we review several ways the Cleveland planners integrated political judgment and initiative with professionally sound analysis. Just how did the staff take advantage of the opportunities they faced? Articulating a cogent, equity-oriented public voice, these planners took their studies far beyond the City Planning Commission's meeting room.

Finally, in Chapter 15, we consider problems of ethics and evaluation. We realize quickly that issues of ethics in planning are pervasive, immediately practical, and badly in need of attention. We reject any attempt to reduce the complexity of the cases to simple ethical maxims. Instead, we find that the cases can help us to appreciate the richness of actual ethical questions as they arise in practice: to spread information or to withhold it? to fulfill an obligation to the mayor or one to the people of the city? to work with other agency staff *sub rosa* or not? to bring necessarily imperfect project analyses into the public realm or not?

We offer the cases of Part One and the following chapters to pose a series of practical and political issues. Just how can the typical ambiguity of local planning mandates provide opportunities and not just paralysis for equity-oriented planners? How can the typical complexity of local government provide still other opportunities and not just project delays? When politicians, private developers, agency directors, and neighborhood leaders face an uncertain future, how can planners' proposals make a difference?

We stress again what we said in our Preface: planners cannot single-handedly change the landscape and political economy of our cities. We should not ask planners to do what only broader social movements can accomplish. But planners can make more of a difference in the face of inequality, poverty, and human suffering than we now expect. So we should not ignore the real possibilities that equity-oriented planners have in their day-to-day work simply because they cannot do as much as we might like. In these chapters, accordingly, we begin to identify widespread opportunities for equity-oriented work. We wish to raise the stakes, to ask more of planning practitioners, academics, and students alike.

Wishing most of all to point to the practical opportunities planners face in complex political settings, however, we pay little attention to the national and international political–economic forces that influence our cities. Interested particularly in how one planning staff *can* pursue an equity agenda effectively while another staff in the same political–economic context does not, we assume, but do not explore, the relevance of encompassing political–economic pressures that shape the stages on which planners work.

As significantly, we use "equity planning" here as a shorthand to refer to planning efforts that pay particular attention to the needs of poor and vulnerable populations, populations also likely to suffer the burdens of racial and sexual discrimination, both institutional and personal.[1] But we do not examine the

---

[1]Born of the desire to serve the urban poor, equity planning and "advocacy planning" are siblings—related but distinct. For a discussion of advocacy planning, see Paul Davidoff, "Advocacy and Pluralism in Planning," *Journal of the American Institute of Planners* 31 (1965): 596–615; and Lisa

notion of "equity" systematically, as philosophers might, for the Cleveland planners referred to "equity planning" colloquially and culturally, not philosophically. Part Two is not the place to assess problems of liberal political theory or moral philosophy involving the relationships (and at times the choices to be made) among equity, fairness, legitimacy, and justice, for example. Like those of political economy, these problems are crucial and demand attention, but they are not the focus of this book.

Some readers may find Part Two's discussion overly optimistic or uncritical, inattentive to the limits and shortcomings of the Cleveland planners' work. We wish to be neither particularly optimistic nor pessimistic nor uncritical, but to clarify institutional and political possibilities, to encourage an articulate, activist, equity-oriented planning practice. Equity-oriented planning, as we understand it, can complement and support, not substitute for, broader political organizing to address urban poverty, community needs, and public policy.

In the context of a planning profession too often wary of political complexity, too often silent in the face of urban poverty, we believe that the Cleveland equity planning experience can be instructive. We look forward to critical analyses that will explore further that intersection where politically articulate and professionally sound planning practice, political–economic pressures, and ethical judgment all meet.

The successes of the Cleveland planners were due not only to their hard work, skill, and persistence, but to institutional openings they exploited.[2] These planners knew that City Hall

---

Peattie, "Politics, Planning, and Categories: Bridging the Gap," in Robert Burchell and George Sternlieb, eds., *Planning Theory in the 1980's* (New Brunswick, N.J.: Center for Urban Policy Research, 1978), pp. 83–93. For earlier discussions of equity planning, see Norman Krumholz, Janice Cogger, and John Linner, "The Cleveland Policy Planning Report," *Journal of the American Institute of Planners* 41 (1975): 298–304; and Norman Krumholz, "A Retrospective View of Equity Planning: Cleveland, 1969–1979," *Journal of the American Planning Association* 48 (1982): 163–74 (with critical commentaries following by Paul Davidoff, Jerome Kaufman, and Lawrence Susskind).

[2]Specific opportunities were peculiar to Cleveland, but these hardly explain the distinctiveness and efficacy of the Planning Commission staff. Consider, for example, Krumholz's ability to hire six new staff members upon coming to town; Mayor Stokes's apparent sympathy for his planners' equity agenda;

was as much a web of networks as it was a rigid hierarchy of control. They knew that power and influence came not just from the leverage of economic wealth but from the support of political coalitions too. In Cleveland the planners found institutional opportunities in several places: the nonmonolithic character of urban politics, the ambiguity of planning mandates and problems, the needs of the powerful for planners' analyses, the nature of publicity and problem formulation in planning, and the organization of planning itself.[3]

THE NONMONOLITHIC CHARACTER OF URBAN POLITICS

Political–economic power in Cleveland was economically concentrated and politically fragmented. The showdown between Mayor Kucinich and the major banks drove the city into bankruptcy, and the transit negotiations pitted the city against a ring of suburban governments. The public housing issue found support from the mayor but resistance from City Council. City agencies met the offer of help from the Planning Commission staff in many ways: the police had little interest in listening to the planners, but the Solid Waste Division came to embrace the staff's assistance.

If we think of city government as a monolith, we mislead ourselves. We risk ignoring the ever-changing needs of politicians and agency directors for support from constituencies. We risk assuming that planners lack access and influence before

---

Homer Wadsworth's willingness to involve the Cleveland Foundation in projects Krumholz sought to push.

[3]The planning literature provides more help with the inventory of available strategies than with an analysis of institutional opportunities. Perhaps the best-known sources—still useful, if dated—are Guy Benveniste, *Politics of Expertise*, 2d ed. (San Francisco: Boyd and Fraser, 1977), and Martin and Carolyn Needleman, *Guerrillas in the Bureaucracy* (New York: Wiley Interscience, 1974). More recent additions to this literature include Bruce McClendon and Ray Quay, *Mastering Change* (Chicago: Planners' Press, 1988); Pierre Clavel, *The Progressive City* (New Brunswick, N.J.: Rutgers University Press, 1986); Barry Checkoway, *Strategic Perspectives on Planning Practice* (Lexington, Mass.: D. C. Heath, 1987); Guy Benveniste, *Mastering the Politics of Planning* (San Francisco: Jossey-Bass, 1989); and John Forester, *Planning in the Face of Power* (Berkeley: University of California Press, 1989).

we have even looked for institutional openings. Krumholz's participation in the mayors' cabinet meetings—to which he initially invited himself, only to become a regular member— suggests what we may miss if we assume powerlessness rather than explore opportunities.

Cleveland's city government gave the planning staff little formal power or influence, yet the very informality necessary to run the government provided the planners with several opportunities to pursue their equity-planning agenda. That informality helped the planners develop ties to agency staff and elected and appointed officials throughout city government. It allowed them to put issues on the public agenda. It allowed them to organize influential coalitions—to advance the lakefront park proposal, the land banking legislation, and the transit negotiating strategies.

Too often, we imagine city agencies as well-oiled bureaucracies in which rigid rules govern work on predefined tasks. In government agencies, outsiders often think, bureaucrats exercise little discretion: problems are well-defined, data are adequate, well-defined techniques are at hand, and rules of procedure eliminate all conflicts. But the Cleveland experience suggests that planning agencies are hardly like that. To stereotype city agencies as "bureaucracies" will most likely obscure more than it reveals.

With few exceptions, the problems of planning are rarely well-defined. Data about the future consequences of today's actions are seldom adequate. Rarely can planners "solve" complex urban problems by using routine methods and procedures. Instead, planners have to interpret problems and their political contexts together, so they can use whatever techniques are at hand in a practical, timely, and politically astute manner. In Cleveland, the networks that linked organizations were as important as the boundaries that separated them.

In the freeway case, had the planners worked as blindered bureaucrats, they might have put the I-290 proposal aside as someone else's responsibility. But no one else was responsible for assessing the project's consequences for Cleveland residents. Seeing both risk and opportunity here, Krumholz reached across organizational boundaries, public and private alike, to develop a planning analysis that assessed I-290's threat to poor city residents, proposed a viable alternative, and strengthened a coalition with more affluent suburban residents also threatened by the proposed route.[4]

Work with other agency staff places demands on planners and provides opportunities too. In every meeting, planners can put in time or try to shape agendas, nurture coalitions, and learn about the priorities and needs of other city actors. The Cleveland planners were hardly cloistered. They built friendships with—and gained the respect of—other professionals, neighborhood and church activists, politicians, confidants of the mayors, and still others. One staff member eventually worked part-time with the Solid Waste Division for six years. Others worked closely with neighborhood organizations. Still others worked with local banks. These planning assignments were largely discretionary, not bureaucratically dictated. Informal ties across bureaucratic boundaries, then, provided information-sharing and coalition-building opportunities for these equity-oriented planners.

Shaping their own work programs and agendas, finding allies in city agencies and community groups, the Cleveland planners began to develop their equity-planning agenda. They found further opportunities to advance their work where they might have least expected them: in the very confusion, ambiguity, and conflict-ridden nature of planning problems.

AMBIGUITIES OF MANDATES AND PROBLEMS

Planners face complexity, not simplicity, in their daily work; conflict, not consensus; moving rather than stationary targets. But because their planning mandates are often deeply ambiguous, planners have opportunities to identify and address equity issues in influential ways.

When the planners worried about the futility of updating the General Plan and went to the Planning Commission for advice and guidance, commission members replied with thoughtful, but contradictory and inconclusive, suggestions. For their

---

[4]Krumholz's inviting sub rosa planning assistance from an engineering firm and from NOACA itself raises important ethical questions, to which we return, but it in no way weakens our central point here: bureaucratic rules and procedures structure, creating as well as constraining, the discretion planners will often have to identify and pursue equity-related problems.

parts, Mayors Stokes, Perk, and Kucinich seemed altogether more concerned about protecting their images (and votes) than with charging the planning staff to get anything in particular done. Under these conditions, the planners had a good deal of freedom—to define an agenda attending to the needs of the poorest in Cleveland, or to languish and muddle along.

For some planners, the lack of a clear mandate would have been confusing, but the Cleveland planners took it as a source of opportunity. For some planners, too, the lack of a clear mandate would no doubt have been positively threatening, for any initiative the staff took would then appear to be "uncalled for"! But the Cleveland planners invoked broader traditions of public service, professionalism, and the ideals of a democratic political culture to legitimate their efforts to expand "choices for those who had few."

The planners prepared a powerful equity-planning statement, the *Cleveland Policy Planning Report*, which served to provide both direction for their own work and provocation for the national planning profession.

The persistent complexity and messiness of most planning problems provide opportunities as well. For just what "the problem" really is in any one case will rarely be clear. Trash dumping at a city park will be seen by some as an economic issue (no funds for clean-up!), by others as an environmental issue (protect the park!), by yet others as a non-issue (the schools come first!), and by still others as a political problem (is the mayor responsible?) Facing this rich ambiguity of problem interpretation every day, planners must not only create a semblance of order but get a job done too. Facing the Euclid Beach or Tower City or People Mover proposals, the planners could well ask: What consequences do these proposals have for the city's poor and vulnerable populations? What public subsidies for private benefits are at stake?

Because virtually any planning problem can be posed in many ways, the ambiguity planners face is an essential rather than incidental part of their work.[5] Even when public options

---

[5]A broad, if thin, literature explores the work of "problem formulation." See, for example, Murray Edelman, *Constructing the Political Spectacle* (Chicago: University of Chicago Press, 1988); Joseph Gusfield, *The Culture of Public Problems* (Chicago: University of Chicago Press, 1981); John Seeley's brilliant "Social Science: Some Probative Problems," in his *Americanization of the Unconscious* (New York: International Science Press, 1967); and the

are severely constrained by relations of power, the planning questions remain: What can and ought to be done? What advantages and disadvantages, virtues and problems, come with each alternative?

We do not mean that regardless of constraints, opportunities will exist. Facing a gun on a dark street, "Your money or your life!" does not promise many alternatives. And when city planners, often desperate for development-spurred tax dollars, face developers pressing for tax abatements and public subsidies, the planners may take the developers to be making the same demand: Your city's money or its economic life.

Yet we too easily *presume* planners' powerlessness and fail to explore the limits and vulnerabilities of the apparently more powerful. We risk resignation just when we need to organize. We need in each case to assess just what negotiating power and leverage we have—which depends significantly on the *needs* of the other—without assuming, before the fact and in every case, that we have no power at all.

Constraints exist, but opportunities do too, even when planning mandates provide little specific guidance for action. When the Cleveland planners examined the tax-delinquency situation, for example, no mandate told them to work to change the state property law. When they documented the progressive deterioration of the lakefront beaches, no clear instructions told them to try to transfer caretaking responsibilities to the state. When they documented the needs of the transit-dependent, they could have filed a report and stopped there, for, again, no instructions or recipes told the planners what to do. These problems of housing, parks, and transportation were poorly defined, messy, open-ended, ambiguous, and therefore open to interpretation and intervention in many ways.

The planners exploited rather than avoided the complexity of these problems. Faced with the challenges of reviewing proposed projects—from a Tower City development to the take-over of Muny Light—and their long-term consequences, the planners could hardly avoid doing research. But research always requires a series of practical choices: what information

---

closely related "Dilemmas in a General Theory of Planning," *Policy Sciences* 4(1973):155–69, by Melvin Webber and Horst Rittel. The discretion planners have to construct problems selectively remains largely unexplored territory. See also Robert B. Reich, ed., *The Power of Public Ideas* (Cambridge, Mass.: Ballinger, 1988).

to pursue, how to assess it, how to report it. So the planners' research presented them with opportunities: to identify needs of vulnerable populations, to examine carefully the false promises of this year's project to "save the downtown," to make information available to the public about the uses and abuses of public subsidies and tax abatements.

A striking use of the Cleveland planners' research involved the issue analysis and speech writing they did for politicians bound for legislative hearings, church basements, annual meetings of civic associations, or NOACA-like board meetings. Few politicians would deliver a planner's speech "blind" or verbatim; yet politicians' on-going needs for articulate, coherent, grounded analyses of issues can nevertheless provide opportunities for planning staff.

A curious example of some success here is suggested by the following effusive and laudatory, if tongue-in-cheek, note Krumholz received from Mayor Stokes:

(letterhead)

CITY OF CLEVELAND

May 17, 1971

Norm!
You are fired as a speech writer! Retired—I should say. Because I cannot believe you have a third excellent speech bubbling within you!
"Federal Housing Policy: A Paper Moon in a Cardboard Sky" is great. I'm not going to change even a comma! I'll deliver it as you wrote it.
Goddammit! You're going to make a Socialist of me yet!!

Sincerely,
[signed]
Carl Stokes

An appreciative, handwritten expression of thanks, this note is a cultural document too. Stokes apparently did not take such speech writing for granted: he seemed surprised that the city's planners could serve him effectively in this way. The speech provides a simple example of planning influence that came not only from organizing information, but from alerting the mayor to the staff's competence, anticipating his needs, reshaping his public image, and articulating directions for housing policy as well.

PUBLICITY AND PROBLEM FORMULATION

This leads us to a central point. When we try to explain how planners can be effective, we often reach too far too fast, thinking about planners as problem-solvers. When we do that, we often ignore the crucial practical work that planners must first do as problem-formulators to pose problems, to shape public attention and decision-making agendas. As problem-posers, planners work as public educators, coalition-builders, and professional-bureaucratic organizers as well.

For when decision-makers need "information," they typically need much more than "the facts," much more than the back-up of computer printouts. They need "information" framed cogently: a succinct and compelling story, one we too easily label "good advice," that will help them interpret the threats and options they face.[6]

Our point is illustrated strikingly by Gardner Ackley, who served as chair of the Council of Economic Advisors from 1964 to 1968. Speaking about the challenges of maintaining access and influence while giving advice to the president of the United States, Ackley argued:

> The single most important requirement for access to power is the ability to write clearly, simply, understandably, giving everything that's necessary but nothing that's extraneous, in sentences of no more than ten words, in words preferably of no more than two syllables, arranged on the page with a lot of space so that you can see the organization of the argument by the arrangement of the space on the page, with dots and indentations and dashes and numbered points, and no solid paragraphs more than about three or four lines long. Then you don't have to read anything two or three times to figure out what it's saying. Very few dependent clauses. Qualifications belong in separate sentences, and qualifications that aren't really relevant to the issue should be omitted.
>
> We knew that this was very important to our influence with the President because we observed it so often. For example, a memorandum would come to the President from the Treasury on some eco-

---

[6]On the importance of stories in medical diagnosis, teaching, and public policy analysis, see Robert Coles, *The Call of Stories: Teaching and the Moral Imagination* (Boston: Houghton Mifflin, 1989); see also Richard Neustadt and Ernest May, *Thinking in Time: The Uses of History for Decision Makers* (New York: Free Press, 1986). Martin Krieger, *Advice and Planning* (Philadelphia: Temple University Press, 1981), provides a philosophical analysis of the character of good advice. Cf. David Wiggins, "Deliberation and Practical Reason," in Joseph Raz, ed., *Practical Reasoning* (Oxford: Oxford University Press, 1978).

nomic question. It was written in paragraphs that were six or eight inches long on the page, single-spaced, right out to the margins; full of long sentences, with a lot of modifying clauses; containing a lot of detail, some of which was pertinent and some of which wasn't. [President Johnson] would look at those things and after about five minutes he'd send them over to the Council and ask, "Would you translate this for me?"[7]

The Cleveland planners knew that they had not only to organize information, but to articulate what it meant. They understood that Mayor Stokes needed not just information to take to the NOACA board, but a cogent negotiating strategy. He needed not just a position, but a forceful story of interests to be protected and served, principles of participation and representation to be honored, a city's and region's future to be developed. Mayor Perk needed not just information concerning the city's parks to face public pressure about the deteriorating lakefront. He needed a crisp, future-oriented story, a plan that accounted for the problem, promised a line of response, and gave a cast of characters realistic parts to play in achieving that response. The Cleveland planners recognized Perk's vulnerability, and they responded with a plan. They devised the plot, managed a supporting task force, procured foundation support for the required expertise, and provided a "here's how we're going to do it" story that Perk proudly presented to the public.

When the private utility continued to threaten Muny Light, the planners provided much more than data for interested reporters, legal counsel, politicians, and the public at large. They researched the history of CEI's actions; they compared rates and services; they devised strategies for the city to protect its interests—and their story was vindicated by the federal Justice Department.

The land banking case teaches the same lesson. The planners built upon their research to propose another "here's what to do" story, and they changed the state of Ohio's property law in the doing. How was this possible? By defining city needs, organizing potential beneficiaries, and articulating strategies too, the planners helped to create the political space to do this work. Long before "solving" any problems, these planners

---

[7]From Erwin C. Hargrove and Samuel A Morley, eds., *The President and the Council of Economic Advisors: Interviews with CEA Chairmen* (Boulder, Colo.: Westview, 1984), pp. 227–28.

worked through coalitions, task forces, the media, and neighborhood groups to formulate problems and solutions, to call both public and decision-makers' attention to equity-related issues of displacement, threatened urban services, transit needs, and more.[8]

THE NEEDS OF THE POWERFUL AND PLANNING OPPORTUNITIES

"The powerful" depend at times on benign public images, at other times on secrecy, here on public acquiescence, there on the control of information. Planners can at times affect those conditions. They might enable public scrutiny of a developer's inflated promises. They might help to publicize alternatives to a privately lucrative but publicly costly construction project. They might support equity-oriented coalitions. In all these ways, planners might counteract established power and press an equity-planning agenda forward.

The influence planners have depends not only on available information, but on the needs and vulnerabilities of many other actors.[9] Developers, banks, mayors, and other politicians are not all-knowing, fully autonomous, and independent. These actors depend on the cooperation of many others to sustain their power, and so they are vulnerable to the organizing of constituencies, clients, neighborhoods, workers, and

---

[8]A truism in planning holds that problem formulation must precede problem solution, but the apparent triviality of that logical relationship has preempted political and sociological research exploring just what planners can do when they formulate, identify, pose, bound, shape, and select "problems." Exploring these apparent synonyms, as Stanley Cavell argues in *Must We Mean What We Say?* (Cambridge: Cambridge University Press, 1976), can help us investigate the practical world of planners' real opportunities. See also George Lakoff and Mark Johnson, *Metaphors We Live By* (Chicago: University of Chicago Press, 1980). Gusfield's *Culture of Public Problems* suggests the fieldwork to be done. For alternative views see Karl Weick, *The Social Psychology of Organizing* (New York: Random House, 1979); and James March and Johann Olsen, eds., *Ambiguity and Choice in Organizations* (Oslo: Universitetsforlaget, 1976).

[9]For a classic modern discussion, see the equation of power and interdependence in J. D. Thompson, *Organizations in Action* (New York: McGraw-Hill, 1967). See also Benveniste, *Politics of Expertise*, and Paulo Freire's notion of "limit situations" in his *Pedagogy of the Oppressed* (New York: Seabury, 1970).

others.[10] In each city, these vulnerabilities will take their own specific shape. In "hot" real estate markets, private developers will be more vulnerable to planners' criticisms of their projects than they would be in other locales. Yet developers more generally are vulnerable to the uncertainties and unpredictabilities of public agency cooperation or resistance, the force of organized public opinion, and still other sources of delay and expense. Politicians elected by narrow margins will be more vulnerable to shifts of public opinion than politicians enjoying more comfortable pluralities. Agency directors facing public pressure will be more vulnerable than those whose actions face less public scrutiny. And so on.

Politicians must worry about their reputations. Corporate actors must worry about influences on their costs of doing business, whether they involve fiscal and regulatory pressures, materials and transport costs, or pressures from the international economy or the shop floor. Government agencies must worry about maintaining favor with those who control their budgets.

All of this "worry" is structurally rooted because these actors are interdependent. No one of them can fully control the others, so they need to keep a watchful eye on a complex and uncertain future. Thus, Cleveland City Council President George Forbes could call for the planners' resignation one week and ask them for materials for a speech a week or two later. Cleveland real estate interests, themselves vulnerable to the uncertainties caused by speculators, came to support the planners' land banking bill. And the powerful suburban governments, vulnerable to the withdrawal of Cleveland's dues and the federal government's support from the regional planning agency, NOACA, had to respond to the Cleveland planners' arguments.

As in Cleveland, planners across the country, we believe, will be able to identify issues of inadequate services, deteriorating housing, and the burden of tax abatements and help get these problems on public agendas, even if they cannot "solve"

---

[10]For an important analysis that begins to explore this point, see Peter Marris's discussion of our metaphors of change in *Meaning and Action*, originally published in 1982 as *Community Planning and Conceptions of Change* (London: Routledge and Kegan Paul, 1987).

them.[11] They can supply the media with timely information and so help others to act. They can help city agencies by providing analyses of options, as the Cleveland planners did with the Solid Waste Division and Muny Light. They can supply community organizations with information about opportunities to make their needs felt. They can provide legislators with cogent information about issues, or supply city officials with the background needed to participate in intergovernmental negotiations, as the Cleveland staff did in the transit and lakefront cases. To know what influence they might have in any specific case, planners must examine closely just how the power of "the powerful" is itself contingent and vulnerable, just what that power requires for its own maintenance.

THE ORGANIZATION OF PLANNING

The planning agency itself provides opportunities of another kind. Over the ten years of his tenure, Krumholz was able to recruit and cultivate a competent, hard-working, and idealistic staff, who supported one another practically and emotionally in their commitment to the equity-planning agenda. Krumholz recalls in Chapter Two that he did his best to nurture an *esprit de corps* among the new people, with frequent late meetings and parties at his home, at Bonner's apartment, and, later, at a large house that five or six of the staff rented together as a sort of commune:

> For many years I would pick up three or four staff members in my city-assigned car—an old police cruiser with the shotgun rack still in place—and we would discuss the issues of the day on our way to work. This "committee on wheels" was more productive of ideas than any other committee I can recall. . . . It was a time of hard work, almost total absorption in the job, and great camaraderie.

---

[11]Planners face greater opportunities to formulate than to "solve" public problems. They will have influence not because they can make public decisions but because they can at times shape the agendas of public decision making. For a lucid analysis, see Steven Lukes, *Power: A Radical View* (New York: Macmillan, 1974). Certainly, many planners have chosen not to pursue an equity-planning agenda. We wish here only to argue that regular, structural opportunities to do equity-oriented work are nevertheless likely to exist in settings all across the country. On political leadership, see Ronald Heifetz and Riley Sinder, "Political Leadership: Managing the Public's Problem Solving," in Reich, *The Power of Public Ideas*, pp. 179–203.

Krumholz recruited a committed, competent, and reasonably congenial staff. But he recruited more than that. In Ernie Bonner he had recruited a manager and an organizer as well as a technically competent analyst. Bonner's internal leadership and administrative abilities became an essential complement to Krumholz's externally oriented work of meeting with politicians, other agency directors, the mayor's cabinet, neighborhood residents, influential business leaders, and others.

Central to our whole story, of course, is the fact that Krumholz, as the city planning director, was committed to developing and pursuing an equity-planning agenda. His professional encouragement of the staff's work was second in importance only to his shielding and protection of that work. When Council President Forbes attacked the planners on television, Krumholz "took the heat" rather than stifling his staff's work. For many years, too, significantly, the Planning Commission also supported the staff's pursuit of equity-related goals.

Creating the equity agenda together also created a more critical, cohesive, and determined staff. No one has been as insightful about this as Charles Hoch:

> What Krumholz did was go about creating a community—a moral community of reform and resistance—in the midst of a bureaucracy. This was not a private, provincial community, but a public and cosmopolitan community based on strong ties of loyalty, reciprocity, democracy, and commitments to social justice. The social ties that made up this community enabled members to persist, take on risky tasks, pursue a difficult mission, and create the integration of political wisdom and technical smarts that made for effective results.
>
> Krumholz was so different as a leader because instead of commanding he nurtured, instead of shedding responsibilty he embraced it, instead of concentrating control he dispersed it. When he responds to such interpretations by pointing to the important contributions of his staff, this is not just testimony to modesty but an accurate assessment of the community required to make his contributions to planning effective. So the combination of strategic and equity-focused effectiveness was rooted in the formation and maintenance of the staff's "community." Furthermore, the public goals planners hope to fulfill probably cannot be realized without some sort of community like the one Krumholz helped found.[12]

---

[12]Letter to Forester, October 14, 1988. Cf. David Kertzer, *Ritual, Politics, and Power* (New Haven: Yale University Press, 1988).

14

To Be Professionally Effective, Be Politically Articulate

> The promise of [innovative planning is] to keep curiosity and open-mindedness alive throughout the government and . . . produce a flow of valuable new ideas, of which every government has a chronic shortage. . . . The important thing in each jurisdiction will be the systematic search for ideas already in the public domain but likely to be ignored by existing operating agencies. Competence for the invention-oriented planning practitioner will consist largely of a taste for reading and conversing widely (though with discipline), and a capacity to show imagination in applying the ideas he finds to the setting of his own jurisdiction. The plain fact is that, except within certain narrow specialties, no one else seems to do this in most American state and local governments.
>
> —Alan A. Altshuler,
> *The City Planning
> Process* (1965)

To play an effective role in the messy world of urban politics, planners have to be professionally able, organizationally astute, and, most of all, politically articulate. In Cleveland, developing that professionally sound and politically articulate planning voice did not mean back-room deal making. It meant actively anticipating and counteracting threats to Cleveland's vulnerable populations. It meant articulating a vision of a better Cleveland, a city of more services and less poverty, a city of greater choice and less dependency, a city of adequate shelter not only downtown but all across town. Being politically articulate planners meant defining issues and setting agendas, working on problems before being invited to do so. It meant knowing ahead of time that politicians and city department staff would often be too busy, too uncertain, too self-interested, to get involved in some issues—and that this would produce opportunities for the planners to make a difference. Develop-

225

ing an articulate equity-oriented planning voice in Cleveland meant negotiating to serve the interests of the poor, but it meant much more than that, too: building trust and the planners' reputation, providing technical assistance, developing strong ties to the media to inform public opinion, at times leaking information to oppositional figures, drafting legislation, again and again bringing technical analysis to bear on issues of public costs, benefits, and well-being.

The Cleveland cases suggest that planners in other localities too can nurture and inform public debate, expect and respect differences, listen carefully, build cooperation, and work both aggressively and professionally to defend the interests of those least organized in our society. But they need not deny or regret political debate, dread or mystify political and economic conflict, or long for an apolitical society wiped clean of conflicts of interests and values. For if the truism that "planning is political" means anything, it means that planners will inevitably work within a web of political relationships. If they ignore those relationships, planners will virtually assure their own ineffectiveness.

ANTICIPATING PROBLEMS AND ORGANIZING SUPPORT

Many of the "new staff" Krumholz hired came to Cleveland to do equity-oriented work. Once on the job, they seemed painfully aware of the costs of their own inaction in the face of the city's business as usual. All around them, politicians pressed typically narrow agendas, developers lobbied for political support and favors, agencies suffered the effects of political pressures and patronage appointments, and city policies were shaped by the influence of local business elites.

Had the planners been less interventionist than they were, absentee landlords who had abandoned buildings would have held the city hostage all the more. Local construction interests might have procured contracts for white elephants like the Downtown People Mover and enriched themselves at public expense. Illegal dumpers might still be using the lakefront as a dump.

But the planners did take initiative and act. They did not wait for someone to bring a full-blown problem to the Planning

Commission before they went to work. The staff anticipated problems, studied them, typically took their results to the mayor, and argued for various strategies of response. A passage in a letter from Krumholz to Forester makes the point best. Asked to speculate about how a random day during his tenure as planning director might have differed from another city planning director's day, Krumholz began:

> I might begin my day with a breakfast meeting with some of my staff to review things or just because it's fun. J. Doe might begin with a breakfast with the Chamber of Commerce for exactly the same reasons. If there's a hot item on the local agenda I might be invited to breakfast with the Chamber's people, but as a potential adversary. For example, if their hot proposal is a domed stadium (it is, in Cleveland), I would have prepared studies challenging the financing (because it's going to take much public subsidy) and the site location (because it will displace a local market used extensively by the black community). They would want to quiet down my noisy questioning. J. Doe would take a supportively quiet position and adopt the public posture that there's nothing to comment on until legislation is formally placed before the Planning Commission. Of course, by that time, it's all over. I would try to stop or reshape the issue (and others) long before it came up in the form of legislation.

"Of course, by that time, it's all over." That simple line could serve as the epigraph for this entire book. It captures a view of professional action set in a real-time political context.

Amplifying Krumholz's point, Mayor Perk's law director, James B. Davis, provides us with a City Hall insider's account of the Cleveland planners' influence in local government. Asked how Krumholz and the planning staff fit into the daily operations of City Hall, Davis said:

> He didn't fit into it at all; he was not on anybody's game plan; he was not on anybody's chart. The city planning director had no role [in City Hall's decision-making processes] on paper, but Norm managed to have a major role anyhow. . . . [He] was a pretty good politician. He made himself enormously useful on a host of issues to whichever mayor it was. He could assemble more information, faster, and more tightly compressed on paper, than anybody else.
>   And whenever a mayor needed some help, some immediate guidance, some policy paper on something, and had the wit to ask for it, Norm would be there the next day, with the thing all done. I'm overstating a little bit, but his turn-around time was fantastically fast and they knew that. And in many cases he had anticipated what they were going to be doing anyway, and he had something all ready for them. He could do things for them that nobody else in City Hall could; that was his political way of getting his foot in the mayor's office. . . .

> He could see things coming up over the horizon that would be major issues for the city . . . be it a stadium contract, whatever . . . those were not things that he needed to be given any special invitation about. He could see them coming. He had a host of ways of knowing these things were coming up, and he would start to investigate.

In the same interview (October 31, 1987), Davis spoke of the scope of planning under Krumholz's tenure: "Norm's perception was that . . . [a physical planning agenda] was important, . . . but he was vastly more concerned with the absolutely critical issues of running the city, which were financial, and [with] the financial impact on the city of anything that moved. . . . He was concerned with all the big new projects that would come floating through the city of Cleveland, and this was where he was not only a think tank but sort of an OMB [Office of Management and Budget] for City Hall. He probably better than anybody had a sense of what meaningful things could be done with a city budget, and he went through it with a fine-tooth comb, . . . trying to get the most bang for the city out of the buck. Now, he was not part of the [budget process] in any formal way, but he had his own involvement with it."

SHAPING THE NEW AGENDA

Arriving in Cleveland, Krumholz asked for his planners' analysis of the Euclid Beach rezoning proposal.[1] His staff's analysis was terse: The Council's for it, the mayor's been noncommittal, and, the implication seemed to be, "the merits" are unfortunately beside the point. When past experience has convinced a staff that their opposition to a project would be futile, the planners might reasonably limit their resistance to the proposal so they can work productively on more promising issues. Yet this reasonable and practical judgment has a deeper political significance. For here the experience of past powerlessness recreates future powerlessness—even if, ironically, this happens without any *present* exercise of influence, without any explicit threats, deals, pressure, or warnings.[2] In the Euclid

---

[1]For another account of the problems associated with "getting going," see Allan B. Jacobs, *Making City Planning Work* (Chicago: American Society of Planning Officials, 1978).

[2]For an extended analysis, see Steven Lukes, *Power: A Radical View* (New York: Macmillan, 1974). See also John Gaventa, *Power and Powerlessness*

Beach case, the planners' accommodation to the politics of zoning not only pre-empted their analysis but reflected a more pervasive professional malaise and cynicism that Krumholz and the new staff would soon work hard to change.

Krumholz's history in Pittsburgh had been instructive. He saw how strong directors with differing senses of the planning agency's mission achieved substantially different results. Cal Hamilton appeared to pay less attention to politics and decision making than to getting the models right; John Mauro apparently did just the opposite. Krumholz had been impressed by Mauro's engaged style of work, if not always by his particular objectives.

Krumholz tried to assemble a planning staff that fit professional analysis into political contexts, that brought analysis to bear upon political decisions, that worked aggressively within, through, and around the decision-making processes of the city by using competent analyses at every possible step. Together, Krumholz and Bonner developed a new style in the Planning Commission. Knowing that analysis or politics alone could lead to the staff's undoing, they believed that professional analysis articulated cogently and persistently in the political process could enhance the planning staff's credibility, respect, and practical influence. It *is* necessary, Krumholz argues, to keep saying the same thing over and over if you want anyone to notice. This includes talking at local meetings, in county and state testimony, in speeches to the profession, in op-ed pieces, in interviews with local reporters, in speeches written for the mayor, and so on.

Struck by Mauro's patience in press briefings, Krumholz echoes Mauro's practical point: "You can have the best ideas in the world; you can do the most careful analysis of an issue; you can write it up in the most brilliant style possible; but if you don't get it in the papers, no one will know it has been done. And if no one knows about it, you might as well not have done it." Krumholz came to Cleveland with the clear sense, based on his work under Mauro, that planners could play important educational roles in the public realm.

(Urbana: University of Illinois Press, 1980). In an interview (October 31, 1987), journalist Roldo Bartimole pointed to the self-censorship of planning staffs and the challenge of an equity-planning leadership to end this by setting the context for the staff to do their work and to speak articulately to equity concerns.

Yet the planning staff that Krumholz inherited in 1969 was hardly prepared to launch a politically engaged, equity-oriented, interventionist planning strategy. Only by choosing projects in the planners' new work program, and by hiring new staff when he could do so, could Krumholz begin to change the posture of city planning in Cleveland. Building on the best of his inherited staff and adding new professionals, Krumholz moved to redefine the political direction, raise the public profile, and improve the professional reputation of the whole planning operation.[3]

The Cleveland planners' production of the equity-oriented *Policy Planning Report* was the most visible sign of the new agenda. With the *Report*, the planners formally and publicly expressed their commitments to equity concerns and identified problems they hoped to tackle. The months of passionate and searching arguments that went into it also reaffirmed the staff's commitments—not just to the equity agenda, but to one another too. Publicizing the *Report* through official channels and the media also helped the planners find like-minded allies in the city.

BUILDING A REPUTATION FOR
PRACTICAL, EQUITY-ORIENTED ANALYSIS

To influence action in City Hall, the Cleveland planners had to raise their profile, to show what they could do. They needed to complement their principled focus—on the vulnerability of those Cleveland citizens "with few choices"—with an articulate and public planning voice that could express the concerns of those citizens. Bonner, Cogger, Wright, and Krumholz worked, accordingly, to make their professional planning analyses increasingly public. Krumholz puts the problem this way:

---

[3]For analyses of psychological and social–psychological aspects of professional interactions and self-limiting strategies of information suppression, unilateral control, self-fulfilling projection, and defensive behavior, among others, see Howell Baum, *The Invisible Bureaucracy* (New York: Oxford University Press, 1987); and the work of Donald Schon and Chris Argyris: for example, *Theory in Practice: Increasing Professional Effectiveness* (San Francisco: Jossey Bass, 1974). On the influence of race, see Thomas Kochman, *Black and White Styles in Conflict* (Chicago: University of Chicago Press, 1981).

It is important to gain and hold the confidence of political and business leaders. If you alienate enough powerful people, you jeopardize your recommendations, the reputation of the planning agency, and your job. At the same time, it seemed to me that we had the responsibility to represent the best interests of the people of Cleveland as we saw them. We went about doing that in a cordial but nondeferential way, without compromising the facts of a case or our professional integrity. A good way to do this was to project an air of professional and technical competence and an apolitical, conservative, even skeptical public stance. The stance was built by always speaking soberly, using numbers when we had them to describe and quantify the issue, and wearing conservative suits and ties.

Articulate staff analysis served the mayors, other agencies, and community organizations alike.[4]

Krumholz's staff needed not just to calculate correctly, but to inspire confidence. With Charlie Volz as the trusted link to the Solid Waste Division, the planners could analyze the division's financial and service-delivery problems. With Layton Washburn as the old friend of Parks Commissioner Nagy, the planners could pursue the lakefront parks proposal. That a politics of personal networks mattered here did not make the technical merits of proposals irrelevant—far from it. But confidence in the staff was crucial. Without it, no report or memo, presentation, argument, or telephone call can be trusted, and without trust, the real merits of a planner's analysis will never get the attention they deserve.[5]

The Cleveland staff knew that every day's work would not

---

[4]The transit negotiations, suggests Michael J. Hoffman (then working for Cuyahoga County), showed "how a hard-working, knowledgeable bureaucracy, with a steadfast director, can affect policy decisions in the public sector. . . . Only city planning had a plan; it backed that plan with sound data; then it fought off assaults with the accuracy of its figures that others were unable to refute. . . . What was achieved was substantial, and would not otherwise have occurred, because the poor had no other advocates" (letter to Forester, June 6, 1988).

[5]Compare Krumholz's strategic advice to equity planners: Frame "recommendations in data, analysis, and written hand-outs so everybody (especially the media) gets it straight. Become the *professional* and maintain that image. . . . While everybody else in City Hall was *political*, we were *professional*. As a result, we were considered the neutral experts in many areas, aiding our influence and providing protection against political threats" (letter to Forester, June 13, 1986). Howell Baum writes: "Unless [planners] respond to the political environment, they are unlikely to have influence. However, if they appear overtly political, they will be indistinguishable from other, explicitly political actors and will be unlikely to have any special influence" (letter to Forester, April 4, 1988).

only address a given project, this site or that parcel or that proposal, but that it would also strengthen or weaken their own reputation because of its timeliness, acuity, and style. Participating in the daily round of meetings and telephone conversations, planners recreate their agency's reputation as they speak articulately or not, provide relevant data or do not, appreciate the pressures on others or ignore them, and so on. In any given presentation, staff need both to present a cogent analysis of "the facts" and to present themselves in a way that will get them a hearing tomorrow, that will build trust and credibility, that will establish their own potential influence and competence. This is simple common sense, but too often that sense is neither so common nor so simple.[6]

Planners must balance tomorrow's continuing need for cooperation, coalition building, and information gathering with today's need to support or oppose a particular project. Working today with community residents, agency staff, politicians, and developers who may be passionately focused on a given project, the planners nevertheless have to try not just to get results in the short term, but to build long-term relationships too. In each day's work, planners face the challenge of maintaining what we may call their "strategic position." Meeting that challenge, the Cleveland cases suggest, takes time, sensitivity, political judgment, and negotiating skill as well. The Police Department's rejection of the planners' assistance, for example, provides a warning. When planners focus on issues but ignore the working relationships that will make their work consequential, they are likely to guarantee their own uselessness.

PRACTICAL RHETORIC AND PUBLICITY

The Cleveland experience should persuade us that professional planning is far more political craft than laboratory science. No matter how rigorous a project analysis, no matter how

---

[6]As planners produce whatever results they do today, they simultaneously reproduce, strengthening or weakening, the social relationships necessary to produce anything else tomorrow. For analysis of the simultaneously productive and reproductive character of planning practice, see John Forester, *Planning in the Face of Power* (Berkeley: University of California Press, 1989). For a closely related account dealing with recent European theories of hegemony and discourse, see Maarten Hajer, *City Politics: Hegemonic Projects and Discourse* (Brookfield, Vt.: Avebury, 1989).

brilliant the results or recommendations, the planner's inevitable work of *articulating* that analysis—gauging when, how, to whom, and to what ends to express the issues—is an activity that is simultaneously professional and political.

Heard in a highly political world, the planners' words mattered. Krumholz has argued that a city planner who believes that solutions lie in comprehensive "central planning" of our national economy would be wise to avoid publicly stating that in so many words. Those words in our society are so nearly taboo that they are almost undiscussable; the ideas at stake would be "dragged down" by the words. But, he suggests, the discussion *can* proceed if conveyed in different words. Muny Light, then, is not to be saved because it represents a triumph of public power over the private sector, but because it is a city asset that should be retained because it makes good business sense. Krumholz has speculated that Mayor Kucinich's downfall was triggered in part by his refusal to modify his political style and language. To have implied that Brock Weir, the CEO of the Cleveland Trust Bank was a vampire sucking the blood of the people of Cleveland was somewhat imprudent, especially since Weir was key to the decision by local banks to call or roll over the city's notes.

Choosing one's words carefully, Krumholz argues, is just as important inside as outside government. In advice giving, argument, not deference, is needed inside the mayor's cabinet as well as inside the planning agency. But the terms of the arguments "must not preclude future agreements." To develop trust with other city agencies, criticisms of those agencies' policies must be "gentle but revealing," Krumholz says, giving the mayor an opportunity to resolve a disagreement among "competent old friends"—both agency directors.

Professional posture had direct political benefits in Cleveland: an aura of publicly recognized legitimacy that strengthened the planners' hand. Confronted by a glowering Jim Stanton upset about public housing hearings or attacked in the press for their positions on development projects, the planners' appeal to professional principles appeared both to shield them and to refocus public attention on the equity issues at hand. What better political protection for planners than their appeal, not to expertise, but to their public and professional mandate, their traditional public-serving mission?

The planners' concern with their own practical voice

reached down to the most rudimentary reports they wrote for Planning Commission meetings. In those reports the staff wrote for the broader public and the press as well as for commission members and the files. To begin building an aura of professional competence, Krumholz points out, the planners adopted, beginning with the Euclid Beach issue, "a standard reporting format for issue review, analysis, and recommendation. This written document clearly set out the facts of each case under review, the staff's evaluation and discussion, a recommended course of action for the commission, and the reasons for the recommendation. The format was simple, straightforward, and consistent. It provided a clear history of the issue for incorporation into the official commission minutes as well as a convenient handout to newspaper and television reporters" (Chapter 4). Presenting the facts of the case, the staff's evaluation, and recommendations for action, these previously mundane reports now enabled professional analysis to serve a broader political function: public education through the mass media.[7] Planning Commission hearings served the planners less as havens from the political world than as settings in which to put pressing issues on the public agenda.

The reports to the Planning Commission, Krumholz notes, "did not emphasize any conflicts that arose within staff discussions. If views conflicted, and they frequently did, we tried to iron them out within our staff discussions and present a unified position to the world. We tried to avoid qualifying statements or uncertainty, preferring instead simple and straightforward themes." The Cleveland staff hoped to make themselves heard in an arena characterized by complexity, little time, poor data, and much conflict. In such settings, they sought to present professional recommendations as cogently as possible, as a prelude to, rather than as a substitute for, further debate.

The issue here is a poorly appreciated yet crucial problem of rhetoric. Planners who hope to pursue an equity agenda must speak and write as well as think and calculate. They must develop an articulate voice, organizing attention to issues and maintaining credibility even when data are inadequate and

---

[7]For an early view of planning as an instrument of civic education, see Thomas Schlereth, "Burnham's *Plan* and Moody's Manual: City Planning as Progressive Reform," in Donald Krueckeberg, ed., *The American Planner* (New York: Methuen, 1983).

tempers are short. They must face the challenge of being persuasive without being manipulative. They must face uncertainty without being paralyzed by it. Faced with the real complexity of housing or transit or service delivery problems, they must select which issues to focus upon and which to put aside. They must be articulate organizers as well as clear-thinking analysts. Gauging what to say and what not to say, when and how to speak to be understood, whether to be challenging or not, encouraging or not—all these are practical problems of rhetoric, of speech and writing, that call for subtle political judgments, for a working political literacy, in daily planning practice.[8]

RELATIONS WITH THE MEDIA

In part, of course, the Cleveland planners' ability to call attention to equity issues depended on the mutually beneficial relationships they nurtured with the local media. The planners could give local journalists and reporters timely information, data, and analysis as only insiders could. In turn, those journalists and reporters provided a broad forum for issues the planners wanted to place on the public agenda and a growing measure of credibility for the staff as well. Without ensuring victories on particular issues, good relations with the media allowed a politically literate planning staff to educate the public about urban issues in a more general way—and perhaps also to set the context for future debates about projects. In a

---

[8]These issues of rhetoric extend far beyond matters of simple persuasion, "communication," or clarity, for they involve deeply political choices about the ways problems and strategies of response are to be seen, if they are to be seen at all. For analyses of the rhetorical character of work in law and economics respectively, see J. B. White, "Rhetoric and Law: The Arts of Cultural and Communal Life," in his *Heracles' Bow: Essays on the Rhetoric and Poetics of Law* (Madison: University of Wisconsin Press, 1985); and Donald N. McCloskey, *The Rhetoric of Economics* (Madison: University of Wisconsin Press, 1986). For a discussion of policy and planning analysis, see Giandomenico Majone, *Evidence, Argument and Persuasion in the Policy Process* (New Haven: Yale University Press, 1989) chs. 1 and 2. For three very different analyses of political talk, see Joseph Gusfield, *The Culture of Public Problems* (Chicago: University of Chicago Press, 1981); Murray Edelman, *Political Language* (New York: Academic Press, 1977); and Benjamin Barber, *Strong Democracy* (Berkeley: University of California Press, 1984). For applications to planning, see Forester, *Planning in the Face of Power*.

setting where lucrative private deals were likely to be made by construction interests, law firms, and politicians, the Cleveland planners bet that cooperation with the media would generally tend to be boondoggle-exposing and public-protecting, whereas secrecy would protect the already powerful. They hoped, too, that media attention would dignify the planning staff as serious professional actors simply by covering their actions and reporting their analyses as newsworthy.

We should ask, then, what would happen if planners across the country took public education seriously as they presented their analyses of the issues of the day before planning boards and commissions? The pedagogic quality of planning analyses would surely improve under the pressure of public scrutiny. The visibility and status of planning staff would most likely increase too—as would, we suspect, the overall difficulty of private raids on the public purse.

Nevertheless, relationships with the media are always politically complex and risky. Krumholz relates several cases in which he gave information to the press at some personal risk. In the People Mover case, to take the most striking example, Krumholz gave information to journalists in the hope of bringing the inflated promises of the project to public attention— even though he felt he could not do this publicly in his official capacity.

If planners can at times exert influence through the media, though, so too can the press create public expectations of planners. The planners can come to be seen as haughty and distant or as down-to-earth and pragmatic, as in the pocket of local politicians or as speaking consistently to broader interests within the city.

Press and television coverage of planning issues increasingly has a political significance of its own. For if we hope for a civic life richer than one dictated by deals made in smoke-filled back rooms, we can appreciate that city planners' pursuit of visibility and publicity is a political good in itself. In a democratic culture particularly, public discussion of projects and decisions can educate and empower the citizens of the political community we call the city. Such "political talk," Benjamin Barber writes, "is not talk *about* the world; it is talk that makes and remakes the world."[9]

---

[9]Barber, *Strong Democracy*, p. 177 (italics in original).

In the freeway case, press coverage and attention contributed to a political climate in which senatorial candidate (and governor) Rhodes came to pledge that he would never force a highway on a community that did not want it. The media's coverage of downtown development disputes brought the planners' analyses of tax abatement strategies to the public's attention. The media's exposure of CEI's strategies to buy out Muny Light also enabled the planners' work to enrich public debate. Had Krumholz and his staff not carefully worked with local journalists and reporters, they would have missed, if not squandered, important opportunities that lay before them.

Yet access to the media will hardly help if the planners have nothing to say. When issues pressed, budgets were limited, and too little staff time was available, the Cleveland planners sought help at times from outside expertise. How they did that in the case of the freeway fight raises provocative practical and ethical questions.

STRENGTHENING PLANNING ANALYSES BY USING OUTSIDE EXPERTISE

In the freeway case, the planners built alliances with the staff of the very organization whose highway proposals they were trying to stop. Krumholz recalls his strategy:

> We wanted to deepen [the division between the NOACA board and its planning staff] and use the NOACA planning staff for our own purposes—in effect, to supplement our own staff at City Hall. That was not as difficult as it may sound. Many members of the NOACA staff had already quietly indicated that they were on the city's side in the controversy. . . . They had already prepared and recommended other courses of action that the board had rejected. Many were idealistic and liberal professional planners; I wanted them as allies. (Chapter 5)

The NOACA planning staff had no decision-making authority, and Krumholz did not try to undermine or subvert NOACA from the inside by lobbying its staff. But NOACA's planners had equity concerns of their own.[10] They offered

---

[10]Recall that the NOACA board had minimal representation of Cleveland residents, the freeway proposals threatened to have an extensive impact upon poor residents of the city, and some NOACA board members had said openly that they were not even familiar with the areas through which the

information and expertise to help Krumholz improve the quality of his staff's alternative route proposal. This political alliance between planners in contending agencies allowed the city planning staff more ably and publicly to press the facts of the case, to assess viable alternatives, and to show the costs and impacts of proposed routes.

What might have happened had Krumholz's staff only assessed the implications of the I-290 proposal? Without the expertise to explore real alternatives, they could have done little planning. Had they paid attention only to the likely consequences of the proposed route, the planners might have chronicled a story of urban displacement instead of acting effectively to prevent it.

Wishing to explore freeway alternatives that were less socially damaging, Krumholz organized a planning team composed of public planners and private engineers. His staff's reputation had enabled sympathetic professionals throughout the city and county to identify themselves as allies—and Krumholz used their help and protected their confidentiality. He recalls, "I have found through the years and on many different issues that it is often possible to get excellent professional assistance from staff members of outside agencies who are angry about or disappointed by their own agency's decisions. If you are visible and publicly identified with a position these professionals favor, they may be very helpful, but always on a *sub rosa* basis, because to be identified in this work might cost them their jobs" (Chapter 5).

Krumholz had also obtained the *pro bono* services of transportation engineers from a local firm. To supplement a city staff's capabilities in this way is unconventional, no doubt, yet still principled (since the planners were seeking to protect the welfare of the city against suburban power)—whether or not it was indeed justified.[11] Krumholz had to make an ethical judg-

---

proposed route ran. Is it surprising that NOACA staff members (or outsiders) questioned the soundness of the routes adopted by the NOACA board or the board's very legitimacy?

[11]For a sustained analysis of a "democratic" conception of bureaucratic responsibility and an assessment of information leaking by public servants, see John Burke's instructive and nuanced *Bureaucratic Responsibility* (Baltimore: Johns Hopkins University Press, 1986). Burke writes, for example: "If superiors in the organizational hierarchy or legislators were blocking access to information necessary for informed political choice, then bureaucratic action to remedy this situation would be in order" (p. 113). Yet "a

ment that would have supremely practical effects: in the interests of calling public attention to the I-290 proposal and workable alternatives, should he welcome, and work to organize, professional support, even if it came from a private firm or NOACA itself?

Krumholz does not spell out his ethical reasoning in Chapter 5, but two possibilities come easily to mind. The first, generally utilitarian, argument might take an expected increase in welfare due to stopping the freeway (preventing massive displacement) to outweigh the possible harm to social trust brought about by cooperation with the engineering firm. The second argument might recognize a conflict of obligations between two public trusts, with the obligation to avoid *sub rosa* work giving way here to the obligation to protect the interests of populations who are relatively unorganized, underrepresented, and otherwise inadequately protected by existing decision-making processes. Each of these arguments could, of course, be contested. Here we wish not so much to defend the decision as to make another point: the necessity for planners to make deeply practical, ethical judgments seems inescapable. If that weak claim is true, then planning education hamstrings students of planning if it does not prepare them to think through the challenges such judgments and choices present.[12]

CONCLUSION

The model of apolitical planning dies hard, in part because we have too few examples of exemplary equity-oriented planning

---

democratic approach does not propose some abstract or unqualified demand for information disclosure. . . . In addition to recognizing obligations to aid the process of political choice, a responsible official must always consider his normal duties—his promise to fulfill his official tasks and those of the broader hierarchical order in which they are set—in determining what he can do by way of remedy. By following this institutionally cognizant course, the bureaucrat will generally find that the legitimate need of the agency or organization for non-disclosure enters into his judgment about whether to act. Balancing these respective demands is necessary because the claims for non-disclosure made by superiors may be spurious or self-serving or, in contrast, the interests served by disclosure may be relatively weak" (p. 68).

[12]For detailed treatments of these problems, see Burke, *Bureaucratic Responsibility*, and Dennis Thompson, *Political Ethics and Public Office* (Cambridge: Harvard University Press, 1987).

that weaves together professional work, political vision, and organizational pragmatism. The Cleveland planners provide us with such examples, warts and all. Committed to serving those poor and vulnerable citizens whom "business as usual" promised to neglect, the Cleveland planners anticipated the play of private power, sweetheart deals, and bids for costly public subsidies.

As they worked with community leaders or mayoral advisors, with agency staff or specially created single-issue task forces, the Cleveland planners were able to develop an articulate, largely public, equity-oriented voice that integrated professional analysis and political initiative. They did not sacrifice professional integrity to political pressure. Instead, their work teaches us that had they not given voice to the equity-planning agenda, had they not pinpointed the vulnerability of the transit-dependent, had they not actively protected taxpayers facing ill-conceived infrastructure projects, the planners would have had far less to show for their professional work. The Cleveland planning experience demonstrates the possibilities of a politically astute, articulate, and effective equity-planning practice.

15

Evaluation, Ethics, and Traps

Politics concerns matters that might well be other than they are; it concerns the question, "what shall we do?" Insofar as it directs itself toward matters that cannot be changed, it is misguided and will fail. . . . Thus the political theorist . . . delineates, one might say, "what has to be accepted as given" from "what is to be done." . . .

The political theorist is thus always a teacher as much as an observer or contemplator. . . . The distinguishing of necessities from possibilities is less like the drawing of a line than like a *Gestalt* switch: a reconceptualization of familiar details so that realities we feel we have always known suddenly become visible for the first time, familiar things suddenly take on a new aspect.

—Hanna Pitkin,
Fortune Is a Woman
(1984)

We suspect that many other planners have been doing similar but more quiet work: resisting massive projects that threatened the public welfare, calling attention to public opportunities, seeking to inject high quality analysis into political decision processes. Unfortunately, though, many planners, and most of the public at large, never see much of the most important work that planners around the country do because their work often involves preventing or resisting public-threatening boondoggles, schemes for private enrichment at public expense, or projects that are just poorly planned and designed. Who can see the monstrosity that was never built? Who knows that these specific millions of tax dollars in a city's budget might have been unnecessarily given away? Who really knows that the transit fare might have been twice what it is, had the planning staff not aggressively intervened? As planners, we can hardly afford to have such invisible work go unrecognized and unappreciated. In the planning profession and the academy too, we need to tell the story of such work, to recognize and indeed honor it, whether it occurs in rural townships or our largest metropolitan areas.

To remember that planners must look beyond a narrow focus on physical planning is only to reiterate what everyone should learn in their first week in planning school: there is no physical planning without people planning, no planning without social, political, and economic dimensions. Likewise, social, political, and economic plans have spatial and physical impacts, and planners can bring their skills to bear in such analyses. Accordingly, we argue not against physical planning, but against an overly site-focused vision of planning that distracts attention from the organizational processes through which planners can make a difference. An active and pragmatic, physically attentive and politically astute planning practice *is* possible. By recounting cases that begin to show how much is possible, this book, we hope, will encourage many planners to think more expansively about their work and act more effectively as well. By learning from one another's experiences and those of the Cleveland planners, today's planners may recognize opportunities where previously they saw only constraints.

How exactly do we "learn from experience"? We do not just have experience, we have experience *of something.* "Experience" is a joke that theory plays on history. Descending from abstract theory to the apparently firm ground of concrete history, we soon learn that experience is endless, seamless, directionless, sometimes eye-opening, sometimes tiresome and irrelevant. Without a sense of direction, we will walk backward rather than forward. Without a broad sense of purpose, our knowledge of historical experience may never seem to matter. Without a set of pressing questions, we may review our past without ever fashioning answers to the problems facing us today.

So if history, or some particular set of experiences, is to inform our practice today and tomorrow, we are back to blending ingredients: history and theory together can teach us about the world. History without theory gives us an overcooked goulash of facts. Theory without history gives us exquisite sauces and spices with little underneath—and we leave hungry and frustrated. By itself, theory gives us relationships of categories without actors; by itself, history gives us a plentitude of actors, but no clear relationships.

The joke that theory plays on history—the facts! *which facts?!*—gets played two ways. No appeal to history is possible without theory, for in recounting a potentially endless history, choices must be made, and these reflect the story-tellers' theories of what matters and how political life actually works. But no appeal to theory is possible without history either, for in telling any abstract theoretical story, content must be filled in, and that content must do justice to real people in real places in real time.

Accordingly, our review of the Cleveland planning experience has been far from a random recounting of events. We have chosen experiences that suggest possibilities for success and failure, possible relationships with many other urban political actors, possible ways of integrating political judgment and professional expertise. We wish to make the Cleveland planning experience accessible, but in necessarily selective ways.

In this book, our blend of history and theory has been heavy on pragmatism, light on the language of structure, class, and political economy. We have gone easy on class analysis, for example, because we wish particularly to explore planners' discretion within the setting of the political economy of Cleveland. Our focus has been on questions of practice and agency within a structural setting rather than on questions of structural change across larger contexts.

But the analysis of practice and the analysis of structure are not altogether separable. Any powerful analysis of planning practice should surely address the possibility of structural change, and the relationships between a person's practice and a society's structure are complex.[1] A powerful analysis of practice must also address how intervention is possible, how practitioners may build relationships with the press or community members or agency personnel, how planners might use information in various professional and simultaneously political ways.

So we need an analysis that treats class structure, for example, not as a static constraint but as a set of social relationships that shape access, control, initiative, and belief. We need an

---

[1]See, for example, the essays in Karin Knorr-Cetina and Aaron Cicourel, eds., *Advances in Social Theory and Methodology: Toward an Integration of Micro- and Macro-Sociologies* (Boston: Routledge and Kegan Paul, 1981); Anthony Giddens, *The Constitution of Society* (Berkeley: University of California Press, 1984).

analysis that is dialectical so that structural relationships can be understood to constitute the issues that planners face—as when wealthier suburban governments attempt to railroad, quite literally, the poorer city of Cleveland. When construction interests lobby for road-building schemes or people mover demonstration projects, when large developers seek tax abatements that directly threaten the provision of services to low-income city neighborhoods, relations of political–economic class then frame planners' actions and their opportunities for intervention. Class relations do not just limit those possibilities; rather, they provide the stage on which the political drama of urban political life unfolds.

EVALUATING PLANNING PRACTICE

Throughout this book, we have wrestled with the problem of evaluation: just what counts as success? How much of a difference made is a success, and how much is a failure? Is the language of success and failure even appropriate when the results of planners' work are subject to the influence of so many others?

The Cleveland planners had no recipe to follow in doing their work. Krumholz worked to assemble a highly competent and socially committed staff. They won some battles and lost others. They looked for opportunities to intervene—acting as entrepreneurs—and responded to issues that others brought to them. Their planning was often contingent, dependent on external circumstances to provide opportunity, support, the possibility of useful intervention. Yet their work was both visionary and pragmatic; it was principled but not dogmatic, coherent but not rigid, activist but not overly aggressive.

We should consider three ways of answering the question of evaluation, each limited but useful.[2] First, we can ask about

---

[2]For a collection of conference papers discussing the problems of evaluating planning efforts, see Ian Masser, ed., *Evaluating Urban Planning Efforts: Approaches to Policy Analysis* (Aldershot, Eng.: Gower, 1983); for a worried account of two typical but unacceptable approaches to the problem, one epistemologically promising (following Popper) but naively unrealistic, and the other dubiously instructive but pragmatically apt, see Eric Reade, "Monitoring in Planning," in the Masser volume.

the *traditional form* of what the planners did. How did they fulfill the terms of their job descriptions? Were their reports competent and timely? Were they easily subject to political influence, simply "hired guns," or did they act professionally? Was their professionalism detached and unresponsive or born of working relationships with others throughout the city? The approach here is somewhat Platonic; given an intuition about an idealized planning practice, how did the Cleveland planners measure up?

Second, we can ask about the *consequences* of their work, the solutions they fashioned to the problems they faced. Working on regional transportation issues, just how did they succeed in rerouting a proposed freeway that threatened massive displacement? Were they able to achieve benefits for Cleveland residents—with respect to parks, to services, to access, to tax savings? The approach here is consequentialist: who got what as a result of the planners' work?

Third, we can ask about the *qualities of action and judgment* that we find in the Cleveland planning experience. Without abstracting "Planning" from the encompassing political world of which it is an integral part, how might we assess the practical virtues, or lack of them, in the planners' work? The approach here is Aristotelian; we wish to learn about the character of action and practice. We might appreciate a planner's courage and take heart from it, be strengthened by it, even if such courage went unrewarded in a particular case.

Taken in its most traditional form, the Cleveland planning experience can be both criticized and praised. Surely it is to be praised for bringing cogent analyses of development proposals before the Planning Commission, even in the face of overwhelming opposition from City Council. The commission staff may have had their eyes open to the political environment around them, but they persisted in providing a high level of professional analysis and reportage—for three mayors and their agency directors.

Yet the staff might be criticized too for lacking an equally aggressive posture when it came to traditional physical planning. Layton Washburn and other older staff members continued to work on physical planning issues, but this traditional focus never seemed to have the same public profile that the work of the newer staff had. The work of the newer staff did have extensive physical implications nevertheless, relating to parks, transport routes, downtown construction, and housing abandonment, for example.

From a strictly consequentialist point of view, benefits and costs are difficult to tabulate in any but the roughest sense. Transforming the lakefront parks from neglected garbage-dumping sites to parklands supported by the state of Ohio and visited by millions of Ohio citizens each year seems a reasonably clear success story for the planners. Helping other agencies save public monies and improve services must also represent an efficient use of staff time and energy. Stimulating the revision of the Ohio property laws to enable cities to land-bank abandoned properties similarly appears to be a beneficial political accomplishment, even if some Ohio cities might misuse their new prerogatives. Lowering transit fares for the elderly in the face of powerful suburban opposition is another benefit, one difficult to compare, for example, with the assistance rendered to the anti–People Mover forces that ultimately stopped this likely white elephant from being built in Cleveland's downtown.

These accomplishments and others took time and resources, of course, and their evaluation depends in part on making relevant comparisons. What else might the staff have done with the same resources? Did the staff's lack of close contact with the business community—a potential criticism—mean that they achieved fewer good outcomes than they might have? What have other planning departments accomplished with the same resources, under roughly similar conditions? In large part, we simply do not know. But if we hope to evaluate the success and failure of planners' efforts in any consequentialist way, we need to know.

The Cleveland staff also practiced with a verve that is itself instructive.[3] No doubt other planning staffs around the country have worked in similar ways that have gone unrecognized. Their stories need to be told. The Cleveland work we can report upon here simply provides a window through which we can see the possibilities of an activist, equity-oriented, and public-

---

[3]In these concluding chapters, "staff" often refers primarily to the newer staff members hired by Krumholz, though Layton Washburn is an obvious exception: he was integrally involved in many of the cases we have recounted here.

serving planning practice. We do not claim that very much was unique to Cleveland. Quite the contrary. The qualities that the Cleveland planners exemplified can be (and to some extent already have been, we believe) exemplified in other cities, larger and smaller alike. The qualities we have in mind are not recipe-like strategies; they are, rather, a more diffuse set of *practical virtues* that the staff manifested in their conduct.

The Cleveland planners were *persistent*. They dug in. With Krumholz's encouragement, support, and protection, the staff worked on projects for many years. There were very few "quick fixes," Operation Snow-Bird and the neighborhood improvement program notwithstanding.

The Cleveland planners *built relationships* with other agencies, with politicians, with neighborhood groups. Krumholz became a regular at the various mayors' cabinet meetings and so transformed the expectations of other agency directors and the mayor's staff. Janice Cogger and others worked closely with neighborhood organizations. Several members of the staff developed close relationships with the community organizers working for the Catholic diocese.

The planners *enlarged the scope of their mission* well beyond that of plan making. With a larger, equity-oriented sense of possibility and relevance, the planning staff became a practical, analytical resource for the city administration. The political patronage system had not had "analytical competence" high on its list of job requirements. Ordinarily, we might think that planners would have less influence under conditions of political patronage than in an administration that valued professional analysis and competence. But the Cleveland case suggests that the opposite may be true as well—especially when an activist director can anticipate the uncertainties and risks that the city will face and bring his or her staff's work quietly but quickly to bear on those issues.

Developing an equity-oriented think tank in City Hall was not Krumholz's explicit intention, but that was the result of his hiring decisions. Bonner, Wright, Cogger, Linner, Miller, and others filled an analytic vacuum in City Hall. Particularly under the Perk administration, their *professional expertise became a relative advantage* within city government, so that in the transit negotiations, for example, Krumholz's staff could substantially shape the agenda and resist the city's capitulation to pressures from suburban politicians. Here professional expertise was not only used by those with political power; it was a source of political power itself.

Krumholz *knew the value of making information public,* as we argued in the last chapter. He trusted the public he might reach through the local press to oppose private developers demanding needless public subsidies. He trusted the public to defend Muny Light against machinations and manipulations of the private utility owners bent on taking it over. Yet his trust in Cleveland residents did not stop him from opposing the city's racist elements. That strong but critical trust led the Planning Commission and the press to develop strikingly good relationships.

The Cleveland planning staff also worked to keep each other honest, debating and arguing at length about their work program and strategies, the differences they tried to make from day to day. They adopted the uncomfortable strategy of seeking to speak truth to power, and so they depended heavily on protection from their director.[4] While the larger cultural ambiance of the recent 1960s buoyed their efforts, the realities of Cleveland in the 1970s could quickly and easily have chewed them up. The staff supported one another in important ways. Several of them lived together, and more partied together, even if the new staff and the older staff were divided. Many of the staff had *integrated their professional work into their personal, political lives.* Had they not done so, surely burnout would have taken a far higher toll than it did.

STOKING THE FIRES:
THE ABILITY TO GO ON

Planning students and faculty who have heard about the Cleveland experience often ask how the staff managed to keep at it. The odds against them were great, and they had very little power. The problems of urban poverty were and continue to be enormous. How did they keep going? Why didn't they burn out, give up, lose hope?

Krumholz and the newer members of his staff turned the

---

[4]Raphaël Fischler notes that such protection implies that the planning director (somehow and already) "had acquired enough authority to be able to shield his staff" (letter to Forester, January 17, 1989).

question into the answer. Precisely because the odds were so long, because the need was so great, because working against the grain of established power was so important, the staff persisted and lent each other support and solidarity to "fight the good fight."

Krumholz and his staff often struck a more pragmatic chord too, saying, in effect, You win some and you lose some. What else is new? When you win, it can be exhilarating and carry you through the losses. You keep trying and do the best you can.

At times, Krumholz hits a lighter note: "Look, this work is fun," he argues. City government is full of interesting people, and there are wonderful people to work with throughout the city, even if others are corrupt, self-aggrandizing, out only to enrich themselves at the city's expense. When the public welfare is at stake, when planners can work with many people to try to improve the lot of those in need, the work can be intrinsically enjoyable even if the hours are long, the problems ill-defined and ambiguous, and the level of tension and conflict great.

Krumholz argues that the nature of the work has a sustaining character too. Planners are not widget-makers. They are trying to reshape the future of our cities, the future possibilities of all the residents of our cities and regions. Their work is as potentially creative as it is ambiguous—indeed, with less ambiguity, perhaps less creativity would be possible. With each project analysis, planners can enlarge and educate public thinking about the future or constrict and stifle it. Neither planners nor the great majority of other actors in the urban environment can have complete control over their work, however, and planners must be able to draw satisfaction from a job well done even if they cannot control the ultimate outcomes of development, urban reinvestment, inflation, or unemployment. Planners can draw strength from a tradition that is deeply promisory, a tradition that calls for practical imagination, for the rethinking of urban possibilities, for an articulation of public well-being in the face of obvious threats to that common welfare. The substance and promise of the work itself matter. In Cleveland, the planning staff did not let one another forget that, and they drew strength from their traditional and professional ideals just as they recognized the massive obstacles that stood in their way.

THE INADEQUACY OF DESCRIPTIVE
POLITICAL LABELS

The Cleveland experience shows us how inadequately our traditional political language describes an activist planning practice. Were the efforts of Krumholz's staff liberal, radical, or conservative? None of these labels helps very much.[5] They fought to protect city residents from displacement, and in doing so they took on the powerful county engineer, Burt Porter. Here they sought not social revolution but the maintenance of a status quo, the prevention of displacement, the continued ability of low-income residents to live without yet one more massive disruption of their lives. That this planning effort was aligned with upper income groups seeking to defend their property values hardly lessens the value of the planners' work. When the planners managed to turn the city's lakefront property over to the state of Ohio for maintenance, was this a radical or politically suicidal move? Hardly, but it did conserve the public resource of a magnificent lakefront and prevent its exclusively private exploitation.[6]

When they called public attention to the control of development and investment by the few, the Cleveland planners might have been considered radical pragmatists or radical democrats. Yet those same actions sought explicitly to protect the lives, neighborhoods, and opportunities of the great mass of

---

[5]Recall Daniel Bell's self-identification, "I think it not amiss to say that I am a socialist in economics, a liberal in politics, and a conservative in culture. Many persons might find this statement puzzling, assuming that if a person is a radical in one realm, he is a radical in all others; and conversely, if he is a conservative in one realm, then he must be a conservative in the others as well. Such an assumption mis-reads, both sociologically and morally, the nature of these different realms." *The Cultural Contradictions of Capitalism* (New York: Basic Books, 1978), pp. xi–xii.

[6]In a letter to Krumholz of November 10, 1988, Charles Hoch offers a related reading: "I would argue that you were not really advocate planners, that is, identifying with a client and representing their interests in a partisan manner. This would have meant political suicide and greatly reduced opportunities for influencing decisions. Instead of advocating for partisan interests, you advocated for a more politically inclusive system. You did not pit the weak against the strong, but rather pointed to the lack of fairness in public policies which favored the strong over the weak. Your effort was therefore conservative instead of radical: restoring a fair balance, rather than inciting a revolution. Hence, you were able to obtain bipartisan support for reforms that were redistributive because of the way you had framed the problem and its solutions."

Cleveland's poor from the assaults of others—and so the planners were surely conservatives as well.

When the planning staff analyzed proposed public expenditures or tax abatements, was such work liberal, conservative, or radical? Does the question even make much sense? To perform such analysis in City Hall is an elementary fiscal responsibility: why should a public body give away taxpayers' dollars needlessly? Yet the analysis of tax abatements called into question fundamental public–private and political–economic relationships.

Krumholz's staff was concerned with poverty, economic opportunity, and the lack of a democratic voice. These concerns are traditional, yet potentially radical too. The staff did not seek to nationalize Standard Oil of Ohio; they worked to protect the people of Cleveland from those—the owners of the private utility, for example—whose private gain threatened the broader public welfare.

The Cleveland planners' experience teaches us that these political labels do planners a double disservice. First, if aspiring planners think that their explicit concern for the poor and unorganized is "radical" in the creeping colloquial sense of "extreme, politically dangerous, and impractical," they have been snookered, their imaginations stifled, their sense of practical possibilities severely cramped. Second, much that can be tarred with the brush of "radical and impractical" can be defended as quite traditional, even life-conserving, culturally conservative in its own right. What distinguished this staff was not a political label but its *politically articulate competence*, its commitment to making analyses public early on, and its activist, initiative-taking style of problem-formulation and intervention.

But we can do more than criticize the inadequacy of our political language. We can suggest ways to evaluate planning practice without trying to pigeonhole it into a political category. We should not judge planners' efforts by asking whether the structure of the urban economy has changed or whether that economy has been transformed. This would make about as much sense as holding farmers accountable for the weather. Structural changes lie beyond the reach of local planners, and asking the wrong questions when we evaluate planners' practice signals our own failure more than any failure of the planners at work.

As a beginning, we suggest a series of questions with which to evaluate planning practice, in part because we recognize that the unique history of each city, each community, must provide the context for any one analysis. Does the planning staff have a reputation within city government for doing timely, literate, and competent work on issues facing city decision-makers? Does the planning staff have sufficiently close relationships with the press, civic associations, and community organizations so that information flows in multiple channels back and forth? Does the planning staff have a role in shaping the agendas of public decision making and public opinion, bringing timely warnings of threatening projects to the public's attention? Does the planning director, at least, have access to the mayor and other agency directors on a regular rather than ad hoc basis? Does the planning director envision the scope of the staff's activity to be economic as well as physical, social as well as aesthetic, service- and implementation-oriented as well as symbolic? Does the planning staff routinely scrutinize the effects of project proposals and opportunities upon the city and region's poor and unorganized people? Do the planners build relationships within city government and throughout the community so that coalitions can be formed, complex conflicts effectively mediated, implementation carried through?

These questions will never have simple answers, but they must be asked. Expanding the scope of planners' traditional practice is often an option, but this option will be lost if planners do not look for it. An expanded scope, however, does not simply mean "more work." We mean to point to opportunities for the more effective use of staff time, to accomplish more in less time, not simply to add to the already long list of planners' responsibilities.

Let us consider now several lessons about ethics that the Cleveland experience provides.

THE ETHICAL CHARACTER OF DAILY PLANNING PRACTICE

Too often we bring to planning a pasta-machine theory of ethics: we think that if we feed the dough of experience into the machine of ethical theory and turn the crank, out will come the one right answer, what colloquially we call "the ethical thing to do." This view produces what we can call "solution sickness"—the frustrated feeling that since ethics rarely produces solutions, it cannot be of much use. If ethical thinking is blind to the world of politics and pragmatism, then ethics, it seems, asks us to be saints and martyrs, not planners.

"Ethics" is not a tool to be used. When we speak of ethics in planning, we refer to a capacity to argue about what to do, to a capacity to think about, evaluate, and judge alternative courses of action. We should prize ethical thinking in planning not because it will magically promote consensus or coherence in the field, but because it can help us understand more sensitively just what is at stake in public decision processes and in our own actions. To put it simply, by enriching our capacities for judgment and questioning, ethical thinking can help us become more insightful evaluators and analysts, better planners, better actors.

Ethical thinking concerns ends and means alike. If planners are to pursue something they regard as "the public interest," surely they should have some articulate conception of what that involves.[7] When devoting attention to the needs of the poor, planners can do better than explain such attention as

---

[7]Krumholz frequently appeals to the "public interest," a concept that has come under scathing attack from pluralist political theorists, but which may be enjoying a resurgence of interest as a result of the reawakening of public philosophy and classically republican political theories: see, e.g., William Sullivan, *Reconstructing Public Philosophy* (Berkeley: University of California Press, 1986), and Robert Bellah et al., *Habits of the Heart: Individualism and Commitment in American Life* (Berkeley: University of California Press, 1985). Krumholz's appeal to "the public interest" should be read in the context of apparent threats to the public coffers from private individuals seeking personal gain. He writes as a planner and not as a philosopher. His appeal to the public interest poses two practical philosophical questions. First, is it possible to evaluate planning efforts without some particular conception of the public good? Second, when does the trickle-down theory of private gain promoting public well-being simply not work—not in economic theory but in urban practice? For the thin theory of democracy fueling attacks on the notion of public interest, see Benjamin Barber, *Strong Democracy* (Berkeley: University of California Press, 1984). For a devastating critique that leads to suspect the apparently more coherent notion of private interest that is supposed to free us from the ambiguities of the public interest, see Michael Rogin, "Non-Partisanship and the Group Interest," in Philip Green and Sanford Levinson, eds., *Power and Community: Dissenting Essays in Political Science* (New York: Vintage, 1970), pp. 112–41.

a personal preference—they can justify that attention, that concern, with ethical arguments that educate the public just as they provide a rationale for the planners' efforts.[8]

Yet ethical thinking is also about action, alternatives, and choices, about what to do now and next. It is about right action. As long as we think that "ethics" is about arcane theory or irrelevant situations or concocted dilemmas, we blind ourselves; we close our eyes as we try to walk across a busy street. General ethical theory cannot tell us where to go, any more than it can tell us who we are. Yet if we bring it to bear on the situations we face, ethical theory and argument can certainly help us understand what we are doing and may yet do, what qualities in the world we wish to preserve and enhance.

So we should ask planning professionals and educators to help future generations of planners anticipate problems of choosing, deciding, judging, evaluating, recommending—by drawing upon the repertoires of ethical argument and debate.[9] Planning curricula ignore questions of ethics at their own risk. Ignoring these questions surely weakens rather than strengthens planning students. In Cleveland, the planners (or at least the newer staff) argued incessantly about what to do. The policy seminars too structured an interagency forum in which staff

---

[8]The fact that ethical theories are hotly disputed diminishes their importance no more or less than intense debates in physics and astronomy diminish arguments and theories in those fields. In both ethics and physics, critical arguments advance the fields. For a touch of humility regarding the claims of Physical Science, see Hilary Putnam, "The Corroboration of Theories," in Ted Honderich and Myles Burnyeat, eds., *Philosophy As It Is* (New York: Penguin, 1979). See also Frank Fischer, *Politics, Values, and Public Policy: The Problem of Methodology* (Boulder, Colo.: Westview, 1980).

[9]We treat ethical theory here not as a matter of philosophical knowledge, but as a way to think about, interpret, and assess questions of value, significance, obligation, and right. Planning is fundamentally a value-laden, value-permeated, value-driven profession. Planning analyses that were value-free would be quite literally worth nothing. Yet most planners have been educated by social scientists with little concern for issues of practice and the demands of practical judgment, social scientists who have "solved" problems of evaluation, recommendation, and prescription by fiat—by simply ruling these problems out of court (out of the university). That may make life simpler for social scientists, but it evades the questions planners confront daily: what to do and why? See Martin Wachs, ed., *Ethics in Planning* (New Brunswick, N.J.: Center for Urban Policy Research, 1985).

across the city could debate the practical ethical questions of what should be done.[10]

We should not forget that ethical debate and argument in practice can educate planners and enlarge their senses of responsibility. We should not focus so heavily on the decisions to be made—the decision to recommend for or against a project, for example—that we fail to appreciate the argumentative process within the staff that informs practical decisions.[11]

We are not suggesting that planners immerse themselves in philosophical debates. If philosophers are trying to write the score—to give an account of justice, for example—planners are performers who must judge what to perform and how to do it. During the People Mover episode, Krumholz read two ethical scripts, one suggesting that his professional obligation was to Mayor Perk and the mayor's personal directives, the other suggesting a countervailing obligation to fight a project that promised to hurt the residents of Cleveland. Krumholz decided to follow the second: to act for the city's residents at the cost of counteracting his boss's wishes.

Analogously, musical scores do not perform themselves; musicians perform and must interpret any composer's work. Likewise, ethical theories do not make decisions; people do. To plan in the absence of considered ethical argument may well produce only the cacophony of an orchestra trying to play

---

[10]It is striking how little we seem to know about such ethical or normative "what should be done" arguments in practice. What, for example, might enable a staff to explore such questions more powerfully, more insightfully? What knowledge and skill can help here? If we cannot now answer these questions, what would we need to do to explore answers? See Frank Fischer and John Forester, eds., *Confronting Values in Policy Analysis: The Politics of Criteria* (Beverly Hills: Sage, 1987).

[11]Henry Shue writes, "Many political philosophers who genuinely would like to see implications for public affairs drawn from their reflections seem to believe that their own job as philosophers is finished when they have formulated and passed around some abstract principle of equality, justice, liberty, property, or such. Any fool, the working assumption seems to be, can then apply the principle to whatever concrete case bothers him; add the relevant facts, stir to a sticky consistency, and bake in a preheated oven. Yet merely selecting the relevant facts is a difficult and eminently philosophical task. It is, in any case, not a matter of pawing through piles of discrete facts and finding those marked "relevant," but a matter of examining entire alternative conceptions . . . and judging how to structure the whole business." "The Geography of Justice: Beitz's Critique of Skepticism and Statism," *Ethics* 92 (1982): 710. Cf. Barber, *Strong Democracy*, pp. 178–98.

without music. With stunning soloists or with an authoritarian conductor able to coordinate the instrumentalists, such an orchestra might at times make music that someone would wish to listen to. With exceptional staff members acting on their own or with a supremely gifted administrator integrating typically diverse talents and personalities, the planning staff's results might also be interesting. But, ordinarily, we wouldn't bet on it.

We can do better than gamble ethically on "stars" to plan well. We can articulate and debate planning strategies and justifications, ethical positions. Such debate can enrich our vision, further our understanding of practical possibilities, and hone our sense of practical choices as well. We must do more than have all planning students debate the purposes and goals of the profession. They must examine practice situations much more carefully. They must debate the conditions under which planners should leak information or withhold it, discourage or encourage the participation of affected publics, build coalitions or remain cloistered within the planning commission's walls.

The challenge of the Cleveland experience is to have us treat ethics *as if we were in practice*—whether we are now in practice or in the schools—and so to probe the possibilities of practice, the possibilities of fulfilling our obligations to many people, the possibilities of enlarging our sense of mission and real capacity. We must pursue these questions of ethics not with philosophical detachment but with judicious engagement as we explore the issues we come to as we complete the sentence, "When we are planning, we might——." This means treating ethical arguments as quite ordinary, but no less important for that fact. The point is not to make ethical argument either esoteric or mundane—just better. And that can happen only if we no longer treat issues of ethics as other-worldly, as removed from practice, as the terrain of abstract philosophers. We need to bring ethics home, to demystify it, to appreciate ethical argument as it appears in everyday practice, and as it might be refined and developed more powerfully in that practice.

THE PRACTICAL PARADOX OF PROFESSIONAL STYLE

Let us turn finally to a trap that too often catches planners despite their best intentions. The Cleveland experience helps us to move beyond a perplexing paradox, one we will call *the practical paradox of professional style.*

The gist of the paradox is quite simple: "neutral" action in a world of severe inequality reproduces that inequality. When public resources can either be channeled to serve the poor or be appropriated to enrich the already affluent, planning neutrality, even planners' silence, will help the strong take from the weak.[12] Good intentions, when blind to the context of action, can lead directly to bad results. When planners refuse to press for redistributive goals, they too often allow a status quo of poverty and powerlessness to remain unchanged.[13] Worse still, any claim by planners to be "above politics"—to separate or isolate their professional work from issues of empowerment, service provision, and distributive equity—will often seem pathetically irrelevant, and indeed self-defeating, in a context of great imbalances of political–economic power. Planners can begin with noble intentions but end up with reactionary results. Here's how the trap works.

Planners enter their profession not just to begin careers but to serve the larger society, including those most in need of jobs, food, and shelter. These young professionals have often chosen planning careers even though other, more financially rewarding options existed. They hope to achieve a measure of personal security while doing work that contributes to the improvement of the lives of others around them.

---

[12]James Davis, Mayor Perk's law director, remarked in an interview (October 31, 1987) that the city's assets were like a beached whale and much of the city's politics involved wealthy elites sneaking down to the shore to carve blubber from the stranded animal.

[13]Economic growth fueled by private investment *can* mitigate poverty (if not political powerlessness), but planners are likely to fail altogether to meet these problems if they put all their hopes on promoting economic growth. Promoting growth should be one of a repertoire of planning strategies, not the only strategy. In the absence of others—resisting unnecessary tax abatements, resisting "white elephant" infrastructure projects, targeting neighborhood services and infrastructure improvements, saving and protecting public assets from private appropriation, and so on—planners who are blind to redistributive strategies will simply allow existing inequalities to remain, or worsen, as the affluent and organized capitalize on their strengths and the poor and less politically organized suffer the consequences. See Todd Swanstrom, *The Crisis of Growth Politics: Cleveland, Kucinich, and the Challenge of Urban Populism* (Philadelphia: Temple University Press, 1985); and Susan S. Fainstein et al., *Restructuring the City: The Political Economy of Urban Redevelopment* (New York: Longman, 1983).

Once at work in a fully political world, planners come to see that the implementation of their ideas and the results of their efforts depend on institutional relationships of power, capital, race, and public involvement. These planners are not social engineers working in an immaculate, temperature-controlled laboratory. They work in the midst of political complexity they could barely have imagined, within political structures that seem routinely to ignore those most in need, whether they are children, the elderly, single women heads of households, or others.

Then, without substantial political power of their own, many planners feel threatened by political pressures. A mayor or city council president who wants to ensure re-election, for example, may try to manipulate the planners' work program. Or a well heeled developer may manipulate information to try to push a project through without careful planning review. Under these all too typical conditions, planners often feel that "politics" gets in the way of their professional work. Attempting as a result to put politics aside, some planners hope to concentrate strictly on "the intrinsic merits" of the proposals at hand. It may seem too risky and too "political," if not distracting, to cultivate ties to the press, to neighborhood leaders, and to the mayor's advisors. Yet when such "putting politics aside" by planners means ignoring their audiences and their role in shaping public decision-making agendas, disaster can follow.

These politics-avoiding planners are likely to isolate themselves and subvert their own influence as a result. They are likely to write in a style that only other professionals will understand. They are likely to present the results of their analyses to key actors *after* the important, though perhaps informal, decisions have been made. As a result, their work risks being rigorous but useless, technically superb but unheeded, analytically precise but off-target. These analysts will have aimed high and scored low. Despite the care with which they do their work, they serve very few people. Rather than guiding future action and policy formation, their work will too often be effectively silent, and silently ignored, for their results will not have had a real hearing, even if they are "on file" somewhere. The pursuit of an apolitical, detached, professional style here produces failure, not competence.

In this scenario, noble aspirations and public-regarding legal mandates alike result in frustration, cynicism, professional isolation, and inefficacy. Worse still, the planners' operative silence becomes a form of complicity with the established relations of political–economic power. Tragically, this professional silence betrays the very intentions that many planners originally sought to honor in their daily work.[14]

But this paradox need not impoverish planning. There is nothing inevitable about it. It is not some existential part of the planner's human condition. Instead, it hinges on an unnecessary assumption that the Cleveland planners clearly challenged: the assumption that political judgments have little place in professional practice.

The practical paradox of setting out to achieve one goal but serving its opposite can be dissolved once we understand that the task of planners is not simply to perform an analysis in their heads or on paper, but to get that analysis across, to organize others' attention to possible actions, to articulate and communicate that analysis, to educate an audience who can make a difference. Otherwise, of course, we are left with a conception of planning in which planning, virtually by definition, will make no difference!

In a political world, time is short, conflict is rampant, agendas are long, and the powerful have the initiative and do not wait for the unorganized to organize and make their wishes felt.[15] To fail to respond to the political structuring of public agendas means effectively to be silent. And to be silent as a

---

[14]No wonder that research into the psychological make-up of planners finds complex patterns of response to the political character of planning tasks and organizations. See Howell Baum, *The Invisible Bureaucracy* (New York: Oxford University Press, 1987).

[15]We try here to move beyond Richard Foglesong's provocative *Planning the Capitalist City: The Colonial Era to the 1920's* (Princeton: Princeton University Press, 1986). Foglesong argues that because planners were limited by existing relations of power, they reproduced those relations of power. But it's hard to know what to make of this claim. We are interested too in the planners' relationships to the powerful and powerless, and we hope to clarify the practical options planners have to strengthen or weaken the prerogatives of private capital, for example. To clarify this point, we can distinguish analyses of planning practice as a political and strategic activity from analyses of planning as an institution within a political economy. Planning as an institution may well be generally system-preserving even as system-transforming directions in planning practice still exist. Foglesong seeks to give a historical account of the former aspects, while we seek to give a relatively more microscopic historical account of the possibilities of a systemically critical yet effective and progressive planning practice.

public servant entrusted with the responsibility of city planning in a thoroughly political world is to resign oneself to the
prevailing politics in that world, to condone a status quo in
which "might" and raw power make "right" and apparent justice. Silence and self-isolation become the quiet voices of complicity.

If planners must not only analyze problems but express
themselves persuasively, not only calculate correctly but communicate effectively, not only think clearly but talk cogently
and write compellingly—then they must act with a political
literacy, as noted in the previous chapter, that has barely been
discussed in the planning and policy professions. Politically
literate planners know how to present focused analyses in
language that others can understand. They know they must
present those analyses on time, in whatever time is available,
whenever they can get a hearing. Knowing they must present
those accounts to audiences who will not always listen closely,
those planners think carefully, as the Cleveland planners did,
about how to teach that audience about important issues at
hand. Politically literate and articulate planners thus seek to be
effective educators every bit as much as rigorous analysts or
problem-solvers. They must be instructive and persuasive organizers—or risk having their best analyses sideswiped by
demagoguery, by the worst sort of political rhetoric, by the
narrowest greed and self-interest.

The Cleveland planners were politically articulate and
professionally effective as a result. They recognized, as we
have argued, that their every analysis shaped not only an immediate project but more enduring public expectations and the
reputation of the staff. They came to speak truth to power—
sometimes winning, sometimes losing, sometimes creating
policies and options they had hardly envisioned—and they
worked closely with other agencies, neighborhood residents,
and politicians as well. Their actions are now history, but the
lessons of their work remain to shape our collective future.

INDEX